LEGAL RESEARCH METHODS
Principles and Practicalities

LEGAL RESEARCH METHODS
Principles and Practicalities

Edited by

LAURA CAHILLANE
JENNIFER SCHWEPPE

Published by
Clarus Press Ltd,
Griffith Campus,
South Circular Road,
Dublin 8.

Typeset by
Deanta Global Publishing Services Limited

Printed by
SPRINT Books
Dublin

ISBN
978-1-905536-76-4

All rights reserved. No part of this publication may be reproduced, or transmitted in any form or by any means, including recording and photocopying, without the written permission of the copyright holder, application for which should be addressed to the publisher. Written permission should also be obtained before any part of the publication is stored in a retrieval system of any nature.

Disclaimer
Whilst every effort has been made to ensure that the contents of this book are accurate, neither the publisher or author can accept responsibility for any errors or omissions or loss occasioned to any person acting or refraining from acting as result of any material in this publication.

Copyright © Cahillane and Schweppe 2016

Preface

This collection arose out of a conference hosted by the School of Law in the University of Limerick in October 2014. The conference aimed to provide information on methods and methodologies in legal research in the context of the growth of PhD and post graduate research generally in law. While students are generally skilled at research they are sometimes unable to articulate their chosen method and thus the methodology section of a thesis becomes a daunting prospect.

The conference aimed to address this fear by providing a hitherto absent forum for researchers and supervisors to discuss current issues in relation to legal research and encouraged discussion and debate on the varying methodological approaches in the field.

The feedback from the event was such that it was decided to publish this collection in the hope that it will be an aid to post graduate students, early-career researchers and those interested in navigating the, sometimes murky, waters of legal research.

We are grateful to the contributors and attendees at that event for their valuable input and meaningful exchange of ideas.

We would like to thank all of the authors who have contributed to this collection for their thoughtful and engaging contributions. We would also like to thank the School of Law at the University of Limerick, and particularly the Head of School, Professor Shane Kilcommins for all the support for the project.

Laura Cahillane & Jennifer Schweppe
17 May 2016

Short Table of Contents

Preface v

Detailed Table of Contents ix

Author Biographies xiii

    Legal Research Methodologies: Framing the Context 1
    Laura Cahillane and Jennifer Schweppe

1. Doctrinal Legal Method (Black-Letterism): Assumptions, Commitments and Shortcomings 7
    Shane Kilcommins

2. Doctrinal Analysis: The Real 'Law in Action' 21
    Rónán Kennedy

3. The Comparative Method in Legal Research: The Art of Justifying Choices 39
    Marie-Luce Paris

4. The Use of History in Law – Avoiding the Pitfalls 57
    Laura Cahillane

5. Legal Material and Historical Research 71
    Thomas Mohr

6. Community-Based Research 89
    Mary Rogan

7. Socio-Legal Methodology: Conceptual Underpinnings, Justifications and Practical Pitfalls 107
    Darren O'Donovan

8. Getting Down and Dirty: The Case for Empirical Legal Research ... 131
    Michael Doherty

9. Participatory Research: Some Provocations for Doctoral Students in Law 149
    Fiona de Londras

10. Empirical Studies in Contract – The Way Forward 163
    Sally Wheeler

11. An Introduction to Research Ethics in Legal Scholarship 187
    Hope Davidson and Jennifer Schweppe

Index 203

Detailed Table of Contents

Preface v
Short Table of Contents vii
Author Biographies xiii

Legal Research Methodologies: Framing the Context 1

1. **Doctrinal Legal Method (Black-Letterism): Assumptions, Commitments and Shortcomings** 7
    - I – Introduction 7
    - II – The Properties Underpinning a Doctrinal Legal Approach 9
    - III – So What is Good About Such a Methodology? 13
    - IV – What are the Dangers? 14
    - V – Conclusion 18

2. **Doctrinal Analysis: The Real 'Law in Action'** 21
    - I – The Continuing Importance of Doctrinal Analysis 22
    - II – Doing Doctrinal Analysis Properly 30

3. **The Comparative Method in Legal Research: The Art of Justifying Choices** 39
    - I – Introduction 39
    - II – Theoretical Core of Comparative Law: Meaning and Purpose 42
    - III – Method of Comparative Law *Stricto Sensu*: Deconstructing the Comparative Analysis 48
    - IV – Conclusion 55

4. **The Use of History in Law – Avoiding the Pitfalls** 57
    - I – Introduction 57
    - II – The Beginnings of using History in Legal Thought: Savigny and Maine 58
    - III – Internal v External Legal Histories 61
    - IV – Things to Avoid 63
    - V – Things to Remember 67

5. Legal Material and Historical Research 71
    I – Introduction 71
    II – Using Primary Sources 72
    III – Secondary Sources 81
    IV – Conclusion 86

6. Community-Based Research 89
    I – Community Engagement 90
    II – Community-Based Research 92
    III – Community-Based Research in Law: Pros and Cons 94
    IV – Practical Reflections on Community-Based Research 99
    V – Practical Matters and Community-Based Research 103
    VI – Conclusion: The Potential of Community-Based Research 104

7. Socio-Legal Methodology: Conceptual Underpinnings, Justifications and Practical Pitfalls 107
    I – Defining Socio-Legal Methodology 108
    II – Framing Socio-Legal Research Questions 110
    III – Theme 1: Critiquing Closure — Doctrinal and Socio-Legal Scholarship 112
    IV – Theme 2: Working Inside Out — Interactions between Socio-Legal Scholarship and the Doctrinal Method 114
    V – Theme 3: Closing the Gap — Law in the Books versus Law in Action 116
    VI – Theme 4: Legal Pluralism and Overlapping Normative Orders 118
    VII – Theme 5: Legal Consciousness and Person-Centred Research 120
    VIII – The Challenges of Socio-Legal Methodology 122
    IX – The Pitfalls of Socio-Legal Research 126
    X – Conclusion 128

8. Getting Down and Dirty: The Case for Empirical Legal Research 131
    I – Introduction 131
    II – Why Empirical Research? 131
    III – Why not? 136

Detailed Table of Contents

    IV – What do I Mean? 137
    V – Examples: Out in the Field 141
    VI – Conclusions: What Next? 145

9. Participatory Research: Some Provocations for Doctoral Students in Law 149
    I – Why Do Participatory Research? 150
    II – Which Participants? 154
    III – What Form of Participation? 157
    IV – Reaching 'Personal' Information 158
    V – Acquiring 'Hard To Reach' Information 160
    VI – Enhancing Depth of Knowledge 161
    VII – Determining Importance of Issues 161
    VIII – Acquiring Generalisable Information 161
    IX – Conclusion 162

10. Empirical Studies in Contract – The Way Forward 163
    I – Introduction 163
    II – The First Group — In the Steps of Stewart Macaulay 165
    III – The Second Group — Following Ian Macneil 178
    IV – Conclusion 184

11. An Introduction to Research Ethics in Legal Scholarship 187
    I – Introduction 187
    II – Context 187
    III – A Brief History of Research Ethics 188
    IV – Applying for Research Ethics Approval 193
    V – Conclusion 202

Index 203

Author Biographies

Shane Kilcommins is head of the School of Law, University of Limerick. He is a graduate of the University of Limerick, (BA in Law and European Studies, 1994) the University of Wales, Aberystwyth (PhD 1999), and UCC (MA in Teaching and Learning, 2007). He joined the Law School in UL as a professor in 2014. He lectures in evidence law, jurisprudence, penology and employment law. He has co-authored various funded research reports on discrimination, victims of crime and integrative learning. He is co-editor of the Criminal Law Online Journal and is book editor for the Irish Journal of Legal Studies. He acted as deputy editor of the Judicial Studies Institute Journal between 2007 and 2010. He is recipient of a number of prizes and scholarships including the President's Prize for excellence in teaching at University College Cork in 2006; and a Fulbright scholarship to undertake research in the US in 2008. He has acted as co-director for the Centre for Criminal Justice and Human Rights at UCC, and is currently a director of the Association for Criminal Justice Research and Development. His book publications include *The Introduction of Community Service Orders* (Barry Rose Law Publishers 2003) *Alcohol, Society and Law* (Barry Rose Law Publishers 2002) (co-editor), *Crime, Punishment and the Search for Order in Ireland* (IPA, 2004) (co-author), *Terrorism, Rights and the Rule of Law* (Willan 2008), *Criminal Law in Ireland* (Clarus Press 2010) (co-author) and *Regulatory Crime in Ireland* (First Law 2010) (co-editor). He has written various articles on penology and criminal justice in the Irish Jurist, the Holdsworth Law Review, the Juridical Review, Criminology and Criminal Justice, the Irish Probation Journal, Administration, the International Journal of Insurance Law, Irish Current Law Statutes Annotated, Cambrian Law Review, the European Journal of Criminology, International Review of Victimology the Irish Tax Review, the Mountbatten Journal of Legal Studies and the Journal of Higher Education.

Rónán Kennedy is a lecturer in the School of Law, NUI Galway. He holds a degree in commerce and a higher diploma in systems analysis from University College Galway, an LL.B. with first class honours from the National University of Ireland, Galway, an LL.M. from New York University and a Ph.D. from University College London. He also studied for the degree of Barrister-at-Law in the King's Inns and was called to the Bar of Ireland in 2003. He worked as a programmer, systems analyst and network administrator from 1993 to 2000. He was Executive Legal Officer to the Chief Justice of Ireland, Mr Justice Ronan Keane, from 2000 to 2004. During this time, he was editor of "The Supreme Court of Ireland: A History", first editor of the

Judicial Studies Institute Journal from 2001 to 2003, and was involved in a number of initiatives to expand the use of information technology in the courts. Before coming to the Law Faculty in NUI, Galway, he taught environmental law and public international law in the University of Limerick. He was the co-ordinator of the LL.M. in Law, Technology and Governance from 2008 to 2014 and was Associate Head for Development and Promotion for the School from April 2009 to April 2010. His research focuses on the relationship between information and communications technology and environmental regulation.

Marie-Luce Paris is Assistant Professor in law at UCD Sutherland School of Law, University College Dublin. Marie-Luce's primary research interests are in comparative constitutional law and politics, global constitutionalism, European public and human rights law. She has also an interest in legal education. Her work has been published in the Yearbook of European Law, German Law Journal, Irish Journal of European Law, Irish Jurist and Revue Internationale de Droit Comparé. Her lastest publication is a book co-edited with Professor John Bell (Cambridge University) entitled Rights-Based Constitutional Review — Constitutional Courts in a Changing Landscape (Edward Elgar 2016). She has held research visiting positions at the University of California, Davis School of Law (USA), and the Australian National University Centre for European Studies (Canberra, Australia).

Marie-Luce received her legal education at Université Panthéon-Assas (Paris II), where she was awarded her PhD, funded by the French Ministry for Higher Education and Research, for her work on The Implementation of the European Convention on Human Rights by the United Kingdom. She obtained her professional qualification as a Barrister-at-Law from the Ecole D'Avocats Du Barreau De La Cour D'Appel De Paris, and worked as a trainee in law firms and at the Commercial Court in Paris. Marie-Luce joined UCD School of Law to teach in, and later direct, the BCL Law with French Law and dual degree BCL/Maîtrise programmes which aim at training UCD law students to the French civil law system. Marie-Luce teaches on a number of undergraduate and graduate courses which include ECHR Law, Comparative Constitutional Law, and French Constitutional Law.

Laura Cahillane is a lecturer in the School of Law, University of Limerick. She is a first class honours graduate of UCC (BCL (Law and French) 2007, LLM (by Research) 2008, PhD 2012, PGCTHLE 2013). Her Research Masters examined the topic of disciplining judges and her PhD, for which she was awarded an IRCHSS Government of Ireland Scholarship, considered the drafting of the 1922 Irish Free State Constitution. Laura undertook a Post-Doctoral Fellowship in UCC and held lectureships in UCC and DCU before joining the School of Law at UL. Currently, she is co-director of the Law Plus degree and teaches Constitutional and Administrative Law. She is on the editorial committee of the Judicial Studies Institute Journal. Her research interests lie in the areas of Constitutional Law, Legal History, Judicial Politics and Comparative Law and she has published nationally and internationally in these areas. She is a frequent contributor to the media on legal and constitutional issues and has advised the Oireachtas on law reform. Recent publications include *Drafting the Irish Free State Constitution* (MUP 2016) and *Judges, Politics, and the Irish Constitution*, with Gallen and Hickey (MUP forthcoming).

Thomas Mohr is a lecturer at the School of Law, University College Dublin. He is honorary secretary of the Irish Legal History Society and book review editor of the Irish Jurist, Ireland's oldest law journal. His publications on Irish legal history range from the medieval brehon law to the law of the independent Irish state in the 20th century. His latest publication is *Guardian of the Treaty – The Privy Council Appeal and Irish Sovereignty* (Four Courts Press, 2016). This concerns an important aspect of the Irish Free State's relationship with the British Empire in the inter-war years.

Mary Rogan LL.B, BCL (Oxf), PhD, MA (Higher Education) (DIT), PGDip (Statistics), Barrister-at-Law (King's Inns) is Associate Professor at the School of Law, Trinity College Dublin. She researches in the areas of prison law and prison policymaking and is the author of *Prison Policy in Ireland: Politics, Penal-Welfarism and Political Imprisonment* (Routledge, 2011), and *Prison Law* (Bloomsbury Professional, 2014). She is a barrister with expertise in prison law. Dr Rogan was awarded a European Research Council Starting Grant worth €1.5million in 2015 for a project entitled 'Prisons: the rule of law, accountability and rights'. She has also received funding from the European Commission and Irish Research Council for projects on imprisonment, pre-trial detention, and law and social change. She was appointed by the Minister for Justice and Equality to chair an Implementation and Oversight Group on reforms to penal policy in 2015. She is also a member of the Central Statistics Office's Expert Group on Crime Statistics. Dr Rogan is a representative of Ireland on the International Penal and Penitentiary Foundation. She is a member of the Board of the Irish Association for the Social Integration of Offenders, and is a former

Chairperson of the Irish Penal Reform Trust. Mary established and ran the community-based learning module, 'Law and Society' while working at Dublin Institute of Technology. She has also jointly supervised a PhD with an NGO partner, the Irish Penal Reform Trust.

Darren O'Donovan is a Senior Lecturer at La Trobe University, Melbourne, Australia. He was previously Lecturer in Law at University College Cork, Ireland from where he also obtained his PhD on housing rights and the Travelling Community. His research interests are in administrative law and human rights, and he is the author of *Law and Public Administration in Ireland* (Clarus Press, 2015) (with Dr Fiona Donson). Darren has published widely on issues of public governance and human rights, including recent articles in Public Law and International Journal of Discrimination and the Law.

Michael Doherty is Professor of Law and Head of the Department of Law at Maynooth University. He lectures and researches in the areas of employment and labour law, industrial relations (especially the role of trade unions) and social partnership, as well as in EU labour law and policy. He has published widely in national and international outlets on these topics (including in the European Law Journal, Industrial Law Journal, King's Law Journal, and Work, Employment & Society) and has presented his work at numerous domestic and international conferences. His work has focused, in particular, on collective employment rights, employee representation at work, the role of trade unions and the role of social pacts in socio-economic governance. He has worked on a number of projects for the European Commission as part of European-wide research networks and as co-investigator on a major, EU-funded project on public procurement. He sits on the editorial board of a number of national and international journals, including Employee Relations, the Journal of Law and Politics and the Irish Employment Law Journal and acts as a reviewer for many more (including Economic and Industrial Democracy and the Dublin University Law Journal). He is a frequent media contributor on labour market issues and is a National Rapporteur on Employment Law to the International Academy of Comparative Law.

Fiona de Londras joined Birmingham Law School as the inaugural Chair in Global Legal Studies in the summer of 2015, following time as a professor at Durham and lecturer at UCD. Fiona's research and teaching are in the fields of human rights and comparative constitutional law with a particular focus on counter-terrorism. She is the joint editor-in-chief of the Irish Yearbook of International Law and co-editor of Legal Studies, the journal of the Society of Legal Scholars of the UK and Ireland. She is also a member

Author Biographies

of the Executive Committee of the Society of Legal Scholars, and a member of the advisory boards of the Centre for Comparative and European Constitutional Studies at the University of Copenhagen, the UCC Department and Faculty of Law, and the Centre for Global Public Law at Koc University, Turkey. In 2009, Fiona founded Human Rights in Ireland, a collaborative academic blog with a focus on human rights issues in Ireland and on Irish scholarship about human rights theory, practice, law and politics.

Sally Wheeler is Professor of Law at Queen's University Belfast. Prior to taking up her position at QUB she worked at Birkbeck and the University of Leeds. She edits the Northern Ireland Legal Quarterly and in 2012, became a Fellow of the Academy of Social Sciences. In 2013 she was elected to the Royal Irish Academy. She is the Director of the Institute of Governance and conducts research on corporate social responsibility. Her publications include *Corporations and the Third Way* (Hart 2002) and *Reservation of Title Clauses: Impact and Implications* (Clarendon Press 1991).

Hope Davidson was awarded a BA in History from TCD in 1992, and was admitted to the Roll of Solicitors in 1996. She practiced in Dublin for ten years in the defence of claims against hospitals, in public liability, employer liability and clinical negligence. She was accredited as a Mediator in 2009 and has sat for a number of years on the Mental Health Tribunals. She completed a Masters in Health and Care Law in UCC in 2014 for which achieved First Class Honours, her minor thesis was on the reform of the law in relation to voluntary psychiatric patients. She is continuing her research in the area of healthcare decision-making and incapacity in UL under the supervision of Dr. Eimear Spain and Jennifer Schweppe and her PhD thesis is entitled 'Decision-making in dementia care: autonomy, capacity and the doctrine of informed consent.' She won the Dean's Award for 'Best Paper' at the AHSS Postgraduate Conference 2015 and a PhD Scholarship to the IALT Annual Conference 2015. Her research interests include human rights, medical ethics and mental health and mental capacity law.

Jennifer Schweppe is a lecturer in law at the University of Limerick. She was the President of the Irish Association of Law Teachers for 2009-2010. She completed a Graduate Diploma in Academic Practice at the University of Limerick, and won the Small Group Teaching Award at the University of Limerick in 2010. She was awarded a National Award for Excellence in Teaching by the National Academy for the Integration of Research, Teaching and Learning (NAIRTL) in 2011 and was a finalist for the European Award for Excellence in Teaching in the Humanities and Social Sciences in 2012. Her research interests lie in the areas of hate crime and abortion law. Her work in the area of hate crime looks at the criminalisation of bias motivation, and explores the potential of introducing hate crime offences in an Irish context. She is co-editor of two major collections in the area of hate crime, including *The Globalization of Hate: Internationalising Hate Crime?* (Oxford University Press 2016) and has published in the Journal of Hate Studies, the Oxford Handbook Online in Criminology and Criminal Justice, the Northern Ireland Legal Quarterly and the Irish Jurist. She is co-director of the International Network for Hate Studies and is also founder and co-Director of the University of Limerick-based Hate and Hostility Research Group, the only academic research group in Ireland dedicated to exploring and understanding hate crime in an Irish context. Her work in the area of hate crime has been funded by the Irish Research Council, the Irish Council for Civil Liberties and the European Union.

Introduction

Legal Research Methodologies: Framing the Context

Laura CAHILLANE *and Jennifer* SCHWEPPE

To say that research methods and research methodologies are part of the hidden curriculum in the undergraduate law programme in Ireland is to perhaps overstate its presence. While in other disciplines, students are taught at the earliest stages in their University education *how* research is conducted within that discipline, in law schools, we prefer to discuss the *why*, *what* and *when* of research: indeed, anything other than the *how*. We do, of course, instruct students on the mechanics of research – where is the library, how do we access legal databases, why Google is not always your friend when conducting legal research – as well as discussing the processes of digesting and analysing case law and the technicalities of the legislative process. Thus, when a student enters a graduate programme and starts engaging in graduate research, they are rarely if ever conversant in the methods and methodologies of legal research.

Even at completion of graduate studies, until recently, discussing methodology was dismissed as not really something that lawyers *did* and was dealt with in a rather cursory manner at the early stages of a thesis. Take, for example, the discussion of methodology in the PhD of arguably the finest legal mind in a generation in Ireland:

> Standard research methodology has been employed. The major constitutional cases from this period have been examined in detail; frequent reference is made to parliamentary debates, books and learned journals and extensive use has been made of important archival material.[1]

Not only is this the entire extent of the discussion of the author's methodology, but there is no context given to it, no sources to justify its use, nor even a name ascribed to what this 'standard research methodology' is. Nor was this thesis published a terribly long time ago: indeed, it dates only to 2001.

---

[1] G Hogan, 'Development of Judicial Review of Legislation and Irish Constitutional Law 1929–1941' (PhD thesis, Trinity College Dublin 2001).

Of course, such a formula was entirely acceptable at the time and widely used. In fact, many legal theses did not mention methodology at all.

In the intervening years, rather than being relegated to a perfunctory mention in the introductory part of a PhD thesis, a description and discussion of the methodology employed in the research is seen as one of its core elements. Indeed, one of the first things that is asked of a graduate student is: discuss and describe your methodology. Furthermore, a significant part of many PhD viva examinations is now spent discussing the methodology, and often the result will hinge on the strength or otherwise of this section. But how are students expected to describe or defend their methodology when they have never been instructed in or even introduced to fundamental principles of legal methodologies in a formal manner? Though some students will have been exposed to qualitative and quantitative research methods in other disciplines as part of the undergraduate programme, they are often unable to articulate how legal research is conducted – though of course, they are perfectly capable of engaging in it. Further, while they may be fully competent in qualitative and quantitative methods from studying, for example, sociology, they are often unaware of the particular strictures, theoretical frameworks and complexities associated with legal research.

In October 2014, the School of Law at the University of Limerick hosted a seminar on research methods in law to demystify and contextualise research methods for Irish graduate students. Speakers were asked, not only to describe and analyse the particular method they themselves are expert in, but also to highlight some of the practicalities and pitfalls associated with that method. Is it, for example, even acceptable today to engage in pure doctrinal research, or do we all need to be engaging in socio-legal analysis? Can the inclusion of a section on the history of the legal principle under scrutiny allow the author to justifiably state that they are engaging in historical analysis? And what *is* socio-legal research anyway? The general consensus was that the discussion was so useful that it warranted a follow-up edited collection. That aspiration has been realised in the form of this volume.

This collection of essays draws largely from the papers at that conference, and aims to introduce graduate students to the theoretical frameworks utilised in diverse methodologies, as well as the 'how to' in each case. Some of the advantages and disadvantages to each method are also discussed, with authors often taking an opportunity highlight what they consider to be excellent examples of the utilisation of a particular methodology.

Shane Kilcommins begins by looking at what was traditionally regarded as 'standard legal methodology' – that is doctrinal methodology. He points out that, while this methodology is often very useful and indeed most suitable for certain types of legal research, very often students simply do not know how to explain what it is they are doing. Attempts to articulate the methodology often appear to lack rigour or depth. In order to avoid this and to help readers to better understand what doctrinal methodology actually consists of, this chapter attempts to unpack its assumptions, commitments, and foundational claims. He also demonstrates that, while in recent years, black-letterism has attracted pejorative undertones and is sometimes regarded as not sophisticated enough for high quality legal research, it also has its place and, when used appropriately, it has much to commend it.

In his chapter, Rónán Kennedy begins by agreeing that, while the doctrinal method has been criticised, as the working method of the judiciary and at the core of the traditional legal curriculum, it cannot be ignored. Describing the doctrinal method as complex, multi-layered and distinctive (as well as confusing, flawed and difficult to explain), he goes on to analyse its advantages and disadvantages before, in Part 2, explaining how to conduct doctrinal analysis , outlining the three steps which should be taken in doing so. He then addresses the question of how to frame a research question which is suitable to the method, and describes a number of recent examples of doctrinal research projects in Ireland as good examples of the use of the method.

The next method under analysis is the comparative method. Given that there is no agreed definition on what the method of comparative law is, Marie-Luce Paris aims not to propose a comprehensive theory on the comparative method nor to offer *the* definitive method for comparative legal research but rather to provide a critical explanation of the main conceptual tools on how the issue of method in comparative law has been approached. She first addresses the theoretical core of comparative law, outlining an account of its meaning and purpose. She then goes on to explore what is meant by the comparative method and outlines two different methods proposed by Kamba and de Cruz. She further observes that, aside from determining the intellectual framework for the research, there are further practical challenges to engaging in research utilising this method.

These challenges are not, however, insurmountable, and as the author observes, the use of comparative law is no longer marginal, but pervades scholarship.

Laura Cahillane then considers the use of history in legal research. She considers the work of two great legal historians in order to demonstrate the potential dangers involved with such a method. She then examines the debate surrounding the use of internal and external legal history, and points out various pitfalls to avoid when conducting historical legal research. Her chapter concludes that using a legal historical methodology can be a very worthwhile pursuit, provided one is aware of the dangers and how to avoid them.

Thomas Mohr continues on the theme of history and law, noting that, unlike some of the other methodologies, students are generally well versed in the connection between the fields of law and history from an early stage in their studies, and he observes that legal scholars cannot avoid engagement with historical legal methodologies. To assist researchers with this process, and to ensure that it is done in a methodologically sound manner, he explains that the primary challenge will be finding and evaluating sources. In an Irish context, where much of the State's archives were destroyed in a fire in 1922, this may be particularly challenging. However, state records are just one source for the legal historian, and he provides a detailed account of both the primary and secondary sources available for this type of research, concluding that, while challenges exist in using this methodology, they are not insuperable.

In the next chapter, Mary Rogan examines the relatively new domain of community-based research. She observes that, whilst this type of research is attractive at a policy level to funders, policy makers and senior administrators in higher education, practical barriers exist within the academy. Describing community-based research, she observes that it is particularly suitable for legal scholars, noting that the potential audience will include those who struggle to vindicate theoretical rights of access to justice. She explains the pros and cons of this type of research, and then reflects on her own experience in the field. She concludes that, when done correctly, community-based research has the potential for real impact, with researchers having an opportunity to make changes in both policy and practice which is, surely, the aim of most legal scholars.

The remaining chapters in the book deal to some extent or another with socio-legal methods and methodologies. Darren O'Donovan begins this section by looking at the position of law in relation to the general social sciences and, having located this methodological school, he goes on to analyse the benefits in this particular approach. He discusses five major strands of socio-legal research and looks at how they seek to make distinctive contributions to knowledge Finally, he addresses the fear that students sometimes have around this particular methodology that by engaging in it they are no longer engaged in 'legal' research. The chapter is also intended as a practical guide, assisting the reader in negotiating the central pitfalls of adopting a socio-legal approach.

In his chapter, Michael Doherty makes a 'call to arms' to researchers to engage in empirical legal research. With an undergraduate degree in law and a PhD in sociology, his particular experience in this regard, which he recounts in the chapter, is both informative and compelling. He outlines why engaging in empirical research benefits the researcher, both from the perspective of the research itself as well as the skills set she acquires. He highlights some of the issues that require consideration in designing a research question and methodology, using his own experiences as mini case studies. He concludes by offering some recommendations to institutions, law schools and researchers as to how empirical legal research can be better supported in the future.

Using a framework which examines the role of participatory research in legal research, Fiona de Londras explores some of the key forms of participatory research that are available to students, first outlining some of the key circumstances in which engaging in participatory research is particularly useful. She then points to some of the key questions to ask when determining *who* your research participants should be, and goes on to highlight some of the key issues to consider when asking what *form* of participation is most useful to your research. She concludes by observing that, whilst participatory research is a valuable means of ensuring your research makes an original contribution to knowledge, it should only be conducted where the research enquiry justifies the methodology, and where the process and participants are engaged with in a careful manner.

In the penultimate chapter, Sally Wheeler examines the particular issue of empirical studies in contract law. This chapter focuses on scholarly work on the use of empirical methods in contract law and points to some further avenues of exploration. She analyses the foundational work of Stewart Macauley and Ian Macneil, and the studies which rely on their work to explore not only the manner in which empirical studies can be utilised in contract law, but also to identify research methods that are replicable by lone scholars or postgraduate students. She concludes by highlighting areas which remain unexplored, including how gender or socio-economic status impact on contract negotiation.

Prior to engaging in the type of work described in the latter part of this text, researchers should secure research ethics approval from their institution. In the final chapter of the book, Hope Davidson and Jennifer Schweppe briefly set out a history of research ethics and its role in research in a humanities context, before providing some practical advice on how to apply for institutional ethics approval.

CHAPTER 1

Doctrinal Legal Method (Black-Letterism): Assumptions, Commitments and Shortcomings

Shane KILCOMMINS*

'You come in here with a head full of mush and you leave thinking like a lawyer'.Professor Kingsfield, The Paper Chase (1973)

1 – INTRODUCTION

It has always struck me when asking postgraduate law students to write research proposals in which they should work through the core elements – question, structure, methodology, originality/location in the literature – how challenging they find the process of articulating their methodologies. The issue of methodology is a difficult one for lawyers for a variety of reasons: we are not ordinarily exposed to quantitative and qualitative methods at undergraduate level, and we are often reluctant (initially at least) to engage with sociological, conceptual or standpoint accounts. Whilst many of these concerns are understandable given the heavy emphasis on conventionalism at undergraduate level (though this is being ameliorated in recent years), it seems clear that these gaps extend to even the most fundamental of methodologies for lawyers – doctrinal legal method. Consider, for example, the following attempts at articulating this methodology:

– A doctrinal methodology will be applied to evaluate the…rules…

– The project will involve doctrinal legal analysis. Various provisions of the Constitution…will be examined…Furthermore, case law... will be considered.

– This project will…examine the legislation from a legal doctrinal point of view, consisting of an examination of the statutory provisions involved.

---

* Professor Shane Kilcommins is Head of the School of Law, University of Limerick.

– Standard legal methods will be used to analyse and synthesise legal sources (case law, legislation, constitutional principles).

Although we can argue over the details of the various representations, they are, to my mind at least, broadly accurate, capturing roughly what most us would outline when we navigate the swampy textual lowlands of legal rules and engage with dense institutional legal practices relating, inter alia, to craft, interpretation, and authority. The principal concern with these statements relates not to their accuracy, but to their depth. Are they sufficient? How will they look to a non-legal observer (who may be an assessor)? Do they appear rigorous? How would they compare with the methodologies offered by postgraduate students in different disciplines?

On the face of it, the explanations look thin, implicitly painting a picture of a method which is simplistic, thickly descriptive, and relatively unskilled, a join-the-dots, 'taxonomic stock-taking'[1] exercise that could be undertaken by any adult with basic knowledge of the English language and some time on his or her hands. And yet, as lawyers, we know this is untrue. We know that law is technocratic, employing rigorous analytical processes, emphasising precision and inductive-deductive logic, but also fidelity to complex institutional practices. If you doubt this, try to remember the first full case you read as a first year law student. Perhaps you too struggled with the dense narrative, the strange presentation, the seemingly endless layers of substantive and procedural rules, the elusive search for the *ratio* and for 'fit' more generally, and with the analysing, distinguishing and synthesising skills demanded of you in interrogating its content.

Those initial struggles allowed you, in time, to pass through a portal – the threshold concept of doctrinal law – enabling you to 'think like a lawyer'. It is the complexity of that learning journey which is not reflected in the statements outlined above. Nor should we expect that it would be captured. For the most part, doctrinal legal methodology is something which is acted upon by us as lawyers but rarely articulated in a systematised way that documents what we do when we seek to accurately posit the law on a particular issue.[2] We all know what doctrinal legal reasoning is (or what it is not), but we rarely examine or reflect upon its overarching principles and throughlines. What follows is a loose attempt to unpack some of the

---

[1] A C Hutchinson, 'Beyond Black-Letterism: Ethics in Law and Legal Education' (1999) 33(3) The International Journal of Legal Education 301, 302.
[2] T Hutchinson and N Duncan, 'Defining and Describing What we Do: Doctrinal Legal Research' (2012) 17 Deakin Law Review 83, 99.

assumptions and commitments that underpin lawyers' efforts at wading through layers of authority, its ordering, and its interpretation.

II – THE PROPERTIES UNDERPINNING A DOCTRINAL LEGAL APPROACH

Doctrinal legal method emphasises coherence and unity. It involves the search for a 'system' of general, logically consistent principles, built up from the study of particular instances. This system is built on empirical and rational foundations. It is loosely *empirical,* in that lawyers work with the raw data of cases and other legal provisions. It is *rationalist,* because it presupposes that the system is logical and internally coherent. As Weinrib suggests, it is an 'immanently intelligible normative practice'.[3] This intelligibility is rooted in logical deductions derived from *a priori* propositions, and the principles of inductive generalisation and analogous reasoning. The basic building block of deductive reasoning is the syllogism in which a conclusion is inferred from two premises.[4] A classic example is as follows:

All men are mortal.

Socrates is a man.

Therefore, Socrates is mortal.

In a legal setting, the deductive syllogism – reasoning from a generalised major premise to a minor factual premise – is dependent upon the establishment of the factual pattern (minor premise) (F), the identification of the relevant legal norm (major premise) (R), and the application of the norm content to the determined fact to produce a particular legitimate conclusion (C). It can be presented as a simple formula: $R + F = C$.[5] The following would look like a syllogistic legal translation of a legal norm relating to vague terms in contract law:[6]

Major Premise: *All contracts with vague terms are void.* (Rule)

Minor Premise: *The contract in the present case has a vague term.* (Fact)

Conclusion: *Therefore, the contract in the present case is void.*

---

[3] E Weinrib, 'The Jurisprudence of Legal Formalism' (1993) 16 Harvard Journal of Law and Public Policy 583.

[4] RJ Aldisert, S Clowney, and JD Peterson, 'Logic for Law Students: How to Think Like a Lawyer' (2007) 69(1) University of Pittsburgh Law Review 1, 3.

[5] R Posner, 'Legal Formalism, Legal Realism, and the Interpretation of Statutes and the Constitution' (1986) 37 Case Western Reserve Law Review 179, 182.

[6] N MacCormick, *Legal Reasoning and Legal Theory* (Clarendon Press 1997) 19-23.

Analogical reasoning attempts to show that the facts of a particular case (F) are substantially similar to those in the binding precedential case (R) and should therefore have a similar outcome (C). Inductive legal logic, in contrast, involves reasoning from the particular to the general to produce a normative assertion. By observing examples of a number of particular instances, a general rule is posited. The more instances produced, the safer it is to rely upon the accuracy of the general rule. It would translate as follows:

> **Premise One:** *A High Court case held that a contract with a vague term was void.*
>
> **Premise Two:** *A second High Court case held that a contract with a vague term was void.*
>
> **Premise Three:** *A third high court case held that a contract with a vague term was void.*
>
> **Conclusion:** *Therefore, all contracts with vague terms are void.*

The important thing about deductive, inductive and analogous reasoning is that the validity of the argument depends purely on logical form. Provided the premises are correct and accurate – taking care to avoid flawed syllogisms or the fallacy of 'hasty generalisations' – and any analogies are relevant, the conclusion will be valid. Of course, in addition to its rationalist morphology, the practices inherent in doctrinal legal reasoning are also *argumentative*, in that they encourage argument about the premises, the analogies, and the extent to which they apply or fit.[7]

Doctrinal legal reasoning also emphasises law's insulated, 'internal point of view'.[8] The coherence of the discipline 'points not outward to a transcendent ideal, but inward to the harmonious interrelationship among the constituents of the structure of justification'.[9] Legal reasoning is autonomous, and there is no need for recourse to non-legal reasons or justifications. Questions and solutions are founded upon distinctly legal materials, demarcated from competing normative claims to truth. In this sense, doctrinal law employs an epistemologically *internal way of knowing*.[10] We 'know' therefore that justifications based on a statutory provision or a valid precedent, for example, are legal reasons that form part of the 'inner logic of law', whilst appeal to

---

[7] R Dworkin, *Law's Empire* (Reprint, Hart Publishing 1998) 130.
[8] G Samuel, *Epistemology and Method in Law* (Ashgate 2003).
[9] Weinrib (n 3) 593.
[10] N Luhmann, *Law as a Social System* (Oxford University Press 2004); Gunther Teubner, *Law as an Autopoietic System* (Basil Blackwell 1992).

the authority of Joyce's *Ulysses* is outside of the law, and cannot form part of its conceptual coherence.

In relying on it as a method for answering a research question, one implicitly takes seriously the *institutions*[11] and concepts through which law expresses its structural coherence. Doctrinal legal method is, for example, premised on valid sources of law which serve to limit the scope of any legal question and its determination; in assessing conduct, legal functionaries cannot stray beyond these ontological sources, the ways in which they are coordinated to each other, and their hierarchical arrangement. This relates not only to law application but also to law creation. This institutionalisation is wholly routinised, given its systematic acceptance by agencies such as courts, legislatures, police, regulatory officers, prosecutors, citizens and so on.[12] The properties of law – particularly the scheme of authority it invokes – demand that it is taken seriously. As MacCormick notes:[13]

> [A]ll persons have reason to take seriously the requirements that law imposes. They have reason to do so whether or not they are personally inclined to endorse the law's requirements as morally desirable or morally obligatory, and whether or not willing to pursue personal preferences where these diverge from what the law requires. There are powerful reasons for conformity, and these can have a daunting reality even for someone who, on good grounds, dissents for fundamental reasons from the state's rules requiring certain conduct.

In relying upon doctrinal legal reasoning as a methodology, one accepts or assumes that law is *normative*, in that it guides and provides reasons for action. It is, in this sense, a unified normative order not premised on systems of predictions, negotiations, incentives, or beliefs.[14] It provides the 'bad man', for example, with an anti-authoritarian, *ex ante* conception of the legal system, permitting him to conduct himself according to knowable rules. It also is a benchmark for the 'good citizen' who seeks to act in good faith by conducting his or her activity in line with a prescribed order.

It is also very *comprehensive* in that it can claim authority to engage in all kinds of regulation: legal systems 'either contain norms which regulate

---

[11] J Raz, *Practical Reasons and Norms* (Reprint, Oxford University Press 1999) 132-148.
[12] N MacCormick, *Institutions of Law: An Essay in Legal Theory* (Oxford University Press 2007) 12-13.
[13] ibid 53.
[14] J Gardner, *Law as a Leap of Faith* (Oxford University Press 2012) 179.

[behaviour] or norm conferring powers to enact norms which if enacted would regulate it'.[15] It is also strongly *authoritative*. It is a system 'which claims supreme authority to interfere with any kind of activity'.[16] Out of the total complexity of a particular social problem, doctrinal legal method helps to distil what is relevant – as least what is relevant according to a legal lens – and make authoritative (and final) declarationns in respect of that problem.[17]

Further, doctrinal legal reasoning is *limiting*, in that it sets boundaries to the extent to which legal functionaries can intervene, and to what can be achieved. All citizens and officials have to operate within 'the rich but nevertheless insulated world of precedents and statutes."[18] It is premised on a Rule of Law framework, which restrains the arbitrary or coercive exercise of executive authority, where a strong state must have respect for and indeed yield to its constraints.[19] Anything not the subject of rules cannot be determined, but may be in the future, and anything subject to rules must operate in ways that are compatible with them.

Doctrinal legal methodology is largely *conservative* ('formal') in that it has a strongly backward-looking orientation; it respects legal institutions, and demands fidelity to existing rules. It is also *innovative* ('grand'), however, given its evaluative aspects and its potential for alteration through rules of change.[20] Dworkin neatly captures this conservative-innovative dynamic: 'propositions of law are not merely descriptive of legal history, in a straight forward way, nor are they simply evaluative in some way divorced from history. They are interpretive of legal history, which combines elements of both description and evaluation but is different from both'.[21]

In relying upon this method to answer a research question, one generally accepts the rationality of the subject area, its location within an institutional context, its internal epistemology, its hierarchical and coordinated features, its encompassing and authoritative embrace, and its pragmatic utility. This acceptance helps to validate its claims to truth. Anyone relying on it is also working on relatively safe ground given that 'the life of the law consists to a

---

[15] Raz (n 11) 51.
[16] ibid 154.
[17] J Bell, 'Legal Research and the Distinctiveness of Comparative Law' in Mark Van Hoecke (ed), *Methodologies of Legal Research* (Hart Publishing 2011) 164.
[18] G Quinn, *Justice and Legal Theory in Ireland* (Oak Tree Press 1995) 6.
[19] C Becarria, *On Crimes and Punishment* (Reprint, Cambridge University Press 1995).
[20] HLA Hart, *The Concept of Law* (Oxford University Press 1961) 63.
[21] R Dworkin, *A Matter of Principle* (Harvard University Press 1985) 147.

very large extent in the guidance both of officials and private individuals by determinate rules which, unlike the application of variable standards, do not require from them a fresh judgment from case to case'.[22]

III – So What Is Good About Such A Methodology?

Despite the pejorative undertones associated with 'black-letterism', it has much to commend it. To begin with, it emphasises the coherence of law's institutional configuration. In specifying the criteria of legal validity and the delegated unity of the legal order, it facilitates conceptual coherency and consistency, giving integrity to law and the decision-making process. What if there were no rules and no reasoning process?[23] There is an important truth in it, in that it reflects what lawyers and legal functionaries actually do. The derivation of legal principles generally occurs through a process of continuous testing, using hypothetical fact patterns or contrasting examples to clarify the scope of rules and reasoning being distilled. Deductive reasoning along the model of syllogism is also a characteristic feature of 'most well-done judicial opinions – that is, the conclusion can be reconstructed as following deductively from a statement of the applicable rule of law and the statement of the facts'.[24] Simplistic as it is, the formula R + F = C is employed in a good many instances in legal reasoning. Its self-referential internal process itself helps to confirm its coherence, to give it a structure of truth.

As a mode of reasoning, it has a practical, pragmatic value; it is not undertaken for its own sake. In a world dominated by association and associative interaction, we need rules – to ensure compliance, to maintain order, and to regulate behaviour along some agreed lines. The uncertainty and insecurity of a more arbitrary or ad hominem decision-making process not linked to rules or stable institutional practices would, in contrast, seem unimaginable. Moreover, the rules themselves, and their application, work most of the time. They are therefore decidedly useful, permitting authoritative resolution of disputes and problem cases.[25] Courts and legislatures also continue to possess the possibility of being the 'last authoritative voice' on all attempts at dispute resolution or settlement (which can provide a practical rebuff to other social,

---

[22] Hart (n 20) 132.
[23] L Fuller, *The Morality of Law* (Yale University Press 1964) 46-91; J Habermas, *Between Facts and Norms* (Reprint, Polity Press 2008) 143.
[24] B Leiter, 'Legal Formalism and Legal Realism: What is the Issue?' (2010) 16 Legal Theory 111.
[25] K Llewellyn and A Adamson Hoebel, *The Cheyenne Way* (University of Oklahoma Press 1983) 290-309.

political or moral methodological claims), and the law continues to regulate the legitimate monopolisation of coercion and violence within states.[26]

The 'withering away' of law and legal reasoning has not occurred and is unlikely to do so given the stakes at play, embedded interests, and the ontological insecurity that it would generate. We continue to argue and seek reform from within the existing paradigm of law and its 'heavy instruments'. Nor have other alternatives to dispute resolution, truth finding, prediction and control proven more acceptable. Reducing social complexity in this way does, for example, 'compensate for the cognitive indeterminacy, motivational insecurity, and limiting coordinating power of moral norms'.[27]

It is also highly technocratic and skilled. Consider, for example, whether a particular fact pattern constitutes harassment. This will involve framing the facts to fit with the institutional requirements of law; distinguishing between civil and criminal considerations; engaging with multiple substantive and procedural legal instruments; and employing skills which emphasise analysis and synthesis, the process of argumentation, the power of reasoning, and the importance of wording. The public nature of this technocracy also facilitates transparency, providing a benchmark for critique, and the possibility of change.

IV – What Are The Dangers?

Employing doctrinal legal methodology to answer a research question also raises the possibility of particular types of criticism. Though you may be very confident that your justifications are nailed on, you should at least be aware of the types of arguments that can be made against its use. The broadest and perhaps most obvious is a moral one – is it sufficient and morally just that a legal finding is valid simply because it follows a deductive logical form? What about the morality of the decision and its contribution to human flourishing? Whether law should be severed from morality, or can be, are difficult questions that have troubled lawyers for a long time. This is not the place to rehash previous jurisprudential attempts or to offer new solutions. Nevertheless, it seems reasonable to suggest that a doctrinal view of law as a means of social regulation provides, at best, an incomplete picture.

Moreover, some would argue that the development of a doctrinal approach can very much be seen as part of the project of modernity whose primary

---

[26] Raz (n 11) 158; Habermas (n 23) 326.
[27] Habermas (n 23) 326.

function was to rid the western world of local, contingent, irrational, and non-objective phenomena.[28] The value of cloaking legal method in a deductive garb are obvious; it will appear objective, value free, rational and fair – reinforcing law's claim to truth. This search for certainty in law has been questioned, some explaining it in psychological terms as nothing more than a childlike need for determinacy.[29] Students, upon entering law school, for example, are told to abandon emotion and empathy - childish and naive characteristics that are out of place for anyone wanting 'to think like a lawyer'. Teachers of law encourage students 'to put away childish things'.[30] The coherency of law thus comes to serve the controlling force occupied by a father for a child.[31] Totalising thought tendencies of this kind should make us suspicious, and at least open to the possibility that situational and subjective experiences may be marginalised by the unitary impulses of such foundational claims.[32]

Many commentators would argue that legal decision-making does not always have an intrinsic order. They 'are not the products of logical parthenogenesis born of pre-existing legal principles but are social events with social causes and consequences'.[33] Law is a social endeavour. This limits the extent to which certainty can be achieved. Because it is social, legal propositions are not verifiable in the same way that empirical propositions are (i.e. the boiling point of water). How, for example, can we be sure that different judges would arrive at the same deductions in any give case? How, particularly in times of rapid social and industrial change, can we guarantee that for every legal dispute there is a fixed antecedent rule already in place which will permit simple, formal syllogising?[34] It will also be possible to confine a particular ruling to its particular facts so as to avoid having to follow it.

The interpretation of legal rules is therefore, in part, based on the predispositions of decision-makers who are not asocial, apolitical or amoral automata. Indeed some commentators would argue that the 'correct legal solution' is usually nothing more than the 'correct ethical and political

---

[28] Z Bauman, *Intimations of Postmodernity* (Routledge 1992) 12.

[29] J Frank, *Law and the Modern Mind* (Princeton University Press 1949) 19.

[30] D Kennedy, *Legal Education and the Reproduction of Hierarchy: A Polemic Against the System* (Afar 1983) 13.

[31] Frank (n 29) 19.

[32] E Spain, *The Role of Emotions in Criminal Law Defences; Duress, Necessity and Lesser Evils* (Cambridge University Press 2011).

[33] F Cohen, 'Transcendental Nonsense and the Functional Approach' (1935) XXXV (6) Columbia Law Review 809, 847.

[34] J Dewey, 'Logical Method and Law' (1924) 10 Cornell Law Quarterly 17, 26.

solution' at a particular point in time.[35] Thus doctrinal legal rationality is a process which is open to manipulation:[36] 'every decision is a choice between different rules which logically fit all past decisions but logically dictate conflicting results in the instance case'.[37] Furthermore, whilst appeal courts mostly concern themselves with the niceties of legal particulars (substantive and procedural rules), trial courts have to contend themselves with facts, and facts by their very nature are elusive. They do not comprise the hard, objective, data of science.[38] Even the traditional sciences rely on particular ways of knowing and organising events and data that are not fixed and absolute,[39] but are influenced by power relations, shared beliefs, and subjective interpretations of collecting and interpreting data.

Law is also based on language — not algebraic concepts — which has by its very nature an 'open texture' that often gives rise to a number of legitimate interpretive choices. Language is not (always) a transparent, objective medium. It is enmeshed in subjective reference points (signifiers) for the both the listener and the speaker[40] that militate against the objectivity of interpretation. There will often be a choice in the rules, principles or standards to apply (and the enforceability of same), or exceptions to invoke, thereby permitting arguments which purportedly follow the logic of legal reasoning to lead in different directions with different outcomes. As Kelman notes: 'In every dispute about the appropriate resolution of a legal controversy, rule like solutions, standard based solutions, and intermediate positions will uncomfortably co-exist, none fully dominating either day to day practice or *a fortiori* justificatory rhetoric'.[41] Black-letterism, therefore, relies on a form of essentialism, when it posits the view that there are essential meanings to words and laws that can be objectively understood through a process of adjudicative neutrality, rather than meanings having to be chosen through a process of interpretive construction.

Moreover, fidelity to the *a priori* principles of the past in some instances will be unsuitable in a contemporary context having regard to changes in cultural, social, political, economic and moral contexts.[42] In this sense, legal rules are

---

[35] Kennedy (n 30) 20.
[36] K Llewellyn, *The Bramble Bush: On Our Law and Its Study* (Oceana 1960) 72-73.
[37] F Cohen, 'The Ethical Basis of Legal Criticism' (1931) 41 Yale Law Journal 201, 215.
[38] J Frank, 'A Plea for Lawyer Schools' (1947) 56(8) Yale Law Journal 1303, 1307.
[39] T Kuhn, *The Structure of Scientific Revolutions* (2nd edn, University of Chicago Press 1970); M Foucault, 'Truth and Power' in P Rainbow (ed), *The Foucault Reader* (Penguin Books 1991).
[40] D Patterson, *Law and Truth* (Oxford University Press 1996) 151-180.
[41] M Kelman, *A Guide to Critical Legal Studies* (Harvard University Press 1987) 17.
[42] R Pound, 'Mechanical Jurisprudence?' (1908) 8 Columbia Law Review 605.

not hermetically sealed from broader considerations.[43] Law is therefore too autopoietic in not giving sufficient thought to context. Too much emphasis on black-letterism and in tracing the celestial lines of development of various legal rules can also divert attention away from engaging in broader discursive analysis of the working of rules, the ideological, economic and socio-political currents running through them, the dynamics of how they change, and the policy and contextual implications for choosing one rule over another. It has also been argued that doctrinal legal reasoning is presentist, seeking to rely on the past to explain the present. This approach 'reassures us (lawyers) that what we do now flows continuously out of our past, out of precedents, traditions, fidelity to statutory and constitutional texts and meanings'.[44] If the lawyer is a monist and a presentist, then the historian is a pluralist (looking for contested meanings), and a contextualist (seeking to understand the past in terms of the past).[45]

Doctrinal legal reasoning can also help inculcate a set of attitudes towards the legal system in society, exhorting in particular its legitimacy on the basis of its neutral nature,[46] whilst ignoring the underlying structural inequalities of power which are imbricated in the cross-currents of society. The ideology of objectivity, egalitarianism and the strict application of rules can mask and mystify law's partiality, particularly its capacity to preserve and maintain the status quo for those in power. Hiding behind the 'false consciousness' of black-letterism are the variety of hierarchical interests that it serves. As Kennedy suggests, 'bias arises because law school teaching makes the choice of hierarchy and domination, which is implicit in the adoption of the rules of property, contract, and tort, look as though it flows from and is required by legal reasoning rather than being a matter of politics and economics'.[47] It also has implications for legal practice, particularly the notion that what lawyers actually do is apolitical and independent, merely following the inner technical logic of the law. This might be reassuring, but it is a denial of the political and social realities of legal practice:

> [B]lack-letterism works as a convenient mode of denial. It enables legal academics and lawyers to engage in what is a highly political and

---

[43] G Edward White, 'From Sociological Jurisprudence to Realism: Jurisprudence and Social Change in Early Twentieth Century America' (1972) 58 Virginia Law Review 999, 1004.
[44] R Gordon, 'Foreword: The Arrival of Critical Historicism' (1997) 49 Stanford Law Review 1023.
[45] ibid.
[46] M Horowitz, *The Transformation of American Law, 1780-1860* (Oxford University Press 1992) 266. See also, W Lapaina, 'Langdell Laughs' (1999) 17(1) Law and History Review 141, 143.
[47] D Kennedy, 'Legal Education as Training for Hierarchy' in D Kairys (ed), *The Politics of Law* (Pantheon Books 1990) 45.

contested arena of social life — namely, law — and to pretend that they are doing so in a largely non-political way. The main advantage of this is that they can go about their daily routines without assuming any political or personal responsibility for what happens in the legal process. However, the insistence that lawyering is a neutral exercise that does not implicate lawyers in any political process or demand from scholars a commitment to any particular ideology is as weak as it is woeful. Such an image is a profoundly conservative and crude understanding of what it is to engage in the business of courts, legislatures and the like.[48]

Feminists would argue, for example, that the theory and practice of law (including doctrinal legal reasoning) is not neutral but has been shaped too much by male-orientated values and concerns (it 'speaks to men' by making 'maleness' the norm for the regulation of human relations). For them, the discourse of law has always been a male discourse that excludes the voice of women.[49] In particular, they seek to highlight the patriarchal ideas that pervade the law (often through 'standpoint epistemology'), and to raise the 'woman question' by examining the variety of different ways in which the law fails to take account of the values of women and how it might disadvantage them.[50] Law, therefore, as a mode of social regulation, may be 'deeply antithetical to the myriad concerns and interests of women'.[51] But black-letterism does not wish to engage in these kinds of debates or controversies about the rules. Rather it wishes to focus exclusively on the rules, assuming that they flow from a sterile, closed, logical system that is neutral and objective. This dogmatism can close us off from the exclusionary values and stereotypes that often underpin rules and can serve to reproduce hierarchies of power.[52]

V – Conclusion

A doctrinal legal approach is an extremely valid, purposeful methodology, which carries both a scholarly and practical currency. It has a long and established history. Its epistemic outlook emphasises the logic of law and the value of reasoning; the normative character of rules; institutional coherency; technocracy; internalism and self-referential validation; the limiting tendencies associated with rule determinism; the 'last authoritative voice'

---

[48] Hutchinson (n 1) 307-08.
[49] S Mullally, 'Feminist Jurisprudence' in Tim Murphy (ed), *Western Jurisprudence* (Thomson Round Hall 2004) 351-85.
[50] S Leahy, 'Bad Laws or Bad Attitudes? Assessing the Impact of Societal Attitudes upon the Conviction Rates for Rape in Ireland' (2014) 14(1) Irish Journal of Applied Social Studies 18.
[51] C Smart, *Feminism and the Power of Law* (Routledge 1989) 164.
[52] M Davies, *Asking the Law Question* (Sweet and Maxwell 1994) 120.

positioning of law; its extensive potential range; legal craft; and the importance of being part of 'an interpretive community'. You can feel very confident in using it to address a legal research question.

In employing it, however, it is important to be aware that its assumptions, commitments, and foundational claims can be challenged. Increasingly law is being viewed through a variety of lenses: history, hermeneutics, sociology, anthropology, political theory, moral philosophy, economics, feminisms, and so on. These are all legitimate standpoints and avenues of enquiry which challenge the perception of law as a unitary and neutral expression of social rules. Legal research in Ireland is altering to reflect more catholic, 'house of intellect', types of enquiry. This trend increasingly incorporates the use of new methods (for example, from history, philosophy, jurisprudence, sociology, English literature, psychology, and quantitative and qualitative methods); greater interdisciplinarity (law and history, law and economics, law and literature, law and sociology, law and politics); a more open embrace of theory (feminisms, critical race theory, etc.); an increased willingness to adopt standpoint perspectives (victims, women, children, persons with a disability, LGBT etc.); and the incorporation of more policy-based analyses into legal curricula. All of these developments offer lawyers more and more opportunities for critical engagement with their subject matters. Thus, whilst we continue to frame subjects in terms of the relevant legal rules (as we must), this momentum opens up possibilities for new types of dialogue. 'Thinking like a lawyer' in the future may mean more than just being skilled at rule handling.

CHAPTER 2

Doctrinal Analysis: The Real 'Law in Action'

Rónán KENNEDY*

INTRODUCTION

Black-letter or doctrinal analysis is the heart of traditional legal research and method. At first glance, it seems to simply involve reading texts and applying rules, and is often misunderstood by those without deep familiarity with it as largely a matter of rote learning and black-and-white outcomes. Although it is often taken for granted or side-lined in favour of recent developments towards more socially-situated approaches to research, it remains an essential tool for the proper conduct of research into the law and for the comprehensive critique of legal regimes and systems.

Despite its seeming simplicity, doctrinal analysis is complex, multi-layered, and distinctive. Although it is difficult to articulate the thought-processes involved, and these are often not explicitly taught or considered in detail in the classroom, it involves a particular perspective on the hermeneutical analysis of texts and a terminology all of its own. It can be criticized as conservative, exclusionary, and relying on obvious (but rarely challenged) myths about the perfectibility of the common law. Nonetheless, as the working method of the judiciary and the core of the traditional legal curriculum, it merits careful consideration and exposition.

This chapter explores the history of doctrinal analysis, recent challenges to its primacy, and how to go about it. It discusses what makes good doctrinal research, how to avoid its shortcomings, and considers how to frame a research question amenable to this type of analysis. It concludes by highlighting recent examples of doctrinal research projects that are good starting points for learning more about this still-important working method.

---

* School of Law, National University of Ireland Galway.

I – THE CONTINUING IMPORTANCE OF DOCTRINAL ANALYSIS

The legal academy is going through a transition from a focus on what is alternatively called 'traditional', 'black letter', or 'doctrinal' analysis[1] to more socially situated, cross-disciplinary, and innovative methods of thinking about, and critiquing, the law. However, this 'social turn' in legal research is by no means easy, uncontested, or completely accepted. In particular, it is a change that is reflected somewhat unevenly in the mainstream legal curriculum, particularly for undergraduates, and is not well understood or accepted by legal practitioners or the judiciary. This chapter examines this uneven transition, sketching its history and defending the continuing importance of doctrinal analysis as a thought process that is specific to the discipline of law. It remains an essential skill to anyone who wishes to work with the law at an intimate level, and demands considerably more rigour and effort than its critics may perceive or its advocates often apply. Although black letter analysis is confusing, flawed, and difficult to explain, it remains at the heart of traditional legal research and method, and should be properly understood and applied in the contexts where it is important, rather than discarded or relegated to a secondary role in legal research and teaching.

Defining Doctrinal Analysis

Doctrinal analysis is complex, multi-layered, and distinctive. It is 'the research process used to identify, analyse and synthesise the content of the law',[2] which Salter and Mason say is

> ... best defined ... as a research methodology that concentrates on seeking to provide a detailed and highly technical commentary upon, and systematic exposition of, the content of legal doctrine. This doctrine is interpreted as if it is a separate, independent and coherent 'system of rules'. The priority is to gather, organise and describe legal rules, and offer commentary upon the emergence and significance of the authoritative legal sources that contain these rules, especially cases.[3]

---

[1] See M Salter and J Mason, *Writing Law Dissertations: An Introduction and Guide to the Conduct of Legal Research* (Pearson Education 2007) 48, for a discussion of the differences between these terms.

[2] T Hutchinson, 'Doctrinal Research: Researching the Jury' in D Watkins and M Burton (eds), *Research Methods in Law* (Routledge 2013) 9.

[3] Salter and Mason (n 1) 49.

According to Van Hoecke,

> [l]egal scholars collect empirical data (statutes, cases, etc.), word hypotheses on their meaning and scope, which they test, using the classic canons of interpretation. In a next stage, they build theories ..., which they test and from which they derive new hypotheses ... Described in this way, doctrinal legal scholarship fits perfectly with the methodology of other disciplines.[4]

Drawing on research from the United States of America,[5] Canada,[6] and Australia,[7] Hutchinson and Duncan highlight how doctrinal research is concerned with organising, systematising, and making coherent the law that emerges from judicial decisions, acknowledging that this can be unsettled and contested but seeking to define what is clear. Far from simple, it requires rigour, creativity, and nuance. It is taught and applied at a variety of levels of complexity, from the relatively straightforward problem-based approach in which undergraduate law students are instructed; to the more explicitly self-justifying writing of the judge; to the high-level synthesis performed by the legal academic.[8] The aim should be to provide 'a coherent, detailed, and nuanced picture of what the law is in any given area'.[9]

Its perspective is internal — seeing the law as autonomous, self-legitimising, and striving towards consistency — and using as its raw materials the work product of the legal system itself: constitutional documents, primary and secondary legislation, recorded court judgments. From these, it seeks to construct and test models of legal reasoning, although what external elements (such as social norms, policy goals, and non-legal perspectives) are included

---

[4] M Van Hoecke, 'Legal Doctrine: Which Method(s) for What Kind of Discipline?' in Mark Van Hoecke (ed), *Methodologies of Legal Research: Which Kind of Method for What Kind of Discipline?* (Bloomsbury 2011) 11.

[5] M Minow, 'Archetypal Legal Scholarship: A Field Guide' (2013) 63 Journal of Legal Education 65.

[6] HW Arthurs, *Law and Learning: Report to the Social Sciences and Humanities Research Council of Canada by the Consultative Group on Research and Education in Law* (Social Sciences and Humanities Research Council of Canada 1983).

[7] Council of Australian Law Deans, 'CALD Statement on the Nature of Legal Research' (October 2005).

[8] T Hutchinson and N Duncan, 'Defining and Describing What We Do: Doctrinal Legal Research' (2012) 17 Deakin Law Review 83, 101–07. See also. D W Vick, 'Interdisciplinarity and the Discipline of Law' (2004) 31 Journal of Law and Society 163, 179.

[9] P J Stancil, 'The Legal Academy as Dinner Party: A (Short) Manifesto on the Necessity of Inter-Interdisciplinary Legal Scholarship' (2011) University of Illinois Law Review 1577, 1584.

in these models is something that changes with time and place.[10] While such a perspective might seem to be at odds with the more contextualised view of law put forward by socio-legal scholars, it ironically finds support in some strands within Critical Legal Studies and Systems Theory.[11]

The academic study of the law in Ireland shares its historical roots, as with much else of its legal traditions, with England.[12] University law schools were initially staffed by, and oriented towards, legal practitioners.[13] It is therefore no surprise that the working methods of these practitioners — the doctrinal approach to law – dominated the research agenda of the early law schools.[14]

This black letter approach was once animated by ideals of objectivity — that legal scholars 'were engaged in the process of discovering true legal principles that stood above and beyond the ordinary sphere of law, or that they were tracing the implications of principles that had been discovered'.[15] This was a formalist perspective, perhaps linked to the rise of liberalism and the free market,[16] which is now largely discarded.

This change perhaps has its roots in the importation of the scientific method (with its emphasis on testable hypotheses and empirical proofs) into the legal academy by the slow and unsteady development of 'law and economics' as a distinct approach, a challenge to traditional legal method which had ramifications beyond the limited initial scope of the field.[17] It can also trace its history back to the 'legal realists' of the 1930s, who explored the extent to which social factors influence and alter what formalist legal theory claimed was a mechanical process, and the 'critical legal studies' movement which came after and had more of a reformist and progressive political and ideological perspective. This loose movement began to use social science

---

[10] C McCrudden, 'Legal Research and the Social Sciences' (2006) 122 Law Quarterly Review 632, 633–35.

[11] ibid 643.

[12] For a historical sketch of the early days of UCD Law School, see WN Osborough, 'The Law School's Early Professoriate' (2011) 46 Irish Jurist (ns) 1, and for a similar sketch of UCG Law's beginnings, see Liam O'Malley, 'Law' in T Foley (ed), *From Queen's College to National University: Essays on the Academic History of QCG/UCG/NUI, Galway* (Four Courts Press 1999).

[13] Vick (n 8) 175.

[14] ibid 177.

[15] E L Rubin, 'The Practice and Discourse of Legal Scholarship' (1988) Michigan Law Review 1835, 1855.

[16] Salter and Mason (n 1) 51.

[17] T S Ulen, 'The Impending Train Wreck in Current Legal Education: How We Might Teach Law as the Scientific Study of Social Governance' (2009) 6 University of St Thomas Law Journal 302, 305–06.

methods as a way of highlighting and removing what they claimed were systematic barriers preventing the disadvantaged from gaining access to legal processes which could vindicate constitutional and legislative guarantees of equality.[18]

Although these perspectives are often misunderstood as taking the view that there is little or no distinction between law and politics, the realists were not, in fact, so dismissive of traditional legal process and reasoning, holding that

> … the rule-bound aspect of judging can function reliably notwithstanding the challenges presented by the skepticism-inducing side, although this is an achievement that must be earned, is never perfectly achieved, and is never guaranteed.[19]

Nonetheless, this negative view of traditional legal scholarship has led to the growth and development of socio-legal approaches to law.[20] Cownie, in her study of the culture of the legal academy in England, concludes that 'pure doctrinal research no longer dominates the legal academy in the way that it used to.'[21] While the Irish legal academy was quite conservative,[22] a similar development seems to have occurred in Ireland,[23] although this has not yet been as clearly documented (or strongly argued) as in other common law jurisdictions, and is perhaps less extensive and important in the work of academics, who are not subject to the funding imperatives that drive much of the research agenda in the United Kingdom.

Done properly, doctrinal legal research can be demanding, useful, and satisfying work, affording the researcher an opportunity to thoroughly map areas of the law that may not have been previously properly explored without leaving the comfort of one's desk (or perhaps seat in the library). It is,

---

[18] J Goldring, 'Babies and Bathwater: Tradition or Progress in Legal Scholarship and Legal Education?' (1987) 17 University of Western Australia Law Review 216, 225. See also, Debra Livingston, 'Round and Round the Bramble Bush: From Legal Realism to Critical Legal Scholarship' (1982) 95 Harvard Law Review 1669, and Brian Z Tamanaha, 'Understanding Legal Realism' (2008) 87 Texas Law Review 731.

[19] Tamanaha (n 18) 732.

[20] W Twining, *Blackstone's Tower: The English Law School* (Stevens & Sons-Sweet & Maxwell 1994) 141–44.

[21] F Cownie, *Legal Academics: Culture and Identities* (Hart Publishing 2004) 58.

[22] T Mohr and J Schweppe, 'Irish Scholarship, Irish Law and the Irish Association of Law Teachers' in Thomas Mohr and Jennifer Schweppe (eds), *30 Years of Legal Scholarship* (Thomson Round Hall 2011) 6–7.

[23] R Byrne, 'Four Thoughts on Legal Writing and Law Reform' in Thomas Mohr and Jennifer Schweppe (eds), *30 Years of Legal Scholarship* (Thomson Reuters 2012) 62.

however, much more than simple 'declaratory' legal research.[24] The doctrinal researcher is not engaged in a simplistic process of discovering basic, incontestable facts, in the fashion of the (now highly contested) stereotype of the disinterested, objective, and plodding scientist who toils in a laboratory in search of natural principles and universal laws. This view of doctrinal research is widespread, particularly amongst those with little training or experience in it. As Becher and Trowler point out, '[Academic lawyers'] scholarly activities are thought to be unexciting and uncreative, comprising of a series of intellectual puzzles scattered among large "areas of description".[25] However, the reality is that the doctrinal legal researcher is an individual, creative force:

> The writer of legal doctrinal criticism is not unrelated to the sociologist, theologian, or philosopher – much of their work is about one's worldview and what, therefore, is desirable societal regulation. The research work is relatively straightforward. The reflection process is the major part of the work and is particularly conducive to original and lateral thought.[26]

The individual is therefore very important in the process of doctrinal research, and, whether or not the researcher is aware of it, her perspective on the world will influence every aspect of her research, not least her choice of method. The purpose of this chapter is to enable the self-aware, reflective researcher to properly understand the advantages and short-comings of this particular research method, to practice it properly, and to think carefully about how and when to engage in it.

Taking Doctrinal Analysis Seriously

Doctrinal analysis is sometimes seen as on the way out — 'now entering its final death throes'[27] according to Bradney — but Cownie's study of English academics (despite her claim that '[w]e are all socio-legal now')[28] shows that it has not yet completely disappeared and is seen by many who engage in socio-legal studies as an essential basis for more 'law in context' or empirical explorations of the law.[29] Indeed, Bradney acknowledges its continued

---

[24] M Pendleton, 'Non-Empirical Discovery in Legal Scholarship–Choosing, Researching and Writing a Traditional Scholarly Article' (2007) Research Methods for Law 159, 162.
[25] T Becher and P Trowler, *Academic Tribes and Territories: Intellectual Inquiry and the Cultures of Disciplines* (Open University Press 1989) 30.
[26] Pendleton (n 24) 163.
[27] A Bradney, 'Law as a Parasitic Discipline' (1998) 25 Journal of Law and Society 71.
[28] F Cownie, 'Researching (Socio) Legal Academics' (2004) 42 Socio-Legal Newsletter 1.
[29] Cownie (n 21) 54–55.

existence,[30] despite circumscribing its utility, and while Twining is sceptical about the need for a 'core' to legal studies,[31] he accepts that rules can be 'necessary and central to the study of law'.[32] As the working method of the judiciary and the core of the traditional legal curriculum,[33] it merits careful consideration and exposition, as 'properly understood and limited, doctrinal analysis is among the very best tools we have for operationalizing our philosophical judgments about what law should be.'[34]

Doctrinal analysis is not based in strong or elaborate theoretical frameworks and is sometimes criticised as under-theorised.[35] It tends to focus on the institutions with authority in the 'machine' of governance.[36] It is positivist in that it relies only on what is demonstrably and clearly known from definitive sources. This leaves significant gaps in our understanding of the legal order, and how it actually functions in practice,[37] but this does not mean that a realist, fact-finding approach will provide an alternative full picture.[38]

Challenges to Doctrinal Analysis

In response to these difficulties, legal scholars have developed a number of different ways of approaching research in law. These are often divided into 'black letter' or 'doctrinal' approaches (which focus on positive laws as a subject of study and attempt to construct a coherent narrative, or recommendations for reform in the interests of coherency, from legislation and case law) and 'law in context' approaches (which move the focus away from law and towards the broader social and political context, within which law may be both the cause and solution to a problem). A realisation that positive law is only one part of the overall story of law reform and development has given rise to an increased focus on interdisciplinary approaches to law,

---

[30] Bradney (n 27) 71.
[31] Twining (n 20) 153.
[32] ibid 176.
[33] According to Jones, it is 'the heart of English law'. Irish law, for all that it has begun to diverge from its Anglo-Saxon origins since 1922, is not yet that different. Gareth Jones, "'Traditional' Legal Scholarship: A Personal View' in PBH Birks (ed), *Pressing Problems in the Law, Vol 2* (Oxford University Press 1996) 11.
[34] Stancil (n 9) 1584.
[35] Goldring (n 18) 221.
[36] P Allott, 'Parliamentary Sovereignty — from Austin to Hart' (1990) 49 The Cambridge Law Journal 377, 380.
[37] Goldring (n 18) 224.
[38] E A Peters, 'Reality and the Language of the Law' (1980) 90 Yale Law Journal 1193, 1194.

which can encompass socio-legal studies, feminist legal studies, critical legal studies and new approaches to international law.[39]

According to Vick, there can be tensions between these points of view, rooted in 'the challenges interdisciplinary legal research pose to widely-accepted notions about the purposes of legal scholarship, the relationship between academic lawyers and the legal profession, and the collective identity of the legal discipline itself.'[40] According to Banakar and Travers, mono-disciplinarians see interdisciplinary work as a threat to their status and prefer to dismiss it.[41] Despite these challenges to doctrinal research,[42] it remains a significant element of legal scholarship.[43]

Advantages and Disadvantages of Doctrinal Legal Research

It is true that '[a]t times doctrinal researchers do no more than "work the rules" in isolation from practice or the theory underlying the rules, and without due consideration for how the rules might be improved or reformed.'[44] However, this weakness can be avoided. Before delving into how to carry out traditional legal research, it is perhaps best to consider its shortcomings,[45] so that it can be completely described and that the researcher who is considering whether to apply it can either decide it is inappropriate or design their project in a way that overcomes or minimises its limitations.

Salter and Mason provide a comprehensive list of advantages and disadvantages[46] which is too long to set out here. Suffice it to say that doctrinal research can be criticized as conservative, exclusionary, and relying on myths about the perfectibility of the common law. It is important to understand that choosing this particular method is an ideological choice, which (implicitly at least) supports a particular way of looking at, interpreting, and engaging with the world: judgment-based approaches to the law focus (obviously) on cases, thereby supporting the notion of the importance of the law in society.[47] If doctrinal analysis is not really 'research'

---

[39] M McConville and Wing Hong Chui, *Research Methods for Law* (Oxford University Press 2007) 5.
[40] Vick (n 8) 164.
[41] R Banakar and M Travers, 'Law, Sociology and Method' in Reza Banakar and Max Travers (eds), *Theory and Method in Socio-Legal Research* (Hart 2005) 6.
[42] S Bartie, 'The Lingering Core of Legal Scholarship' (2010) 30 Legal Studies 345, 356.
[43] ibid 367.
[44] Hutchinson (n 2) 16.
[45] Rubin (n 15) 1838.
[46] Salter and Mason (n 1) 108–18.
[47] P C Kissam, 'The Ideology of the Case Method/Final Examination Law School' (2001) 70 University of Cincinnati Law Review 137, 150.

but merely 'scholarship', as Dickson claims,[48] then this is a significant weakness, particularly if the resulting gaps in the end result are left unexamined.

It is also important to highlight that choosing non-doctrinal methods does not perfect the research process. Although it has been argued that sociological inquiry is essential for legal research,[49] it is important to avoid becoming an 'intellectual voyeur',[50] and to be aware of the risks of empirical legal research, such as an unclear understanding of the nuances, assumptions, biases and limitations of other disciplines; or an overstatement of the reliability of results obtained by quantitative research.[51] Epstein and King have highlighted how

> 'the current state of empirical legal scholarship is deeply flawed. ... [with] ... many proceeding ... with little awareness of, much less compliance with, the rules of inference that guide empirical research in the social and natural sciences';[52]

and Collier warns that the humanities may yield limited benefits to the analysis and critique of law, claiming that 'because of the radically different structures of authority in law and the humanities, the hope that humanistic theory will be able to provide a source of intellectual authority for law is largely a vain one.'[53]

Lawyers should not therefore be so quick to abandon the distinctive methodology of traditional doctrinal analysis. This does not, of course, mean that it should be practised in a single-minded, unreflective way, but rather as a conscious choice, with an awareness of its failings. While doctrinal research carries with it certain ideological choices, and can be conservative, those values might, in fact, be a good match for the researcher's own views. Alternatively, for those of a more critical persuasion, a rigorous doctrinal analysis can be an effective starting point for highlighting how the basic

---

[48] B Dickson, 'Legal Scholarship in Northern Ireland 1980-2010' in Jennifer Schweppe and Thomas Mohr (eds), *30 Years of Legal Scholarship* (Thomson Reuters 2012) 26.
[49] R Cotterrell, 'Why Must Legal Ideas Be Interpreted Sociologically?' (1998) 25 Journal of Law and Society 171.
[50] B Leiter, 'Intellectual Voyeurism in Legal Scholarship' (2013) 4 Yale Journal of Law and the Humanities 4.
[51] Vick (n 8) 185.
[52] L Epstein and Gary King, 'The Rules of Inference' (2002) The University of Chicago Law Review 1, 6.
[53] C W Collier, 'The Use and Abuse of Humanistic Theory in Law: Reexamining the Assumptions of Interdisciplinary Legal Scholarship' (1991) Duke Law Journal 191, 194.

frameworks of the supposedly neutral legal regime align with external ideological perspectives or how the 'law in action' (discovered through some other research method) diverges from the 'law in books' in a way which further increases social disadvantage and discrimination. Either of these can be good routes to what Burrows calls, in his defence of doctrinal scholarship, 'shaping practical decisions affecting the workings of society in general'.[54]

II – Doing Doctrinal Analysis Properly

According to Van Hoecke, legal doctrine is *hermeneutic* (focused on interpreting texts), *argumentative* (resolving different views of those texts), *empirical* (albeit in a confused fashion, with a variety of sources of data), *explanatory* (either following law's long-standing approaches to the creation or discovery of legal rules or the perspective of some external discipline), *axiomatic* (to a very limited extent), *logical* (again, in a limited way), and *normative* (both by describing and promulgating choices about values).[55] A great deal of doctrinal analysis is about reconciling seemingly inconsistent precedents – perhaps to create some over-arching theory of the law, but one that is consistent within itself, not one that is consistent with external values. It uses the traditional sources of law — constitutions, legislation, and case law – as its primary data,[56] and is often criticised for restricting itself to these. The principal (or at least desired) audience for doctrinal scholarship are judges, and it therefore applies the same methodology as they claim to do.[57] (This section does not explore the question of whether the doctrinal method is, in fact, a complete or accurate account of how the courts go about their work. This is a legitimate and interesting issue, but one to which black letter research assumes a positive answer.) In this method, the essential features of the legislation and case law are examined critically and then all the relevant elements are combined or synthesised to establish an arguably correct and complete statement of the law on the matter in hand.[58]

Moving from this broad statement to a precise sequence of operations that can be carried out in a systematic fashion is not easy, however. Van Gestel and Micklitz highlight how doctrinal research varies from jurisdiction to jurisdiction, but draw attention to three key features: reliance on authoritative

---

[54] A Burrows, *Understanding the Law of Obligations: Essays on Contract, Tort and Restitution* (Bloomsbury Publishing 2000) 113.
[55] Van Hoecke (n 4) 4–11.
[56] Hutchinson (n 2) 13.
[57] J Vranken, 'Exciting Times for Legal Scholarship' (2012) 2 Law and Method 42, 43–44.
[58] Hutchinson (n 2) 9–10.

sources, the goal of presenting the law as 'a coherent net of principles, rules, meta-rules and exceptions, at different levels of abstraction', and a re-thinking of rules to avoid the appearance of arbitrary decisions.[59]

Duncan and Hutchinson claim that doctrinal research consists of a two-step process: 'first locating the sources of the law and then interpreting and analysing the text.'[60] Although the first step seems relatively simple, some reflection (or experience in legal research) will quickly show how difficult and complex this can be. The (only) appropriate materials to use are those which are the primary work product of the institutions of the legal system — the courts, legislature, and the executive. (Fortunately, textbooks are central to the doctrinal method;[61] they can also greatly assist in shortening the process of gathering relevant information, but are not always up to date.) While this seems to be a limited selection of sources, a relatively straightforward question in (for example) company law will bring into play an inter-related hierarchy of documents. Leaving aside the situation-specific memorandum, articles and other contractual documents, which may or may not be based on the models available in the Companies Acts, the relevant legislation stretches across many different acts of the Oireachtas, dating from 1963 on, with layers of amendments, together with secondary legislation which emerges from the relevant government departments at a rapid rate and without very much publicity. In addition, there may be many High and Supreme Court decisions, now supplemented by the output of the new Court of Appeal, any of which may be relevant and have to tracked down through a variety of sources and search engines, such as LexisNexis, Westlaw, and the Courts Service's own site. European law becomes increasingly relevant to all areas of Irish law, and the Constitution lurks in the background of even the most private of transactions, with appeals to property rights, fair procedures, and legitimate expectation possible at any time. At the time of writing, of course, the new Companies Act will be brought into force in the very near future, bringing with it the complication of having to consider how this may alter the legal landscape, essentially having to research the same question twice in the context of two bodies of law — one old, encrusted, but well-researched, and the other new, perhaps cleaner, but very under-explored. A good grounding in the basic skills of legal research — locating and obtaining key materials — is essential.

---

[59] R Van Gestel and Hans-Wolfgang Micklitz, 'Revitalizing Doctrinal Legal Research in Europe: What About Methodology?' (2011) 26 <http://cadmus.eui.eu/handle/1814/16825> accessed 6 April 2015.
[60] Hutchinson and Duncan (n 8) 110.
[61] Salter and Mason (n 1) 58.

To understand the complexity of the task, see McGrath's 'The Company Charge Register and the Constitution',[62] which is a good example of how an issue of private law crosses over into public law (and international human rights law) in a challenging way.

Having gathered the raw information, it now must be synthesised and systematised. This second step is also complex. Writing primarily for those who practice law,[63] Gionfriddo puts forward an 'objective' method for synthesising the current state of the law from a variety of decided cases. This must be comprehensive and constantly compared to the overall corpus of decisions. The process begins by considering the explicit statements of judges in arriving at their decisions. These are considered in the overall context of the general area of the law, to determine whether or not they are consistent with generally-agreed principles and approaches. In addition, the detail of what rules are expressed, and how, is important: if judges use the same phrases, then the reader should ask if they are being used to mean the same thing. If they do not, the reader should compare these carefully to see if they have, in fact, the same meaning. The reader should also be alert to the possibility of a 'patchwork' of rules which is necessarily incomplete because the cases which the judges see as necessary for the development of a coherent framework are simply not coming before them for decision. Then, the reader attempts to divine (and test) the implicit rules that are not clearly articulated in the texts of the judgments but seem to underpin the area of law under scrutiny.[64]

To explain the method in more detail, Hofheinz outlines a procedure:

> ... first, identification and synthesis of rules and principles; second, construction of a question set. In the first part of this step you identify the rules and principles (whether judicial, legislative, or constitutional) which governed the resolution of prior problems. ... You must identify the holding of each case dealing with a similar problem, and each black letter rule or principle relied upon by the court in reaching the holding. Synthesis into general statements reflecting the decisions follows, and is commonly organized into a topical outline of such statements. In the second part of this step you must create a question set which requires each fact relevant to evaluation of the outcome (called 'material facts'),

---

[62] N McGrath, 'The Company Charge Register and the Constitution' (2014) 52 Irish Jurist (ns) 20.
[63] J Kent Giofriddo, 'Thinking Like a Lawyer: The Heuristics of Case Synthesis' (2007) 40 Texas Tech Law Review 1, 3.
[64] ibid 10–16.

logically structured to allow efficient analysis of a new problem presenting new facts.

... Material facts being those dispositive of the outcome under current law. Relevant facts are those contextual facts which might be useful to consider if the result indicated by the material facts is not preferred, or if the case is one of first impression and policy analysis is appropriate.[65]

Duncan and Hutchinson query whether this second step can be clearly explained,[66] and it may be that it can only be understood through experience, but it can, perhaps, be structured to a certain extent:

1. *Identify the ratio decidendi in the relevant cases*: What are the material facts? What rule can we extract from these? What will the judge follow in future such cases?

2. *Interpret the legislation*: What is the purpose of the legislation? What are the key phrases and words relevant to the area under consideration? What rules does the legislation create or modify?

3. *Identify the doctrinal issues*: What are the general rules that emerge from the case law and legislation? What are the exceptions to this rule? What are the grey areas and the unanswered questions?

4. *Critique these issues*: Can the entire edifice be made coherent? Are there contradictions within or between different judgments, or between case law and legislation? Are there obvious situations that are not considered?

5. *Identify solutions*: What problems could be resolved by recourse to higher-level policy considerations? Where is legislative intervention required? How can the entirety be made into a coherent, rational whole?

This process must be underpinned by 'systematic rigour and detailed technical analysis based on a thorough, careful and close reading of the meaning and scope of primary sources.'[67] While the process requires a

---

[65] W Hofheinz, 'Legal Analysis' (no date) <www.hofheinzlaw.com/LANLSYS.php> accessed 5 March 2015.
[66] Hutchinson and Duncan (n 8) 111.
[67] Salter and Mason (n 1) 47.

literature review, it is more than this. It also produces more than simply a descriptive overview of the law.[68] It is based on various forms of reasoning — deductive (from the general rule to the specific instance), inductive (from several instances of specific outcomes to the identification of an overall general rule), and by analogy (inductive reasoning applied across problem areas based on arguments of similarity).[69] Creative and nuanced choices are sometimes called for, particularly in applying reasoning by analogy.

The end result should be a framework that 'makes sense'. 'Conceptual confusion'[70] is actively sought out and resolved, either from the author's own resources (by putting forward an alternative formulation of the categories and rules developed by lawmakers) or by appealing to those with greater power (the courts and the legislature) to put matters right at the earliest possible juncture, by giving an authoritative ruling in an appropriate appeal or by passing legislation.

Kelly concludes her discussion of Irish contract law with the hope that the reforms that she suggests will lead to a legal regime that 'will be more logical, certain, fair and commercially convenient, and more in line with the law in most other jurisdictions'.[71] This prescription and goal is common for doctrinal research. If it is not reached, it is up to the researcher to decide whether this is because of inadequate analysis (in which case the process should be restarted at an appropriate point) or whether some perspective external to the law (and relying perhaps on a social research method) would be useful in explaining the lack of coherence or consistency. Black letter approaches can usefully be combined with others,[72] in hybrid research designs that allow the triangulation of findings and the compilation of more comprehensive viewpoints.

While the process might seem mechanical, it is rarely this for anything but the most trivial of legal questions. The process is best thought of as iterative and non-linear: more of a game of snakes and ladders than baking

---

[68] Hutchinson and Duncan (n 8) 111.

[69] ibid. For more on judicial reasoning in the Irish courts, see D M Clarke, 'Judicial Reasoning: Logic, Authority, and The Rule of Law in Irish Courts' (2011) 46 Irish Jurist (ns) 152.

[70] J Donnelly, 'Inherent Jurisdiction and Inherent Powers of Irish Courts' (2009) 2 Judicial Studies Institute Journal 122, 125.

[71] C Kelly, 'Privity of Contract–The Benefits of Reform' (2008) 1 Judicial Studies Institute Journal 146, 170.

[72] See generally, Emerson H Tiller and Frank B Cross, 'What is Legal Doctrine?' (2006) 100 Northwestern University Law Review 517.

a cake. In addition, lawyers will often disagree on particular questions, as issues of interpretation, the precise meaning of language, and the overall policy goals in an area will be regarded differently. If the research is being done in the context of practice or advocacy, facts matter a great deal. Finally, every good lawyer should be aware that only a court can give a final answer to a question of law, and even the most experienced lawyers are sometimes surprised, confused, or annoyed by the decisions of judges in particular cases.

Starting Points for Doctrinal Research

How, then, to frame a research question which is particularly suitable for this method? A general enquiry, such as 'how should the law on charitable donations by private companies be reformed?' might at first seem appropriate, but some further consideration will show how this issue could be approached from a number of a directions, not all of which are doctrinal. The 'should' implies a normative framework, which the doctrinal method will not supply (unless one regards the coherence of the law as something desirable in itself). 'The law on charitable donations' could mean that law as it is to be found in the books, or that law in action, which raises the question of whether a socio-legal enquiry might prove more fruitful.

Rephrasing the question to be more precise and focused on the black letter law will make it more suitable to a doctrinal approach. Salter and Mason claim that the research question should be restricted to questions of law that could be argued before an appellate court, and that questions of politics, morality and ethics are to be excluded.[73] This goes perhaps a little too far and, while the focus should be on the strict letter of the law, there is nonetheless scope for, and perhaps a need of, some form of critique in order for the research to go beyond the strictly descriptive. Therefore, 'external' questions can be used as a means of assessing the adequacy of the law, once its current state has been thoroughly researched and analysed. 'Is the law on charitable donations by private companies adequate in light of concerns regarding transparency?' provides a framework within which the existing law, its rules and categories, can be categorised and critiqued.

There are a number of recent examples of doctrinal research projects in Ireland that are good starting points for further exploration and emulation, although never slavish imitation. As a particularly good example of the doctrinal approach in commercial law (where it is often applied), consider McGrath's article on 'The Certificate of Registration and the Company

---

[73] Salter and Mason (n 1) 62.

Charge Register',[74] which argues that the courts are mistaken in their interpretation of s 104 of the Companies Act 1963. In a similar vein is Biehler's 'Security for Costs: A Reappraisal of Established Principles?',[75] which seeks to reassess the underlying rationales for the law on security for costs in light of recent court decisions. Also in this general area is Ahern's article, 'Directors' Duties: Broadening the Focus Beyond Content to Examine the Accountability Spectrum'[76] which seeks to situate the literature on directors' duties into a broader context of duty, enforcement, liability and remedy.

From a more public or constitutional law perspective, a good example of recent Irish doctrinal research is Cleary's 'Public and Private Law Principles: *Murphy v Attorney General* Reassessed',[77] which argues that the courts have misunderstood the principles set down in this seminal case, and therefore created anomalies which are problematic and should be rectified by reconsidering the public and private elements of the case. Similarly, de Blacam's 'Assessing Procedural Error in Public Law'[78] presents a categorisation of procedural error, explains why these should be distinguished from each other, and how, while O'Reilly's 'Errors of Fact and Errors of Law as Grounds for Judicial Review'[79] presents a similar categorisation, although with a more historical perspective. Another public law example, this time from the criminal law, is Prendergast's 'The Connection between Mental Disorder and the Act of Killing in the Defence of Diminished Responsibility',[80] which 'set[s] out different potential understandings of the connection between mental disorder and killing [and argues] ... that it is important and appropriate for the Court of Criminal Appeal to settle the precise scope of the defence'.[81]

---

[74] N McGrath, 'The Certificate of Registration and the Company Charge Register' (2013) 36 Dublin University Law Journal (ns) 35.

[75] H Biehler, 'Security for Costs: A Reappraisal of Established Principles?' (2012) 36 Dublin University Law Journal (ns) 173.

[76] D Ahern, 'Directors' Duties: Broadening the Focus Beyond Content to Examine the Accountability Spectrum' (2011) 33 Dublin University Law Journal (ns) 116.

[77] N Cleary, 'Public and Private Law Principles: *Murphy v Attorney General* Reassessed' (2011) 34 Dublin University Law Journal (ns) 155.

[78] M de Blacam, 'Assessing Procedural Error in Public Law' (2010) 32 Dublin University Law Journal (ns) 186.

[79] J O'Reilly, 'Errors of Fact and Errors of Law as Grounds for Judicial Review' (2012) 47 Irish Jurist (ns) 1.

[80] D Prendergast, 'The Connection Between Mental Disorder and the Act of Killing in the Defence of Diminished Responsibility' (2013) 49 Irish Jurist (ns) 202.

[81] ibid 203.

All of these share a common concern with properly situating their subject matter within the existing and accepted mapping of the subject area, perhaps adjusting some items to make way for new concepts or highlighting a new portion of territory which has been created or excavated by the activities of the courts. These are very doctrinal in approach. However, as this chapter argues, there is space for doctrinal articles that are nonetheless aware of and relate to the broader social world outside of the courts. Mark de Blacam's 'Official Language and Constitutional Interpretation'[82] is a good example of this, providing both a sophisticated discussion of the meanings of terms such as 'national language' and 'official language' but also placing the consequences of the legal framework which surrounds the Irish language in the context of its social milieu and concludes with two questions, one legal and one 'not obviously so'[83] about these consequences. Similarly, Murray's 'Moving Towards Rights-Based Mental Health Law: The Limits of Legislative Reform' begins with a doctrinal analysis of the Mental Health Act 2001 but concludes that '[i]t is necessary to look beyond the statutory framework at the practical implementation of the legislative provisions to determine the impact of the rights-based model and to begin to address any shortcomings.'[84] Doctrinal research can also be cross-disciplinary or comparative in nature, such as Bell's 'Judges, Fairness and Litigants in Person'.[85]

Appropriate Application of the Doctrinal Method

Researchers in law (and in other disciplines) need to avoid the tendency to treat the law 'as a datum, as fact, unproblematic, and one-dimensional'.[86] Although the doctrinal method is often seen as part of the problem rather than part of the solution to this challenge, it can in fact be an important tool for those who seek to understand, criticise, and improve the law. Law and society are not two distinct spheres of study, and it is not possible to work in one without a good knowledge of the other. A deep exploration of the law is an important grounding for research that deals with social issues and institutions which are intertwined with legal regimes. As Goldring points out, '[w]ithout knowledge of technical rules, no one can gain a proper understanding of the specific operations of the legal order, let alone change them.'[87]

---

[82] M de Blacam, 'Official Language and Constitutional Interpretation' (2014) 52 Irish Jurist (ns) 90.
[83] ibid 113.
[84] C Murray, 'Moving Towards Rights-Based Mental Health Law: The Limits of Legislative Reform' (2013) 49 Irish Jurist (ns) 161.
[85] E Bell, 'Judges, Fairness and Litigants in Person' (2010) 1 Judicial Studies Institute Journal 2.
[86] McCrudden (n 10) 648.
[87] Goldring (n 18) 219.

The application of this method does not need to be tied to out-dated and discredited positivist and formalist paradigms, or notions that the law exists in the ether, awaiting discovery by scholarly astronomers. It is true that '[l]egal doctrine is simply not a self-contained body of knowledge in the 'modern' sense.'[88] However, in order to apply what Floyd calls 'a post-modern sensibility' to 'the rules and principles discerned in opinions',[89] we need first to establish what those 'rules and principles' are, or at least what the courts think they are. It is, of course, possible to determine those rules and principles from observing or interviewing those who actually apply the law. In some instances, that may be more appropriate, particularly where the 'law in action' deviates from 'law in books' to a significant degree, where the legal regime under investigation is largely based on unwritten procedures, non-legal processes (such as economic analyses), or bureaucratic and regulatory discretion. However, where the principal reference point for the structure and functioning of a topic of enquiry is a set of black-letter rules, traditional doctrinal research is an appropriate and very useful research method.

---

[88] T W Floyd, 'Legal Education and the Vision Thing' (1996) 31 Georgia Law Review 853, 870.
[89] ibid.

Chapter 3

The Comparative Method in Legal Research: The Art of Justifying Choices

*Marie-Luce Paris**

The [comparative] method is not complicated. In fact, it is so simple that I have for long hesitated to dignify it with the term 'method'[1]

I – Introduction

Comparative law is a thriving area in the study of the law which has attracted, in the last decades, a growing interest in legal scholarship and legal education.[2] The expanding literature published in quality specialised outlets as well as a steadfast number of research events organised by universities, research institutes and other numerous organisations all attest the phenomenon.[3] It is difficult to find an academic law curriculum which

---

* Dr Marie-Luce Paris is a lecturer in the Sutherland School of Law, University College Dublin.
[1] JC Reitz, 'How to Do Comparative Law?' (1996) 46 American Journal of Comparative Law 617, 635.
[2] The statement is not new. See, for example, WJ Kamba, 'Comparative Law: A Theoretical Framework' (1974) 23 International and Comparative Law Quarterly 485; E Örücü, 'Developing Comparative Law' in E Örücü and D Nelken (eds), *Comparative Law: A Handbook* (Hart 2007) 43. For a selection of works on comparative law (excluding works specifically on methodology), see, among others, K Zweigert and H Kötz, *An Introduction to Comparative Law* (OUP 1998); M Reimann and R Zimmermann, *The Oxford Handbook of Comparative Law* (OUP 2006); E Örücü and D Nelken (eds), *Comparative Law: A Handbook* (Hart 2007); J Smits, *Encyclopaedia of Comparative Law* (2nd edn, Edward Elgar 2012); M Adams and J Bomhoff, *Practice and Theory in Comparative Law* (CUP 2014); M Siems, *Comparative Law* (CUP 2014).
[3] Two of the most prominent (i.e. high impact factor) law journals, namely the American Journal of Comparative Law and the International and Comparative Law Quarterly, contain 'comparative' in their title. The most prominent and oldest organisation dealing with comparative law is the International Academy of Comparative Law founded after the First World War and whose aim is the comparative study of legal systems. At European level, prestigious research centres such as the Max Plank Institute for Comparative and International Private Law in Hamburg, and the Max Plank Institute for Comparative Public Law and International Law in Heidelberg, are good examples. At national level, organisations such as the Society of Legal Scholars (within the UK and Ireland) and its comparative law section, and the domestically-based Irish Society of Comparative Law, promote events and research in comparative law.

does not comprise a course in comparative law in some form, whether as an introductory course in the first years of study, or as a more substantial course at a later stage. A comparative perspective may also be embedded, in a more or less systematic way, in the study of the different subjects of law (i.e. contract law, commercial law, constitutional law, family law, procedural law...). Comparative legal studies are also increasingly being pursued at doctoral level. In a sense, 'we are all comparatists now',[4] or bound to be.

There are various reasons why a legal scholar might want to undertake a research project in comparative law. One of these reasons could be that the scholar wishes 'to give an edge' to her research. It is often the case that a research topic that is not strictly on international law or European law would include a comparative law dimension.[5] This is a valid reason on the face of it. Because the discipline of law is becoming more cosmopolitan in a so-called 'globalised' environment, discarding an external outlook in a doctoral thesis would be perceived as fairly short-sighted and would deprive the work of a more ambitious relevance. As a matter of fact, resorting to comparative law constitutes a strategic choice made by the researcher. Doctoral students have to be strategic in their choices (of topic, supervisors etc.) and now almost all doctoral programmes include a research plan as well as a professional career development plan in an effort to rationalise the whole PhD experience which outcome is geared towards the employability of the graduate student whether in academia or outside of it. The choice of comparative legal studies is itself being dictated by a combination of both the researcher's own interest in the area and her long-term professional plan. The researcher's own interest might be triggered, for example, by an in-country experience as an international exchange student, making her want to retain a connection with the foreign legal system. As a professional, the researcher might wish to pursue comparative law in an academic career or in a non-academic setting such as, for example, in the context of a domestic law reform commission post, or in a job in an

---

[4] W Twining, 'Globalisation and Comparative Law' in Örücü and Nelken (n 2) 84. For a more nuanced view, see Wilson, for whom '(...) comparative law has, more often than not, been seen as an extension of the study of national law' and '[l]ooking at law from a comparative point of view (...) still remains a specialism (...) [and] [i]t cannot yet be said that it has become part and parcel of the orientation of law students or legal scholars, let alone legal practitioners'. See G Wilson 'Comparative Legal Scholarship' in M McConville and W Hong Chui (eds), *Research Methods for Law* (Edinburgh University Press 2007) 87, 101.

[5] Although this observation is not scientifically or statistically proven here.

international or European organisation,[6] or in international law firm requiring technical competences in another legal system. Besides these deliberate reasons, it must be said that resorting to comparative law brings one of the most intellectually challenging experiences in the study of the law. This is due not only to the 'de-parochialising role'[7] of comparative law but also to the imperative for the researcher to reach a high level of abstraction in order to attempt to make sense of the differences and similarities between the legal systems compared and map out solutions to the legal issue under examination.

One would expect that the prominence acquired by comparative law would be associated with the emergence of a solid standard method. That is not the case. Despite a more systematic literature discussing the challenges of an appropriate method in comparative research,[8] there is (still) no definition of what the method of comparative law is, let alone, to some extent, what comparative law is. As Kamba put it in 1974, 'comparative law still lacks a clearly formulated and widely accepted theoretical framework within which specific comparative legal studies and research may be undertaken in a meaningful and effective manner'.[9] More than two decades after that statement, Zweigert and Kötz declared that there was 'very little systematic writing about the method of comparative law'.[10] A few years later, Örücü could still argue that 'the basic problems have remained the same. There is no one definition of what comparative law and comparative method are'.[11] It is not a coincidence then that, in the most recent and exhaustive attempt to shed light on the issue, Samuel does not purport to provide a definitive theory on method, but rather outlines a 'methodological road map' for the research student in comparative law.[12] As in any other area of law, the issue

---

[6] One can think, for instance, of the Research Unit of the European Court of Human Rights which conducts, although on a non-systematic basis, comparative research of the 47 legal systems of the Council of Europe, thereby assisting the Court in bringing more rigour to its comparative work, in relation to the consensus approach in particular. See S Flogaitis, T Swart, J Fraser, *The European Court of Human Rights and its Discontents: Turning Criticism into Strength* (Edward Elgar 2013) 93.

[7] Twining (n 4) 72.

[8] Two of the most recent works on the methodology of comparative law include P Giuseppe Monateri (ed), *Methods of Comparative Law* (Edward Elgar 2012), and G Samuel, *An Introduction to Comparative Law Theory and Method* (Hart 2014). See also M Van Hoecke, *Epistemology and Methodology of Comparative Law* (Hart 2004). Most comparatists nowadays include method as part of their scholarship.

[9] Kamba (n 2) 485.

[10] Zweigert and Kötz (n 2) 33.

[11] Örücü (n 2) 43.

[12] Samuel, 'Concluding Remarks: A Methodological Road Map?' in Samuel (n 8) 173ff.

of method is crucial. And because every legal scholar — as all other lawyers, whether practising lawyers, judges or legislators — will be confronted with foreign legal material, one must be equipped with the basics in this respect. Since the comparative method does not rest on an agreed framework, it is open-ended and will necessarily be 'dictated by the strategy of the comparative lawyer'.[13] This element of strategy is the core of the argument here: the method used by the researcher will be valid only in so far as it is organised and explained. In other words, the researcher in comparative law, while going through the different stages of the comparative analysis, has to set her own parameters of research within the theoretical framework provided in the comparative law literature and has to justify the direction she chooses to give as regards her methodological choices. In short, the researcher has to master the art of justifying her choices about why and how she uses comparative law.

The aim of this chapter is not to propose a comprehensive theory on the comparative method (which will require a more extensive study), nor to offer *the* definitive method for comparative legal research (which, as seen above, is impossible and, in any case, objectionable). Rather I aim to provide a critical explanation of the main conceptual tools on how the issue of method in comparative law has been approached by bringing to the fore the justificatory argument thereby assisting the researcher in refining her own approach. The first part outlines what I call the 'theoretical core' of comparative law, which refers to the meaning and purposes (or functions) of comparative law to the extent that these inform methodological issues. The second part examines the method *per se* and aims at deconstructing the different stages of the process of comparison.

II – THEORETICAL CORE OF COMPARATIVE LAW: MEANING AND PURPOSE

Embarking on a comparative legal project implies addressing a number of questions, namely the 'WH questions': What does comparative law mean? Why does one undertake it? How can one carry out a valuable and effective comparison? These questions have been the subject of numerous theoretical expositions about the interrelationship between the meaning, purpose and method of comparative law. These expositions have generated what I term a 'theoretical core' about comparative law, that is, a body of theoretical

---

[13] Örücü (n 2) 48.

knowledge that can be taught and learned about comparative law.[14] The object of the following developments is to provide a concise account of the meaning and purpose of comparative law, before explaining what is envisaged as its method.

Meaning of Comparative Law

Simply stated, comparative law means the application of the comparative technique to the field of law. However, the definition is not as straightforward as it seems, since it requires addressing a set of subsequent questions, such as, what is understood by law? what is comparison? and indeed, is comparative law reducible to a technique?[15] This has entailed an interesting epistemological debate around the issue of whether comparative law is simply a process to be applied to the discipline of law, or a distinct branch with its own knowledge content and purpose — in other words, whether comparative law is a legal method or a legal science in its own right.

Method or Science?

The understanding of comparative law as a science dates back to the formative stage, when early 20th century scholars would argue that the object of comparative law was the 'discovery of concepts and principles common to all "civilised" systems of law, that is to say, universal concepts and principles which constitute what [could be] called *droit idéal relatif* or an ideal relative law. At the time, for the proponents of such a meaning, the object of comparative law had 'a purely scientific object', which was to explain the 'causes which underlie the origin, development and extinction of legal institutions'.[16] Comparative law would then be regarded as detached from the different branches of law to constitute its own branch of legal scholarship and appear as 'a science of knowledge with its own separate sphere; an independent science, producing theoretical distillate'.[17]

However, this has long been questioned, with one of the main reasons being that comparative law has no defined subject matter and does not produce any rules or principles of law — even if it is correct to assume that using

---

[14] In addition to the examination of these questions, the theoretical core arguably includes the corpus of knowledge about legal families and the one relating to the historical development of comparative law.

[15] Even if the name 'comparative law' is not uncontroversial. Some other expressions have been used as better reflecting what comparative law actually is, such as the 'comparative study of law' or 'comparative legal study and research' (Kamba (n 2) 487), or 'comparative analysis of law' or 'comparative legal studies' (Örücü (n 2) 46-47).

[16] Kamba (n 2) 488.

[17] Örücü (n 2) 44.

comparative law may assist in drafting or changing rules in national, European or international law. Comparative law is not a legal system or a set of norms applicable in a particular field or territory. Some voices have insisted that the subject of comparative law would be better off in finding its audience by 'penetrating other subjects of law than [by] trying to assert its own continued independence'.[18] Today, it is generally agreed that comparative law is actually a method and dissenting 'voices questioning the fashioning of comparative law as method remain largely marginal'.[19]

Method and Knowledge Progression
There is more to comparative law than the mere application of a technique though. Comparative law is an ambitious intellectual activity which has law as its object and comparison as its process.[20] Deconstructing the approach proposed by Samuel — that of 'a process in which the comparatist takes several objects in order to study them within a "scientific" framework in which the object (...) being studied is viewed in terms of the "other" [and] it is the contrast between the domestic and the "other" that generates knowledge progression'[21] — one can see the key correlation between method and knowledge progression. Comparative law is not simply acquiring knowledge of another legal system; it is not 'an introduction to French, English, German, Chinese or whatever law'.[22] It is not either applying a comparative dimension via another research method in law. According to Samuel, it is 'not a particular form of legal history, or legal philosophy or theory, or sociology of law', although it can be combined with the use of other research methods in law such as the historical method or the socio-legal method, for example.[23] As 'a method of looking at law',[24] comparative law aims at reaching 'higher grounds' in the sense that it is not limited to the understanding of another legal system, and the better understanding of the researcher's own legal system. It also aims at understanding the discipline of law, not just in its technicalities, but also in its epistemological and ontological dimensions by critically reflecting on

---

[18] B Markesinis, 'Comparative Law: A Subject in Search of an Audience' (1990) 53 Modern Law Review 1, 21. As Markesinis put it, 'the comparative method may have more of a future by penetrating other subjects than by trying to assert its own continued independence under the unconvincing title of comparative law'.
[19] See the positions of Pierre Legrand and Alan Watson cited in Simone Glanert, 'Method?' in Monateri (n 8) 63.
[20] Zweigert and Kötz cited in Örücü (n 2) 44.
[21] Samuel (n 8) 11.
[22] ibid 10.
[23] ibid. See Chapters 4 and 5 of this collection for the historical method, and Chapter 7 for the socio-legal method.
[24] Örücü (n 2) 46.

the origin, nature and limits of the law itself. In other words, the comparative enterprise aims at fulfilling 'the essential task of furthering the universal knowledge and understanding of the phenomenon of law'.[25] The comparative method thus inscribes itself in a scientific framework aimed at knowledge progression. In that respect, several scholars have viewed comparative law as a stand-alone discipline, or as the 'critical method of legal science'.[26] Because it is capable of generating its own knowledge about law, comparative law can acquire its substance and become 'an elected field of research', where the confrontation of the different tools and methodologies at use arguably results in the development of analytical thinking about the law, and 'produce a growing body of critical understanding, a framework for thinkable thoughts and global strategies'.[27]

When one is clear that comparative law is an integrated intellectual process carrying its potentialities as regards the contours of the legal discipline, one has to ask herself why she is resorting to it and why is comparative law relevant to her project.

Purpose of Comparative Law

Determining the purpose of one's comparative legal project is key since it largely dictates the method of comparison. The reasons for resorting to comparative law are diverse since these reasons very much depend on who undertakes the comparative legal research — whether a scholar, a policy or law-maker, or a judge — arguably all animated by the common endeavour of making the law better.

Diversity of Purposes

Comparatists have identified an array of purposes attributed to comparative law. For instance, for Örücü, these objectives may range from 'aiding law reform and policy development, providing a tool of research to reach a universal theory of law, giving a critical perspective to students and an aid to international law practice, facilitating international unification and harmonisation of laws, helping courts to fill gaps in the law and even working

---

[25] Örücü (n 2) 44; Samuel (n 8) 25.
[26] Örücü (n 2) 44.
[27] Monateri (n 8) 3. See also, Picard, who claims that comparative law used to be only a method, but has now shaped into a proper area of law, capable of producing a coherent and autonomous body of norms with prescriptive effects; comparative law has thus acquired a substance which envisages law in its generality as detached from the traditional paradigms derived from positive state law. See E Picard, 'La Comparaison en Droit Constitutionnel et en Droit Administratif: Du Droit Comparé comme Méthode au Droit Comparé comme Substance' (2015) 2 Revue Internationale de Droit Comparé 317, 320.

towards the furthering of world peace and tolerance'.[28] In short, these objectives can be of practical, sociological, political and pedagogical nature,[29] depending on the comparatist involved — for example, a policy-maker or legislator would pursue a practical and political objective geared towards law reform and policy development, while a legal academic would pursue a pedagogical objective aimed at providing students with a critical perspective on the domestic legal system by contrasting it with the foreign legal system. The legitimacy of comparative law can be controversial though, notably for its use by courts, including international courts, when they tend to use it as a source of persuasive authority to fill in the gaps in the law.[30]

Contemporary leading comparatists are of the view that comparative law cannot be restricted to practical objectives only. In that regard, comparative academic legal research has arguably a more open-ended objective and the legal scholar enjoys the enviable position of a comparatist who can go about her research without being bound by an imperative of 'result' (i.e. a judgment, a policy, a law) to produce. However, this must be nuanced. Legal research projects, if meaningful, shall tend towards providing findings that can be used in policy-making and /or court (for example, the citation of a scholarly article in a judgment is a proof of academic excellence). Besides, the professionalisation of doctoral studies, especially if benefiting from generous public funding or from private sponsorship, implies a clearly articulated goal of the legal research project. The researcher will need to justify why she is resorting to the comparative law method. This can be explained plainly by stating that the initial hypothesis concerning a particular legal issue will be tested through the comparative method to achieve the expected outcome, and to advance knowledge on the particular legal issue. This can be done from a purely technical perspective (for example, in suggesting solutions to issues in international private law, or in transnational legal issues in general), or from a more policy-based and socially-based perspective (for example, in proposing normatively preferable best practices, theories or policy frameworks etc., with a view to promote legislation, or work towards a project of harmonization or unification of law).

---

[28] Örücü (n 2) 44, 53-56.
[29] ibid.
[30] See M Andenas and D Fairgrieve, 'Intent on Making Mischief: Seven Ways of Using Comparative Law' in Monateri (n 8) 25, 26. See also the use of comparative law by the European Court of Human Rights to rule on the presence or absence of consensus on a particular matter, and as a source of information for European judges in the search for an appropriate answer to a given question. See K Dzehtsiarou, 'Comparative Law in the Reasoning of the European Court of Human Rights' (2010) 10 University College Dublin Law Review 109-40.

To be sure — and in line with the idea of knowledge progression mentioned above — the confrontation of legal rules and institutions of one's own legal system with external legal rules and institutions certainly increases 'intellectual interaction and borrowings',[31] hereby enhancing a capacity for self-reflection. The function of comparative law is then to develop a critical understanding in two respects: first, in respect of the legal systems compared — that is the foreign legal system(s) examined and the researcher's own legal system — and secondly, in respect of the general knowledge of the law and the understanding of the law in context. As a matter of fact, some would argue that law is comparative by nature or, to say it differently, that the process of comparison is ingrained in the discipline of law as per the statement by Sacco who declared that 'comparison begins at home'.[32]

Improving the Law

Certainly comparative law, like any other method of legal research, aims to make suggestions on how the law can be improved. The overarching aim of a quest for 'better law' through the use of comparative law comprises different kinds of objectives as developed by Siems. First, comparative law may help improve law 'technically', which is typical of a 'functional-technical perspective of comparative law' — that is when one looks at two or more legal systems presuming that the law would lead to a similar result, and chooses the best one (for example, the one which provides more legal certainty); secondly, comparative law may help improve a particular social problem or policy, which is typical of a 'socio-legal functionalism' approach to comparative law; thirdly, comparative law may act as a trigger for legal changes, such as 'introducing a new social or economic policy or a re-balancing of group interests', because the foreign law provides a better response to a particular evolution of society.[33]

However, the use of the comparative method in legal research must not transform itself into a systematic quest for *the* better law. The practical and intellectual benefits of resorting to comparative law would be negated if

---

[31] B Markesinis, *The Coming Together of the Common Law and the Civil Law* (Hart 2000) 49.

[32] R Sacco, cited in Samuel (n 8) 20. From an historical point of view, Picard argues that modernity created the necessity to compare laws and legal systems; before then, law equated to justice and came into existence precisely by the confrontation of different legal sources necessarily entailing comparisons. Then, when modern states imposed positivism, law was identified formally by being posed by a sovereign authority; there was thus no need to compare to do justice; comparison was just necessary as a matter of curiosity, for knowledge acquisition, until it became relevant again in modern times. See Picard (n 27) 324.

[33] M Siems, 'Bringing in Foreign Ideas: The Quest for "Better Law" in Implicit Comparative Law' (2014) 9 Journal of Comparative Law 119, 120-24.

definitive cross-cultural statements were made about the quality of legal rules; indeed, one has to resist the 'fascination of ranking legal systems'.[34] Each law is deeply embedded in its historical, social, cultural and economic context, and there is no such thing as 'the better law'. On the contrary, the task of the comparatist is to join forces with other disciplines (for example, economists) in order to cooperate and 'verify the possibility of constructing a meaningful, universal benchmark exempted from partisan preconceptions' about the law.[35] In short, comparative law demands an open and tolerant mind as the path towards a critical mind-set.[36]

III – Method of Comparative Law *Stricto Sensu*: Deconstructing the Comparative Analysis

Since comparative law is by definition process-related, the question of method is clearly of importance. As Samuel puts it, 'any project involving comparative legal studies is particularly method sensitive' since 'different methodological schemes can produce different forms of knowledge'.[37] Outlining a method is a prerequisite before embarking on any meaningful comparative legal research. However, one would be at pains to find prescriptive theories on the matter since 'method remains woefully under-theorized'.[38] It is even the case that comparatists, whether in the private or public law field, are reluctant to promote any specific method and, as Glenn declares, '[t]here is no exclusive method and much to be said about the virtues, and defects, of different methods'.[39] Each author (including this one), or group of authors in a number of edited collections, adds to the mix by exposing her or their view on method.

---

[34] P Giuseppe Monateri, 'Introduction' in Monateri (n 8) 3. See the aberration of the World Bank's 'Doing Business' report, which came to the conclusion that the common law-based systems were superior to the civil law–based systems. See B Fauvarque-Cosson and AJ Kerhuel, 'Is Law an Economic Contest? French Reactions to the Doing Business World Bank Reports and Economic Analysis of the Law' (2009) 57 American Journal of Comparative Law 811.

[35] Monateri (n 8) 3.

[36] See Örücü (n 2) 54-55, where she argues that 'comparative law serves the purpose of broadening the mind of the law student and helps in the development of tolerance' and provides 'the breadth necessary for the development of critical minds'. See also below about the interdisciplinary dimension of legal studies.

[37] Samuel (n 8) 28.

[38] Glanert (n 19) 63.

[39] Patrick Glenn, cited in Glanert (n 19) 62. See also Kamba (n 2) 511, who states that 'it is not possible, nor would it be prudent to attempt to prescribe specific comparative procedures to be followed. The most that one can do is to suggest some broad pointers towards a meaningful technique or techniques'.

The aim then is not to propose an overall theory on the comparative method or to explain, once and for all, how comparative legal research ought to be carried out. Rather the aim is to provide suggestions on how to approach the issue which remains, after all, a matter of choice and strategy of the researcher. Indeed, the lack of consensus over method results in a kind of emancipatory latitude afforded to the researcher and I concur with Glanert who argues that comparatists should be allowed 'to reclaim an agential space as they assume responsibility for their own strategic decisions, instead of reflexively implementing a given methodological agenda'.[40]

One's Research, One's Strategy, One's Method

In general terms, a method is a particular way or procedure for approaching or accomplishing something.[41] In comparative law, these two dimensions of 'approaching' and 'accomplishing' reflect the correlation between the issue of method, on the one hand, and the issue of determining meaning and purpose, on the other hand: a procedure for approaching comparative law necessarily reflects how one envisages comparative law (meaning); a procedure for accomplishing comparative law reflects the goal one wants to achieve by using comparative law (purpose).

In my view, a method or methodology[42] in comparative legal research should aim at organising one's research, that is her approach in selecting material, as well as analysing and exposing her findings. In other words, the researcher has to ask herself what is the intellectual framework for the comparative exercise, and has to pitch the right level of intelligibility for such an exercise. This intellectual flexibility offered to the researcher is both exciting and puzzling.[43] The challenge then is: how much freedom does the comparatist allow herself and how does she deal with the number of practical challenges that will compound the research? The statement by Palmer about a 'sliding

---

[40] Glanert (n 19) 81.
[41] See 'Method', Oxford Dictionaries online <www.oxforddictionaries.com/definition/english/method> accessed 4 March 2016. Oxford English Dictionary online ≤www.oed.com>.. Interestingly, the French definition given in the authoritative dictionary is much more encompassing and includes 'rationalised reasoning with a view to reach a truth (method as different from theory)'; 'a set of logically structured principles, rules and steps which aim to achieve an objective (for example, the scientific method); 'a way or procedure of conducting, in a reasoned manner, an activity or a task, and, by extension, the body of rules which allows for the training in this procedure'.
[42] A methodology is an organised set or system of methods used in a particular area of study or activity. Comparatists often use methodology (or methodologies) when they refer to several methods developed in the field.
[43] See O Kahn-Freund, 'Comparative Law as an Academic Subject' (1966) 82 Law Quarterly Review 40, 41: 'On the professor of comparative law the Gods have bestowed the most dangerous of their gifts, the gift of freedom'.

scale of methods' encapsulates what this is about. By advocating that comparative law should be accessible and flexible, Palmer warns of the necessity to customise one's research: '(...) there is a sliding scale of methods [as opposed to a one size fit for all method] and (...) the best approach will always be adapted in terms of specific purposes of the research, the subjective abilities of the researcher and the affordability of the costs'.[44]

Intellectual Freedom

The application of the comparative technique to the field of law by way of juxtaposing and contrasting the law — generally branches or aspects of it — of two or more legal systems[45] consists of a number of stages. There is no agreement in legal scholarship on the number of these stages. A spectrum of these — from a concise three-staged operation[46] to a detailed eight step process[47] — may assist in framing one's intellectual framework. The first method suggested by Kamba reflects purely intellectual stages which might be conflated in the course of the comparative analysis. Initially, the descriptive phase aims at explaining the legal norms, concepts and institutions in the legal systems compared, and can extend to explaining the socio-economic problems and the legal solutions provided by these systems; then, the second stage seeks to identify the similarities and differences between the legal systems compared; lastly, the explanatory phase aims at providing an account for these similarities and differences, and allows to test the researcher's hypothesis.

The other method suggested by de Cruz is a more detailed 'notice of use' containing both intellectual and practical steps. The following paragraphs propose a number of steps inspired by de Cruz's method of comparison.

1. The first step is the identification and the preliminary phrasing of *the problem*, that is the legal issue which will be explored in the course of the research. The starting point is often intuitive, stemming from the observation of a 'real life' problem that faces individuals in society, or societies as a whole. Most of the time, the idea will require the researcher to do some ground research (for example, in newspapers, in statute books) to identify and translate the 'real life' problem into legal terms. An example would be the issue of the right to water.

---

[44] V Palmer, 'From Lerotholi to Lando: Some Examples of Comparative Law Methodology' (2004) 4 Global Jurist Frontiers 1, 29. See also J Husa, 'About the Methodology of Comparative Law: Some Comments Concerning Wonderland' (2007) Maastricht Faculty of Law Working Paper 5/2007.
[45] Kamba (n 2) 486. See also, Samuel (n 8) 'What is "Comparison"?' 45ff.
[46] Kamba (n 2) 511-12.
[47] P de Cruz, *Comparative Law in A Changing World* (2nd edn, Cavendish 1999) 235-39.

From receiving one's first water charge bill in the post, one might wonder: Why is there now an obligation to pay for water? and why have several hundreds of people taken it to the street to refuse to do so (!)? Is this a first in Ireland, historically speaking? What are the reasons for introducing this tax? Is (access to) water a right? How is the right to have access to water protected by law? The identification of a legal issue might have emerged from these preliminary reflections, either phrased as a tax law issue (for example, the creation of new taxes by the State: legal, economic and social reasons and implications) or as an environmental law issue (for example, the right to water: compliance and enforcement in domestic and international law).

2. The second step is about *the choice of comparators*, that is the identification of the foreign jurisdiction(s), and if possible, the parent legal family to which it or they belong(s). In our example, the researcher might want to examine one or more legal systems about the water tax; if it is one legal system, it might be, for example, the UK because of the familiarity with the language and proximity of the Irish legal tradition with the British legal tradition; if it is more than one legal system, it might be, for example, the UK and France because of the relevance of examining a neighbouring country together with a European continental system in order to give the research a good scope. This is a key stage where the researcher needs to decide on the scope of the research in terms of the number of comparators,[48] and in terms of sub-areas of the legal issue examined (for example, whether she will undertake a systematic comparison or not, whether she will examine institutions and rules of the foreign legal system, or just institutions).[49] The full *research question* should be framed at this stage.

---

[48] A researcher might be trained in more than one legal system. For example, students trained in dual degrees in Irish/English Law and French Law graduate with two law degrees – in that sense, they are both common lawyers and civil lawyers. Their 'own legal system' or 'home jurisdiction' might in fact encompass two legal systems; if later on they embark on comparative legal research, these graduates might wish to expand to a third comparator, that is to a legal system they would consider as 'foreign' in the sense of one in which they were not trained.

[49] One experience shared by a PhD student is that a systematic comparative study is not always possible. For example, about a topic on Costs in Administrative Law in Ireland, a systematic comparison between costs in England and Wales and costs in Ireland would be too large a project to undertake, even in the context of a PhD thesis. Rather, the choice has been made to dedicate some sections of the PhD to the comparative aspects, those which are the most useful to highlight differences in the respective rules in both jurisdictions (i.e. Ireland and England and Wales) in order to usefully analyse and critique a particular set of legal rules. I express my thanks to Irish Research Council Doctoral Scholar, Miriam Keane, for her comments on this.

3. The third step has to do with *research material proper sensu* and, in particular, the strategy to get access to the most relevant, authoritative and up-to-date primary and secondary sources about the foreign jurisdiction(s).[50] The type of sources might be different from those used in the home jurisdiction. In our example, the researcher might need to examine a Tax Code and other administrative regulations if choosing to compare with a continental system. This is another important step in terms of justifying the scope of the comparison. The researcher might decide to only adopt the doctrinal method; most of the time, however, she will expand her study to other methods (for example, the historical method, or the socio-legal method) and, accordingly, look for appropriate sources and material and resort to other kinds of data by, for example, using surveys, interviews, focus groups in empirical studies.[51] This is at this stage that the *interdisciplinarity* of the research needs to be framed.

4. The fourth step is the start of the intellectual process *per se*, that is the *analytical comparison*, where it is suggested to organise the material 'in accordance with headings reflecting the legal philosophy and the ideology of the legal system being investigated', and contrasting it with the home legal system in order to identify a set of similarities and differences between the two (or more) legal systems.[52] This is done by the mapping out of possible answers to address the legal issue by 'comparing carefully the different approaches, bearing in mind possible cultural differences or socio-economic factors, where relevant, and exploring any other non-legal factors',[53] as well as critically analysing the legal principles in terms of their intrinsic meaning. The research question can be refined at this stage.[54]

5. The final step concludes the analytical comparison with the production of *findings*, that is the researcher's conclusions. These should be exposed in 'a comparative framework with caveats, if necessary, and a critical commentary, wherever relevant,

---

[50] The researcher needs a mixture of information and sources such as legislation, case law, official reports, scholarly articles, press articles, etc.
[51] See Chapters 8 to 10 of this collection for more on these methods.
[52] De Cruz (n 47) 237.
[53] ibid 238.
[54] We choose to conflate the several steps proposed by de Cruz in this regard into the single heading of analytical comparison.

and [related] to the original purpose of [the enquiry]'.[55] These conclusions should also be justified 'so that future researchers will be able to see the approach [...] adopted, and why [it was adopted]'.[56]

The different questions that the researcher has to ask herself — namely, how to choose which legal systems to be compared; how to assess, measure and explain similarities and differences between the systems under review; how deep the comparative analysis should be; what weight should comparative law have[57] — are very much about making choices and justifying them. In this regard, one must be aware of the criticisms aimed at comparative research produced by legal academics; they are, in some places, accused of not saying what they do and how they do it; and when they do — say what they do — and venture outside the doctrinal legal method by resorting to cognate disciplines (in social sciences, for example) in order to understand the broader legal, social and cultural context in which law operates, academics are often accused of not doing it properly because they do not apply rigorous standards.[58] Still, the interdisciplinary feature of comparative law has gained more prevalence and researchers are strongly encouraged to use methods of other disciplines than law (for example, sociology, psychology, economy...) in that respect.[59] Leading contemporary comparatists exhort researchers to resort to 'implicit comparative law', which is based on the understanding that there is a necessity to refer to disciplines other than law such as comparative politics, comparative sociology or comparative economics, because these disciplines also deal with questions that compare and evaluate legal differences and arguably present 'the advantage [to be less] hesitant than legal research in making legal and policy recommendations based on cross-country comparisons'.[60] Hence the necessity to explain and justify each step of the research process, namely the stage of the literature review,

---

[55] De Cruz (n 47) 238. This five-step action plan is not meant to appear as such in the research itself. It is, however, important to phrase it as such, since such an action plan might be useful, for example, in funding applications' narratives which often require detailed 'work plans' of one's research project.

[56] ibid.

[57] See also, M Claes and M de Visser, 'Reflections on Comparative Method in European Constitutional Law' in Adams and Bomhoff (n 2) 145.

[58] T Roux, 'Judging the Quality of Legal Research: A Qualified Response to the Demand for Greater Methodological Rigour' (2014) 24 Legal Education Review 173.

[59] See, for example, A Peters and H Schwenke, 'Comparative Law Beyond Post-Modernism' (2000) 49 International and Comparative Law Quarterly 800, 832; J Husa, 'Interdisciplinary Comparative Law: Between Scylla and Charybdis?' 9 (2014) Journal of Comparative Law 28.

[60] Siems (n 33) 144.

the stage of framing the research question, the stage of choosing the comparables and comparators, and the stage of choosing which other method(s) will be used.

Practical Challenges

In addition to putting in place the intellectual framework for the research, the researcher needs to spend time on thinking how she proposes to address two types of practical challenges, namely one of time management and expertise building, and the other of access to, and selection of, information. First, the researcher has to decide how much time she will allocate to acquiring expertise in the foreign legal system, bearing in mind that the time spent on the other legal system is time not spent on keeping up to date with one's own. In other words, the task of becoming a bi(multi)jurist and, if relevant, bi(multi)lingual in one or more other legal systems, has implications, most notably cost implications.

Secondly, as regards the issue of access to sources — legal and non-legal sources — the problem has changed. With the advent of new technologies and the quasi systematic use of online research on the Internet, the issue has morphed from an issue of finding information to one of finding too much of it and having to select the appropriate research material. As Wilson put it, the 'time when the energies of comparative legal scholars were (...) taken up in the search of information [which was] slow and difficult work' has reversed from a shortage to 'a surfeit of information'.[61] While, in theory, there is no more hindrance to a comprehensive and up-to-date research in foreign legal material, in practice, this part of the comparative enterprise will require a careful and rigorous selection. This will include cross-checking references and sources to retain only the most updated and authoritative ones.[62] Besides, 'individuals, groups, institutions and cultures will be judged not for their assiduity in collecting information but for the creative use they make of it'.[63] Both issues of expertise and selection of sources therefore require the elaboration of a strategy as part of the justificatory exercise of the comparative research. Such strategy can be phrased in terms of caveats in the methodology part of the project.

---

[61] Wilson (n 4) 98.
[62] N Witzleb and others, 'Comparative Law and the Internet' (1999) 3 Electronic Journal of Comparative Law 2.
[63] Wilson (n 4) 98.

IV – Conclusion

The use of comparative law is no longer marginal and has largely pervaded legal scholarship. This is due notably to the necessity of understanding the more complex context in which the law operates locally, nationally, and internationally, which has transformed the system of validity of norms and their hierarchy. This is also increasingly related to the urge to address societal concerns. Yet, with no agreement on its meaning (i.e. comparative law as strictly a method or as a discipline in its own right), its purpose (i.e. not one identifiable purpose but a multiplicity of them), or method (i.e. different approaches), comparative law remains an open-ended matter which makes it fascinating but also challenging to deal with.

Since the method for comparative legal research 'needs to be treated as a central element of "legal method"',[64] steps need to be processed according to a framework which explains and justifies the choices made by the researcher. In other words, if one wants her study in comparative law to have scientific value and to contribute to knowledge progression, the method dictates that the researcher has to *expand* her research to the context and variables she thinks are appropriate to the research question, while, at the same time, *limit* it by a rigorous justificatory exercise. This is not (yet again) a definitive method which is provided here, but it is hoped that these lines will contribute to adding another perspective to the numerous studies in the field.

---

[64] Twining (n 4) 84. ·

CHAPTER 4

The Use of History in Law: Avoiding the Pitfalls

*Laura CAHILLANE**

I – INTRODUCTION

There are very few legal theses nowadays which concentrate solely on legal history. However, most legal theses will have aspects of history in them. It is often the first response of a lawyer to trace the history of a particular provision or principle, in order to find its roots or its authority. Often, when beginning a dissertation, the law student will decide that the first (or easiest) task will be to look back over the history of the chosen aspect of the law, from its foundations to its status in the law today. However, while lawyers sometimes feel that history comes naturally to them – judges routinely trace the development of legal principles in their judgments, it is how we teach aspects of the law and often how we write about law – as Reid has warned, it only comes naturally in a certain way.[1] In criticising Chief Justice Earl Warren's comment that 'All lawyers are, of course, in some sense students of legal history', Reid points out that lawyers are interested only in 'the latest interpretation of the rule' and are not worried about the rule in its original context, only 'the net result of [its] evolution, the latest judicial, non-historical appraisal or interpretation of the rule.'[2] Thus, while we may think that a legal historical approach is natural in legal writing, we have to consider the purpose of the approach. There are certain pitfalls and dangers in using a legal history approach and so we must be careful not to be complacent and use history for our own ends. As long as we are aware of the dangers, however, it will be easier to avoid them. In order to illustrate these dangers, we will first take a brief look at the use of history in legal thought.

---

* Dr Laura Cahillane is a lecturer in Constitutional law at the University of Limerick.
[1] J P Reid, 'Law and History' (1993) 27 Loyola Law Review 193, 195.
[2] ibid.

II – The Beginnings of using History in Legal Thought: Savigny and Maine

Rather than trying to trace the use of history in law down through the ages, examining the approaches of different theorists, which, as we shall see later, is something one might be cautioned against doing, I will instead focus on the work of two very influential legal historians: Friedrich Carl von Savigny and Sir Henry Sumner Maine.

Savigny is often credited with being the founder of the school of 'historical jurisprudence'.[3] This school developed in the nineteenth century in response to the 'ahistorical', rationalist natural law approaches which prevailed at the time. These rationalist approaches inspired the move towards codifying the law in various jurisdictions such as Prussia, France and Austria.[4] Savigny disagreed with the process of codification and he argued in his work, *Of the Vocation of our Age for Legislation and Jurisprudence*, that a code which was undertaken too quickly and without proper historical reflection, would obscure the 'moral energies of the nation'.[5] He felt that first, 'the linear lines of descent of the contemporary corpus of legal rules had to be traced before any legal reform along the lines of codification could commence.'[6] This was because, according to Savigny, the material of the law was derived from its entire past and all legal principles have a long past. Which meant that the only way to 'obtain mastery over the internal workings, complexities and nuances of contemporary legal rules', was to examine their past.[7] His method therefore, was 'to trace legal rules, concepts and principles to their roots so as to locate their 'leading axioms''.[8] As David Rabban has put it:

> 'Savigny simply substituted historical research for philosophical analysis as the method for identifying the legal principles from which to deduce a timeless legal structure. ... [His theory] portrayed legal history as an unconscious and inevitable process that revealed the gradual unfolding of the idea of individual freedom.'[9]

---

[3] D Rabban, 'Methodology in Legal History' in A Musson and C Stebbings (eds), *Making Legal History; Approaches and Methodologies* (Cambridge University Press 2012) 94.
[4] JM Kelly, *A Short History of Western Legal Theory* (Oxford University Press 1992) 258ff.
[5] FC Von Savigny, *Of the Vocation of our Age for Legislation and Jurisprudence* (The Lawbook Exchange, Ltd. 1831) 39. Also quoted in S Kilcommins, 'The Historical School of Jurisprudence' in T Murphy (ed), *Western Jurisprudence* (Round Hall 2004) 144, 147.
[6] ibid.
[7] ibid.
[8] ibid.
[9] Rabban (n 3) 94-95.

His central idea, which was later referred to as the *Volksgeist*, was the idea that certain laws are innate to a society — that law is 'shaped by the nation's peculiar soul'.[10] Savigny saw law as something which developed organically with a people, much in the same way as a language develops. Therefore, law is not an abstract set of rules imposed on society but has deep roots in social and economic factors and the attitude of its past and present members of the society. This feeds back into his argument that codification provides mere verbal expression to a body of existing law, whose meaning and content can only be discovered by careful historical investigation.

His theory that the meaning and content of existing bodies of law could be analysed through research into their historical origins and development has been very influential.[11] However, it has a number of shortcomings which will be of relevance to legal historians today. The main problem, as noted by Kilcommins, is that his theory is 'ahistorical in design, compartmentalising huge tracts of history into a neat package of evolution.'[12] Basically, he simplifies something which is actually much more complex than his interpretation of it. His concept of the *Volksgeist* is very unclear — it is not always possible to discern the consciousness of the people. He also over-emphasises the importance of custom and underestimates the role of legislation and crucially, for our purposes, he overstates the role of history, as a teleological method, in interpreting the law. Significantly, his method reads as 'surface narrative which, when scratched, revealed a lack of depth and rigour.'[13] Skimming over history in this way, assuming the progression of time equates to progress, and forming conclusions which are not based on in-depth analysis of the period in time is dangerous. Thus, while he remains significant as one of the first proponents of the legal history approach, the actual approach which Savigny advocated is problematic.

There are certain similarities in the work of Maine, who like Savigny, was opposed to natural law and the utilitarian method. As has been pointed out, 'both jurists also agreed on the importance of Roman law and the merits of analysing legal change through an evolutionary historical lens.'[14] Maine saw himself as a 'scientific historian of legal evolutions', with his analysis

---

[10] Kilcommins (n 5) 148.
[11] JG de Montmorency, 'Friederich Carl von Savigny' in J McDonell and E Mason (eds), *Great Jurists of the World*, (Augustus M. Kelly 1968) 586, and KJ Smith and JPS McLaren, 'History's Living Legacy: An Outline of the 'Modern' Historiography of the Common Law' (2001) 21 Legal Studies 251.
[12] Kilcommins (n 5) 149.
[13] ibid 153.
[14] ibid.

reaching back to primitive Indo-European societies.[15] Smith and McLaren note that from these distant origins, 'Maine purported to demonstrate the emergence of 'progressive' societies from tribalism, customary law and co-ownership ... to one of individualism: famously captured as 'a movement from Status to Contract'.'[16] Maine's theory was that all legal systems evolved in a predetermined, linear trajectory and eventually 'would resemble each other in their maturity.'[17] His scientific historical analysis was based on the notion that societies had to pass through a series of transformative stages, from simple stages at the beginning, which were based on arbitrary commands, through to the era of codes, and eventually, if the society was a 'progressive' one, it would transform into a system which would employ Maine's instruments of legal change: legal fictions, equity and legislation.[18] Gordon has described it as the notion that 'the natural and proper evolution of a society is towards the type of liberal capitalism seen in the advanced Western nations.[19]

Maine's comparative historical analysis may have 'inspired over half a century of scholarship in history and political science',[20] but there are major difficulties with his approach. Smith and McLaren refer to it as 'a form of anthropological Whiggism'.[21] This refers to the view of history as a simple lineage; it involves viewing the past in terms of the 'winners' — the institutions and structures that survived – and assumes that present situations are the ideal result. Rather than investigating how or why things actually happened, it assumes a continued advance and it leads to historical events and concepts being divorced from their context. Maine's evolutionary theory is now classed as a 'narrative of progress', an oversimplification and ahistorical analysis,[22] which simplifies the past and idealises the inexorable march toward the future, progress, and enlightenment. As Kilcommins has put it, 'Plundering history in this manner resulted in the distortion of the complexities and intricacies of earlier societies whilst also leading to a 'complete misapprehension of the relations between the past and the present'.'[23]

---

[15] Smith & McLaren (n 11) 256.
[16] ibid 256-257.
[17] P Stein, *Legal Evolution: The Story of an Idea* (Cambridge University Press 1980) 86.
[18] Kilcommins (n 5) 155.
[19] R Gordon, 'Critical Legal Histories' (1984) 36 Stanford Law Review 57, 59.
[20] Smith & McLaren (n 11) 256. See also, S Collins, *That Noble Science of Politics* (Cambridge University Press 1983) ch 7.
[21] ibid.
[22] Kilcommins (n 5) 165.
[23] ibid, quoting H Butterfield, *The Whig Interpretation of History* (G Bell and Sons 1963) 14.

So, what can we learn from these theorists? Both jurists can be commended for their influence and for promoting the use of history in legal thought and legal writing. However, both made crucial mistakes in their approaches. They both employed 'presentist' or 'Whiggish' histories in attempting to use history to explain developments in the current time. While both claimed to employ a 'scientific' approach, in fact both are guilty of using vague and broad notions and very little pragmatic evidence. They may have had the right idea in promoting the use of history in law but both fell into traps which we now recognise as common pitfalls for legal historians. We will return to these difficulties shortly, but first we must consider another debate in legal historical methodology — the internal versus external legal history debate.

III – INTERNAL V EXTERNAL LEGAL HISTORIES

Lawyers are often criticised by historians for focusing on purely internal approaches to legal history. The internal approach is a doctrinal one, which deals with sources involved in the legal process itself: cases, law reports, legal treatises. It is sometimes referred to, disparagingly, as 'lawyer's history' or 'law office history',[24] and is criticised as giving 'a stark, crabbed, oversimplified picture of the past, developed largely to plead a case.'[25] For example, under this approach, a lawyer will trawl through various historical examples until she finds one that justifies her case or proves her point, notwithstanding the fact that the example might be completely irrelevant when divorced from its context. External legal history, on the other hand, has become much more fashionable and can be described as 'the history of law as embedded in its context, typically its social or economic context.'[26] In as much as the internal approach is described as doctrinal, we can refer to the external approach as looking at the 'law in action' – almost a historical version of the socio-legal approach. As Ibbetson makes clear, 'it is the action that matters. It is the way law operates in society, which seems to have law as the given and its operation as the thing that needs to be examined.'[27] This approach is much closer to the method used by historians in that the law is not studied in isolation but within its social context, and the external legal historian is interested in the effect of that social context.

---

[24] J P Reid (n 1) 197.
[25] S Krislov, 'The Amicus Brief: From Friendship to Advocacy', in Gottfried Dietze (ed), *Essays on the American Constitution* (Prentice Hall 1964) 77.
[26] D Ibbetson, 'What is Legal History a History of?' in A Lewis and M Lobban (eds), *Law and History – Current Legal Issues Vol 6* (UCL 2003) 33.
[27] ibid.

The internal approach has received a lot of bad press in recent years. Morton Horwitz, a leading American legal historian, of the critical school of legal history, has argued that to write lawyers' history 'is to pervert the real function of history by reducing it to the pathetic role of justifying the world as it is'.[28] Another twentieth century legal historian, Roscoe Pound criticised the internal approach for assuming 'that legal change is caused exclusively by legal phenomena and that current legal issues could be decided by logical deductions from past law.'[29] However, these comments are a little harsh and while there may be some basis for the criticism of the way certain types of internal legal history are carried out, there is still a place for doctrinal legal history. In fact, there is nothing wrong with an internal approach — it can be the most useful approach in certain instances, for example, when looking at the history of private law, which often lends itself to such an approach. However, it must be acknowledged that this is the approach being taken, as otherwise, dangerous assumptions can be made about the meanings of past concepts, which without studying them in their context, may not translate easily into modern times. To take a simple example, today we would interpret the words 'secret ballot' to refer to a process involving complete and inviolable secrecy in voting but under the Irish Electoral Act 1923, there were provisions which enabled a voter's ballot paper to be identified. Similarly, the word 'child' could refer to a person under the ages of 12, 16 or 18 depending on the period in time and the context. Therefore, it is important not to impute or assume modern meanings and being cognisant of such a danger will help to avoid it.

Internal history is sometimes criticised for looking at the past through the lens of the present. Michael Lobban has explained how to avoid this by reference to 'the great lesson taught by Milsom', another influential English legal historian. The lesson was that 'legal historians who wanted to understand the 'internal' history of the law — its doctrines and practices — had to attempt to think like a lawyer of the age they were studying. They should not look at past law through the lenses of contemporary legal doctrine.'[30] Lobban explains that for Milsom, 'legal history was therefore a form of intellectual history. In undertaking it, one had to grasp the fact that terms and concepts which hold one meaning for us held a different meaning in different times.'[31]

---

[28] Rabban (n 3) 92.
[29] R Pound, 'The Scope and Purpose of Sociological Jurisprudence III' (1912) 25 HLR 489, 514-15.
[30] M Lobban, 'The Varieties of Legal History' (2012) 5 Revue Électronique d'Histoire du Droit para 14 <www.cliothemis.com/The-Varieties-of-Legal-History>
[31] ibid.

Thus, there is no reason to criticise the internal or doctrinal approach, if used correctly. However, there are those working under that approach who use history selectively for their own ends and this is what has resulted in the criticism and decrease in popularity of the internal approach. But this is not the internal approach proper. In fact, this is what we can properly label the so-called 'lawyer's history' approach. If we separate the concept of 'lawyer's history' from the internal approach, we can identify the approach to be avoided. This is the method which traces universal legal ideas and concepts 'through historic seams of authority in unbroken lineage and the past is enlisted to serve present ends.'[32] In other words, a lawyer's history approach does not respect history but uses examples selectively, often divorced from their context, simply to justify an argument in a case. Thus, an internal or doctrinal approach in itself is not problematic and indeed may be most useful, as long as the practitioner remembers that concepts must be understood in their own contexts, and as long as the advice of Milsom, to avoid the narrow 'lawyer's history' approach, is heeded.

IV – THINGS TO AVOID

Having looked at the methods of early legal historians and the problems with their approaches and taking into account the varying approaches to legal history, there are certain themes which come through and help us to identify the pitfalls in this type of methodology.

Presentism/Whig History

The first snare to avoid is that of presentism, sometimes called Whig history. Both Maine and Savigny were guilty of this and legal historians who came after them, such as Maitland, openly rejected their approach, which was 'a use of the past to tell an evolutionary or teleological story for use ''by modern courts to suit modern facts''.[33] It basically involves an assumption that society is constantly improving and, as a consequence, practices today are better than those of the past. It also involves interpreting the past in a manner consistent with present values rather than those relevant to the time. The term 'Whig history' was coined by Herbert Butterfield, in his 1931 book *The Whig Interpretation of History*,[34] in which he criticised certain English constitutional historians for using the past to

---

[32] P Handler, 'Legal History' in Dawn Watkins and Mandy Burton (eds), *Research Methods in Law* (Routledge 2013) 85.

[33] J Rose, 'Musing on Clio: Why Study the Past, History, and Legal History' (Fifth Annual Rare Books Lecture, Tarlton Law Library, University of Texas School of Law, May 2009) 16, quoting Maitland <http://papers.ssrn.com/sol3/papers.cfm?abstract_id=1411875>.

[34] H Butterfield, *The Whig Interpretation of History* (G Bell & Sons 1931).

justify the present. Butterfield's aim was to point out the dangers of glorifying and distorting the past in order to uphold a particular view of the present. Maitland also referred to such an approach as 'a process of perversion and misunderstanding' and insisted on 'understanding the past on its own terms and in its contemporary context and ideas.'[35] In a similar vein, the well-known British theorist, AV Dicey, was critical of the practice of lawyers who would '[retrieve] the past for normative guidance into a world that "is"',[36] or who believed that the function of the past was to elucidate the present.

In discussing this problem, Lobban refers to the linguistic philosophy of the positivist theorist, HLA Hart, in order to combat a Whiggish approach. Hart argued that 'in order to understand legal ideas, one had to examine the use of particular words in context, to see the linguistic practices of a community.'[37] Lobban points out that the lesson to be learned from Hart and his contemporaries of the Cambridge School is that 'we cannot assume legal notions which were expressed in the past bore the same meanings as they do now.'[38] Lobban feels that keeping this in mind may warn legal historians off a Whiggish approach to the subject.[39] While the term 'Whig history' has certainly become a disparaging criticism of certain types of history, it is quite acceptable to use history to explain developments and to better understand the present. What is important is that an objective approach is maintained and that the interpretation of history is not coloured by the views of the present. Thus, the aspiring legal historian needs to be careful not to use history to simply justify the present or to see history as a constant and linear process.

Law and History as Authority — Lawyers v Historians

Another danger of which legal historians must be aware is seeking to use legal history purely as a source of authority. In order to explain this danger, we need to say a little more on the debate over the different approaches of lawyers and historians. FW Maitland, sometimes referred to as the modern father of English legal history, drew a distinction between the methods of historians and lawyers when using history. Historians operate on the 'logic of evidence', whereas lawyers are only interested in 'the logic of authority'.

---

[35] ibid.
[36] A V Dicey, *Introduction to the Study of the Law of the Constitution* (Macmillan and Co 1885). See also, (10th edn, Macmillan 1959) 22.
[37] Lobban in A Lewis and M Lobban (eds), *Law and History – Current Legal Issues Vol 6* (UCL 2003) 2-3.
[38] ibid 4.
[39] ibid.

Prest puts the theory well in describing how Maitland sees historians and lawyers as operating on 'quite distinct wavelengths, using two different modes of argument'.[40] He states further that:

> Laywers, according to Maitland, are primarily interested in finding legal authorities, the more recent the better, with which to support the cases of their clients. Historians, on the other hand, recognize themselves as bound by no authority, except evidence bearing on the event or phenomena they study; generally speaking, the closer that evidence in time to their subject, the greater its credibility and utility.[41]

Reid has also discussed this difference in approach, arguing that crossing history with law is a dangerous enterprise 'containing more snares than rewards, as it risks confusing the rules of evidence basic to one profession with canons of proof sacrosanct to another.'[42] He points out that 'Lawyers, to function as lawyers, do not have to learn anything of sixteenth-century law, or of the rule's subsequent historical evolution. All that lawyers need care about is the net result of that evolution, the latest judicial nonhistorical appraisal or interpretation of the rule.'[43] Reid accepts that the lawyer and historian both go to the past for evidence but he feels the similarity ends there. He also cites Maitland's argument that while the historian weighs every bit of evidence which comes to hand, the lawyer is only interested in the single authority that will settle the case at hand.[44]

Gough has provided an interesting illustration of this: 'In the English lawyer's view, a judge who applies a law to a fresh case elucidates what was always, potentially as it were, the law on that particular matter.'[45] In other words, the lawyer is interested in the final or 'true' interpretation of the rule whereas a historian will be interested to know what the rule meant to each generation to which it applied. The danger here is that the lawyer, in her search for authority, will 'commingle the current interpretation of the law with the historical interpretation.'[46]

---

[40] W Prest, 'Law for Historians: William Blackstone on Wives, Colonies and Slaves' (2007) 11 Legal History 105.
[41] ibid.
[42] Reid (n 1) 193.
[43] ibid 195.
[44] ibid 196.
[45] J W Gough, *Fundamental Law in English Constitutional History* (Clarendon Press 1985) 6-7.
[46] Reid (n 1) 197.

The greatest danger however, in this search for authority rather than evidence, is highlighted by Reid and it happens when history is used, 'not to learn about the past, but merely to support an outcome.' In most cases, when this approach is employed, the decision has already been formulated and the history is a convenient way of justifying the decision.[47] Gordon refers to this phenomenon as a search for legitimacy: 'It reassures us that what we do now flows continuously out of our past, out of precedents, traditions, fidelity to statutory and Constitutional texts and meanings.'[48] However, just because something happened and was accepted in the past does not give it a legitimacy today. To take such an approach would mean that the law would never change. Take for example, the law on marital rape, which was accepted and upheld through historic precedents for years until the exemption which allowed the practice was finally abolished in 1991.[49] Thus, lawyers have to be very careful in using history as authority or legitimacy for some current legal rule.

History as a Search for Truth

Linked to this is the idea, which lawyers sometimes have, of finding legal 'truth' in the past. Daniel Boorstin has labelled this as a kind of 'legal embryology',[50] which is described as 'a search in the rudimentary forms of the past for the origins and growth of the more fully developed law of the present, often presented as "the inevitable culmination of this process."'[51] Musson and Stebbings have also addressed this:

> 'Legal historians however can show that legal 'truth' is no more in the past than in the present and that a historical framework must take account of a number of different legalities. Indeed, they embrace a different kind of truth – a historical 'truth' that accepts uncertainty and appreciates the contingency of legal authority and the sometimes shaky foundations of the law (which lawyers rarely admit).'[52]

However, some, such as Prest, argue that Maitland and others have overstated the 'propensity of lawyers to misread and misuse history' and have exaggerated the gap between legal and historical reasoning.[53] Personally, I would agree: in my experience, lawyers very often make excellent legal

---

[47] ibid 204.
[48] R Gordon, 'The Arrival of Critical Historicism' (1997) 49 Stan L Rev 1023.
[49] *R v R* [1992] 1 AC 599.
[50] D J Boorstin, 'Tradition and Method in Legal History (1941) 54 HLR 424, 429.
[51] Rabban (n 3) 92.
[52] Musson and Stebbings (n 3) 4.
[53] Prest (n 39) 105.

historians. As Handler has emphasised, it is not necessary to acquire a degree in history in order to employ historical methodologies, as long as legal historians are 'mindful of the ever-present, if not entirely avoidable, risk of being "enticed into carrying concepts and even social frameworks back into periods to which they do not belong".'[54] A useful suggestion by Handler for the aspiring legal historian aiming to avoid these difficulties is to engage in a meaningful dialogue with experts in different fields – sage advice indeed.

V – Things to Remember

To sum up, employing a legal history methodology can be a very useful and rewarding process. However, as with any methodology, there are various matters which must be carefully considered before embarking on such an approach.

First, one must take care not to glorify the past. As legal historians, we have to remain objective and detached. Nostalgia is not the friend of the legal historian! Furthermore, when interpreting history, we have to be aware of our own standpoints and biases. In order to adequately interpret the past, it is first necessary to identify our own perspectives and how these might influence our interpretation. As Prest notes, 'the past is gone forever, and we can never hope to "reconstruct" it in all its complexity. But this does not mean that we are free to treat it as blank canvas for our own creative imaginations or present-day preoccupations to work upon – at least if we aspire to call the result history, not fiction or polemic.'[55] We must endeavour to provide a fair interpretation of legal history. That is, an interpretation which best reflects what contemporary agents understood the law to be.[56]

As we have seen, it is also necessary to avoid an interpretation which sees history as a narrative of progress, as did Maine. As has been noted above, there is an argument that lawyers have a tendency to 'misuse history by attempting to make what is complex and multifaceted into a linear progress'.[57] However, this is also easy to avoid as long as one is aware of the tendency. Karl Marx famously saw history as a march of progress and believed that our experiences would eventually lead to a new and improved future. However, this simplifies history and denigrates and distorts the

---

[54] See Handler (n 32) 96, quoting S F C Milsom, *Historical Foundations of the Common Law* (2nd ed, Butterworths 1981) vi.
[55] Prest in Musson and Stebbings (n 3) 210.
[56] M Lobban, 'Introduction: The Tools and Tasks of the Legal Historian' in M Lobban and A Lewis (eds), *Law and Legal History* (OUP 2004) 1.
[57] ibid 13.

complexities of earlier societies and their practices. We cannot assume that what happens today is somehow better than what happened in the past just because time has moved on. The passage of time does not necessarily equate to improvement in law and society.

We must also consider that, if the past is a foreign country, then it is necessary to learn the language in order to get by. This means learning about the meaning of words, concepts and principles in their own contexts rather than assuming the modern meaning. Gordon gives an example of the meaning of the word 'Liberty' in the eighteenth century as opposed to its modern meaning.[58] Adopting an external approach may avoid this. In fact, Lobban argues that it is only with the aid of the external perspective that we can make sense of the internal developments.[59]

It is also important to avoid prefatory histories. This is a danger in theses and dissertations which are not focused purely on legal history, but which draw on history in some way. As mentioned at the beginning of this chapter, often the first response of a lawyer is to begin her research by tracing the history of her particular subject. However, if this history serves no other purpose than as padding, or as a way of easing into the central question, then it is a prefatory history, which is not useful. Often, all this will do is use up precious word limits. If you intend to introduce your topic by drawing on its history, then make sure the history is relevant to the central question. On the other hand, a relevant historical introduction can be very useful and can contribute significantly to the understanding of the concept at issue.

So, these are all the things to avoid when using history in law, which raises the question of how history should be used. Very simply, history should be used for its own sake. It can be used to demonstrate the conditions of emergence of a particular law or practice, in order to better understand it. It can also be used to demonstrate how thinking might have changed on an issue or even to highlight an injustice. Oliver Wendell Holmes was very careful about his use of history, stating in his work, *Common Law*: 'I shall use the history of our law so far as it is necessary to explain a conception or to interpret a rule, but no further.'[60] Perhaps this approach is a little overly-cautious. Pound was more optimistic about the use of history when he reasoned it should be used to 'illustrate ... how

---

[58] Gordon (n 47) 1025.
[59] Lobban (n 56) 28.
[60] O W Holmes, *Common Law* (American Bar Association 1881) 5.

legal precepts — rules, principles, conceptions and standards — have met concrete situations of fact in organising human society in the past and enabling or helping us to judge how we may deal with such situations with some assurance in the present.'[61] As long as the danger of removing meanings from their original historical setting is avoided, such an enterprise is entirely possible. Handler suggests that one function of legal history is to challenge the assumptions that inform and underpin modern legal scholarship. He points out that: 'It is a commonplace of legal argument to refer to the historical pedigree of a particular rule or institution as an indicator of its strength and value.' In response to this, legal history can serve as a 'useful myth dispelling function ... [by] testing the validity of claims using historical evidence.'[62] Handler also notes that scrutinising past law in its historical context can also reveal errors in current thinking or cause us to question analytical models.[63] History can be used in legal writing in lots of different ways and as long as the advice above is borne in mind, it can be a very worthwhile pursuit.

---

[61] R Pound, 'Introduction' in F Pollock and F W Maitland, *The History of English Law before the time of Edward I* (2nd edn, Washington 1959).
[62] Handler (n 32) 95.
[63] ibid.

Chapter 5

Legal Material and Historical Research

*Thomas MOHR**

I – Introduction

First year law students are introduced to the connection between the fields of law and history soon after they begin their legal studies. For example, they learn that law in most of the former British Empire follows the common law tradition, information that immediately requires a historical introduction in order to make sense. They learn that this tradition focuses on precedents set in the past that require analysis and evaluation. This ensures that their textbooks are filled with historical material that is seldom limited to the introductory chapter. Students become familiar with their country's constitution which also requires a historical introduction to put it into its proper context. Later, they will encounter Equity, an area of law that would be incomprehensible without some knowledge of history. Their introduction to Property Law will begin with explanations of the feudal system and its influence on tenure of land.

Legal scholars cannot avoid some engagement with historical research methodologies, however hard they might try. The purpose of this chapter is to provide researchers with a guide as to how to approach and utilise source material concerning legal history. The main methodological challenge facing researchers examining legal historical material is finding and evaluating the sources. The actual material, once discovered, is largely the same as that used by legal researchers examining other aspects of law. These sources include statutes, case reports, law journals and textbooks. The main source of novelty concerns the use of archive sources. In all cases, the researcher will need to have a good grasp of the historical context behind the relevant source.

This chapter will focus on legal historical source material. Limitations of space ensure that it cannot be a complete and comprehensive guide. Instead, it seeks to offer a short and accessible introduction to actually using this

---

* Dr Thomas Mohr is a lecturer in the School of Law, University College Dublin.

source material. It will focus on legal historical source material that is relevant to the island of Ireland, which was a single jurisdiction until partition in 1920.

There are many challenges that face any researcher who seeks to engage with legal sources that might be considered 'historical' in nature. The first challenges encountered by researchers in the field of Irish legal history include the loss of many archive sources, the absence of any general textbook on Irish legal history, and significant gaps in the secondary sources currently available. These challenges are significant but not insuperable.

II – Using Primary Sources

As mentioned above, the main methodological challenge facing researchers in the field of Irish legal history is actually finding the primary sources. This challenge is not confined to the laborious process of searching through archive documents, in which progress can be slow and the final results uncertain. Finding sources such as old statutes and case reports present their own unique challenges.

Statutes

Early English statutes can be accessed in *The Statutes of the Realm* and *The Statutes at Large* which cover the period between the 13th and 19th centuries.[1] No equivalent to these useful series was ever produced in Ireland. Consequently, the challenges that face the historian attempting to use statutes as historical sources in the field of Irish history are considerable. The most significant are the difficulties in actually accessing many older Irish statutes and determining whether or not particular statutes passed at Westminster actually applied to Ireland.

Statutes were not a feature of early Irish law, popularly known as 'Brehon law'.[2] The institution of having a legislature pass statutes evolved in the 12th and 13th century Anglo Norman settlements in Ireland in parallel to similar

---

[1] The *Statutes of the Realm* (Vols 1-12, Record Commission, 1810-1825) and O Ruffhead, *The Statutes at Large* (Vols 1-18, multiple publishers, 1763-1800).

[2] F Kelly, *Guide to Early Irish Law* (Dublin Institute for Advanced Studies 1988) is the best introductory source to this field and includes a list of all the early Irish law tracts. These tracts were first reproduced in the *Ancient Laws of Ireland* published between 1865 and 1901 in five volumes. These translations have been heavily criticised, for example see DA Binchy, 'The Linguistic and Historical Value of the Irish Law Tracts' (1943) 29 Proc Brit Acad 195, 214. Binchy himself attempted to provide improved translations in his *Corpus Iuris Hibernici* (Dublin Institute for Advanced Studies 1978). A useful companion work is L Breatnach, *A Companion to the Corpus Iuris Hibernici* (Dublin Institute for Advanced Studies 2005).

developments in England.³ It is difficult to define what constituted legislation in medieval Ireland. It is not until the end of the 13th century that the word 'statute' as a description of legislation began to take precedence over such alternatives as 'proviso', 'constitution' 'ordinance', 'writ' or 'mandate'.⁴ For example, the famous 'Statutes' of Kilkenny passed in 1366, intended to halt the adoption of Irish culture by the Anglo Normans, was originally entitled 'ordinaunces et articles'.⁵ The loose and inconsistent use of terminology makes it difficult to distinguish statutes from other medieval legal instruments. This reality renders it impossible to identify a particular measure as the earliest Irish statute without the possibility of dispute. The earliest statute that remains in force in the Republic of Ireland dates from 1293.⁶ Other complicating factors relevant to the application of statute law in late medieval Ireland include the reality that the jurisdiction of the common law only covered parts of the island and the position that most of the native Irish were excluded from access to English law, even within the regions under Crown control.⁷

An additional complication in this area concerns the reality that the 'Lordship of Ireland' created by the Anglo Norman invasion was subject to legislation passed by two legislatures. Statutes enacted in England and Ireland formed part of Irish law throughout the late medieval and early modern periods. Geoffrey Hand concludes: 'It is, in fact, far more difficult to find an English statute of major significance for the development of common law which does not seem to have applied in Ireland than to enumerate those that did'.⁸ Poynings' Act of 1495 (10 Henry VII c.22 (Irl)) brought an additional body of English statutes into Irish law and gave them overriding status over statutes passed by the Irish parliament. Yet there was always a degree of uncertainty as to which English statutes passed at Westminster applied to Ireland and

---

³ WN Osborough, 'The Legislation of the Pre-Union Irish Parliament' in Osborough (ed) *The Irish Statutes, Revised Edition: 3 Edward II to the Union, AD 1310-1800* (Round Hall 1995) (Reprint of edition published London, 1885).

⁴ HG Richardson and GO Sayles, 'The Early Statutes' (1934) 50 LQR 201. AG Donaldson, *The Application in Ireland of English and British Legislation made before 1801* (PhD thesis, Queen's University Belfast 1952) 8-15, and Osborough (n 3) B.

⁵ HG Richardson and GO Sayles, *Parliaments and Councils of Medieval Ireland* (Irish Manuscripts Commission 1947) xix-xx.

⁶ The earliest measure with a definite date to be repealed by the Statute Law Revision Act 2007 was a Charter granted by Henry II to Dublin, 1171-72 (17 & 18 Hen. 2).

⁷ GJ Hand, *English Law in Ireland 1290-1324* (Cambridge University Press 1967) and B Murphy, 'The Status of the Native Irish after 1331' (1967) 2 Irish Jurist 116.

⁸ GJ Hand, 'English Law in Ireland, 1172-1351' (1972) 23(4) NILQ 393, 400.

which did not.⁹ Matters were further complicated by a strong body of opinion in Ireland that maintained that Westminster had no right to extend English statutes to Ireland. For example, in 1698 William Molyneux published a tract entitled *The case of Ireland's being bound by acts of parliament in England, stated,* whose central thesis was actually to deny that Ireland was in any way bound by such statutes.[10] This controversy was a dominant feature of Irish politics in the 18th century and was only brought to a close by the enactment of the Act of Union of 1800 that merged the Irish parliament in Dublin with the United Kingdom parliament at Westminster.[11] The union did not, of course, make statute law enacted for Ireland between 1801 and 1922 identical with that in England and Wales. Legislation was regularly enacted by Westminster for Ireland that did not apply to the rest of the United Kingdom. The phrase 'This Act shall not apply to Ireland' or later 'This Act shall not apply to Northern Ireland' in Westminster legislation has frustrated many researchers for the lack of consistency in its location, sometimes appearing in at the beginning, middle or end of a statute.

Perhaps the feature that has most impeded analysis of the entire corpus of Irish statute law is that there was never a revolutionary event in Irish history that removed a substantial part of it. The great historical landmarks of the twentieth century, partition, the signing of the Anglo Irish Treaty and the creation of the Irish Free Constitution in 1922 and its replacement by the current Constitution of 1937 had little impact on the great majority of existing statute law. Consequently, the number of statutes continued to accumulate over the centuries until it became an unmanageable mass riddled with uncertainty. The main sources of statutes extending to the state established in the 26 counties of the south and west of Ireland are as follows:

>Acts of the English parliament (pre-1707);
>
>Acts of the Irish parliament (pre-1800);
>
>Acts of the British parliament (1707-1800);
>
>Acts of the parliament of the United Kingdom of Great Britain and Ireland (1801-1922);
>
>Acts of the Oireachtas (parliament) of the Irish Free State (1922-1937)

---

⁹ The omnibus provisions of 10 Henry VII c.22 (Irl) created a sense of uncertainty as to which English statutes applied to Ireland. These difficulties were raised by Kennedy CJ in *R (Moore) v O'Hanrahan* [1927] IR 406. See also, Osborough (n 3) E to F.

[10] W Molyneaux, *The Case of Ireland Stated* (1698) and (Reprint, Cadenus Press 1977).

[11] A Lyall, *The Irish House of Lords: A Court of Law in the Eighteenth Century* (Clarus Press 2013).

Acts of the Oireachtas passed after the current Irish Constitution of 1937 came into force.[12]

This neat and tidy list hides a great deal of confusion in identifying which statutes applied to Ireland at various stages in its history. A few examples will suffice to illustrate the challenges facing historians in this field. First, there is considerable uncertainty as to which English statutes were imported by Poynings' Act in 1495.[13] Poynings' Act declared that all statutes 'late made' in England which concerned the 'common and public weal' were to apply in Ireland. It was never entirely clear which statutes were covered by these vague provisions.[14]

Secondly, poor record keeping could create additional uncertainty. Medieval statutes were recorded on statute rolls that were stored at Dublin Castle. Unfortunately, the poor repair of parts of Dublin Castle created storage conditions that were far from ideal. For example, in 1430 it was agreed to try to make basic improvements as 'the books and records are greatly damaged by rain and storms'.[15] Conditions had scarcely improved by 1758 when the Deputy Keeper of the records reported 'the Records daily suffer by Dust and Moisture'.[16] The desire to print a definitive Irish statute book in the early modern period was also defeated by the sheer number of statutes involved. This ensured that only selections of Irish statutes were ever printed in these centuries.[17] In 1885, the Irish Office, a department in the British government, printed all the statutes passed by the pre-Union parliament that were believed to still be in force at the time.[18] The completeness of the list created in 1885 is open to challenge. This uncertainty continues to cause problems in 21st century Ireland. A good example is the Marriage Act (No. 2) 1537, a statute

---

[12] For example, see R Byrne and JP McCutcheon, *Byrne and McCutcheon on the Irish Legal System* (5th edn, Bloomsbury 2007) 434.

[13] 10 Henry VII c.22 (Irl). This statute is named as Poynings Act 1495 in sch II of the Statute Law Revision Act 2007. This title is used in preference to the traditional name of 'Poynings' law' which also used to describe 10 Henry VII c.4 (Irl). The confusion in the use of this term is described in AG Donaldson, *Some Comparative Aspects of Irish Law* (Cambridge University Press 1957) 42-43.

[14] These difficulties were raised by Kennedy CJ in *R (Moore) v O'Hanrahan* [1927] IR 406. See also Osborough (n 3) E - F.

[15] P Crooks, 'Reconstructing the Past: The Case of the Medieval Chancery Rolls' in FM Larkin and NM Dawson (eds), *Lawyers, the Law and History* (Four Courts Press 2013) 291. See also, DB Quinn 'Government Printing and Publication of the Irish Statute in the Sixteenth Century' (1943/1944) 49 Proceedings of the Royal Irish Academy 45, 49.

[16] Herbert Wood, 'The Public Records of Ireland before and after 1922' (1930) 12 Transactions of the Royal Historical Society 17, 26.

[17] Osborough (n 3) F - I. See also, Quinn (n 15).

[18] Osborough (n 3).

that extended the class of relatives prohibited from marrying each other, which fell out of historical memory for centuries only to be unconsciously returned to Irish statute book in 2007.[19]

In the early 20th century, a determined attempt was made to provide a comprehensive record of all Irish statutes passed since 1204. Despite important contributions, this objective remained unfulfilled as the century reached its conclusion.[20] The early years of the 21st century produced additional efforts to fill the remaining gaps.[21] This work provided important assistance to the Statute Law Revision Project launched by the Irish government in 1998 with the objectives of repealing obsolete legislation and bringing greater order to the Irish statute book.[22]

The attempts made to clean out the Augean stables of Irish statute law do provide some assistance to the hapless researcher. For example, legislation revising Irish statute law was passed in 1872, 1878 and 1879 and provides the researcher with details of a large number of Irish statutes that were considered to be in force up to that date. The Statute Law Revision Act (Pre-Union Irish Statutes) Act 1962 represented the first attempt by the self-governing Irish state to fulfil a similar objective. The Statute Law Revision Project that commenced in the 1990s led to the enactment of the Statute Law Revision (Pre-1922) Act 2005 and the Statute Law Revision Acts 2007 and 2015. The 2007 Act repealed all statutes passed before 6 December 1922, with the exception of lists of statutes that were expressly retained. The Statute Law Revision Act 2015 has repealed all statutory instruments passed before 1 January 1821, with the exception of lists of instruments that were

---

[19] Statute Law Revision Act 2007. M Harding, 'The Curious Incident of the Marriage Act (No 2) 1537 and the Irish Statute Book' (2012) 32(1) Legal Studies 78. On the issue of the applicability of British Imperial statutes to the Irish Free State after 1922, see T Mohr 'British Imperial Statutes and Irish Sovereignty: Statutes Passed After the Creation of the Irish Free State' (2011) 32(1) Journal of Legal History 61; 'British Imperial Statutes and Irish Law: Statutes Passed Before the Creation of the Irish Free State' (2010) 31(3) Journal of Legal History 299, and 'The Colonial Laws Validity Act and the Irish Free State' (2008) 43 Irish Jurist 21.

[20] H F Berry (ed), *Statutes and Ordinances and Acts of the Parliament of Ireland, King John to Henry V* (H.M. Stationery Office 1907); *Statute Rolls of the Parliament of Ireland, Reign of Henry VI* (H.M. Stationery Office 1910); *Statute Rolls of the Parliament of Ireland, First to the Twelfth Years of the Reign of King Edward the Fourth* (H.M. Stationery Office 1914). J F Morrissey (ed), *Statute Rolls of the Parliament of Ireland, Twelfth and Thirteenth to the Twenty-First and Twenty-Second Years of the Reign of King Edward the Fourth* (Stationery Office 1939).

[21] P Connolly (ed), *Statute rolls of the Irish parliament, Richard III – Henry VIII* (Irish Manuscripts Commission 2002) and Osborough (n 3). See additional sources detailed in Statute Law Revision Act 2007, s 8.

[22] Statute Law Revision Programme <www.per.gov.ie/en/slrp/> (3 March 2016).

expressly retained. This revising legislation provides invaluable information for the legal historian.[23] In addition, for the first time in Irish history, we now have a comprehensive list of all legislation and statutory instruments currently in force.[24]

Case Reports

Reports of English cases are available from the middle ages onwards. Among the earliest are the 'Year Books' that report cases from the reign of Edward I (1272-1307) until the middle of the reign of Henry VIII (1509-1547). By the Tudor period, numerous authorities were producing law reports. The invention of printing in the early modern period opened a path to providing law reports accessible to a much wider readership. Yet, the practice of producing law reports was slow to take root in Ireland.

Case reporting was not a feature of the early Irish or 'Brehon' legal system.[25] Some of the medieval Irish plea rolls survived the tragic destruction of the Public Record Office in 1922 and provide evidence of Irish cases heard soon after the introduction and consolidation of the common law legal system.[26] Sir John Davies, attorney general of Ireland, published a number of select Irish cases in 1615.[27] G. Gilbert published reports of cases in equity in 1734 that were heard in the Courts of Exchequer and Chancery mostly during the reign of George I (1714-1727).[28] Henry Singleton, who would be appointed chief justice of the Court of Common Pleas in 1740, produced a collection of reports of cases decided in the Courts of Chancery and the Exchequer between 1716 and 1734.[29] Notwithstanding these early efforts, the regular production of case reports in Ireland really began in the 1790s. Law reports produced in this period do, on occasion, include reports of cases from as far back as the middle of the 18th century.

---

[23] Two additional measures, the Statute Law Revision Act 2009 and Statute Law Revision Act 2012, cover private Acts.

[24] See, Statute Law Revision Act 2007, sch 1 and Statute Law Revision Act 2015, sch 1.

[25] See F Kelly, *A Guide to Early Irish Law* (Dublin Institute of Advanced Studies 1988) 238-40.

[26] P Connolly, 'The Medieval Irish Plea Rolls – An Introduction' (1995) (Spring) Journal of the Irish Society for Archives 3.

[27] J Davies, *Le Primer Report des Cases & Matters en Ley resolues & adiudges en les Courts del Roy en Ireland* (John Franckton 1615). See also, H H Pawlisch, *Sir John Davies and the Conquest of Ireland: A Study in Legal Imperialism* (Cambridge University Press 1985) and P Brand, 'Sir John Davies: Law Reporter or Self-Publicist' (2008) 43 Irish Jurist 1.

[28] G Gilbert, *Reports of Cases in Equity* (Nutt and Gosling 1734). A second edition was published in the Savoy, London by Henry Lintot in 1742. Printed versions of eighteenth century Irish appeals to the English, later British, Court of King's Bench and House of Lords also survive. See L Redmond, 'Irish Appeals to the House of Lords in the Eighteenth Century' (1966) 23 Analecta Hibernica 245.

[29] A Lyall (ed), *Irish Exchequer Reports, 1716-34* (Selden Society 2009).

No single repository holds all law reports produced in Ireland between the 18th century and the present. Researchers interested in accessing the earliest law reports should try the Berkeley Library at Trinity College Dublin and the library of the Honorable Society of King's Inns. Several attempts have been made to create lists of Irish law reports but all these efforts appear to have been made in ignorance of each other and, perhaps inevitably, none is without error or omission.[30] Many early reports were intended as 'one-offs' covering a set number of years and were not intended as efforts to produce regular law reports. Nevertheless, the ephemeral nature of attempts to produce regular law reports is readily apparent from the most cursory examination of the history of law reporting. The establishment of the Irish Council of Law Reporting in 1866, known as the Incorporated Council of Law Reporting for Ireland since 1891, was an important development in achieving this elusive goal. This institution was responsible for the production of the Irish Reports, Common Law (1867-1878); the Irish Reports, Equity (1867-1878); Law Reports (Ireland) (1878-1893) and the Irish Reports (1894-Present).[31]

There was a substantial expansion in law reporting on both sides of the border in the 20th century. For example, the Northern Ireland Law Reports Bulletin of Judgments (also known as Northern Ireland Judgments Bulletin) began in 1972, the Bulletin of Northern Ireland Law in 1981 and the Irish Law Reports Monthly began publishing in 1981 but also produced selected judgments that go back as far as 1976. It should be remembered that records of unreported judgments are stored in university libraries and in those of professional bodies. Occasional attempts have been made to publish unreported judgments that have subsequently been considered important. Gerard L. Frewen produced a number of volumes containing previously unreported judgments of the Court of Criminal Appeal that go back to 1924.[32] The 1990s saw the production of the Irish Tax Reports that stretch back to 1922.[33] The Irish Association of Law Teachers also spearheaded a number of important initiatives at publishing unreported judgments in the 1980s and 1990s.[34]

---

[30] For example, P O'Higgins, *A Bibliography of Irish Trials and Other Legal Proceedings* (Professional Books 1986). See also, 'The History of Law Reporting in Ireland' (1869) 3 ILTSJ 659, 673; 'Irish Law Reports' (1931) 1 Law Journal (Irish Section) 9 and E G Hall, *The Superior Courts of Law: 'Official Law Reporting in Ireland, 1866-2006* (Incorporated Council of Law Reporting for Ireland 2007).

[31] Hall (n 30).

[32] GL Frewen (ed), *Judgments of the Court of Criminal Appeal 1924-1978* (Incorporated Council of Law Reporting for Ireland 1983). The editing of these reports was later taken over by Eithne Casey. See E Casey (ed), *Judgments of the Court of Criminal Appeal 1984-1989* (Round Hall 1991).

[33] BH Giblin and S Keegan (eds), *Irish Tax Reports – Volume 1* (Butterworth Ireland 1994).

[34] J Aston and M Doyle (eds), *Index to Irish Superior Court Written Judgments, 1976–1982* (IALT 1984) and *Index to Unreported Judgments of the Irish Superior Courts, 1966–1975* (IALT 1990).

The publication of the first of these volumes provided the impetus behind the decision of the Law Library in 1983 to record each written judgment as it issued. This would lay important foundations for the creation of online databases of Irish judgments.[35]

Archive Sources

Archive sources often contain useful records on how particular laws were applied and enforced. They can also reveal confidential material that shaped the drafting of a particular source of law. A seminal event in the history of Irish archives was the explosion and fire at the Irish Public Records Office, located in Dublin's Four Courts, on 30 June 1922 during the opening phase of the Irish civil war. In 1919, Herbert Wood, an archivist who would later be appointed deputy keeper at the Public Records Office, completed a *Guide to the records deposited in the Public Record Office of Ireland*, just three years before the destruction of most of this material.[36] As Wood would later observe: 'The tragedy of 1922 lies in the fact that the method of assembling the public records under one roof was the very means of making such a destruction possible'.[37] Yet, although much was lost in 1922, many sources survived, and new material has been generated since the foundation of the self-governing Irish state.

It is impossible to give an exhaustive account of all archival sources that store legal material. A few general points will have to suffice. The National Archives of Ireland, located on Bishop Street, Dublin, hold a great wealth of material awaiting scrutiny by legal scholars. These include medieval sources that survived the conflagration of 1922. They also store files generated by government departments after 1922. Those of most obvious relevance to legal researchers are Department of Justice papers, Department of the Taoiseach papers, Office of the Attorney General papers and the Office of the Department of the Parliamentary Draftsman papers.

The equivalent institution north of the border is the Public Record Office of Northern Ireland, located in Belfast. This institution stores documents generated by successive governments of Northern Ireland, but also stores other records of legal significance. The first deputy keeper of PRONI was

---

[35] T Mohr and J Schweppe, 'Irish Scholarship, Irish Law and the Irish Association of Law Teachers' in Mohr and Schweppe (eds) *Thirty Years of Legal Scholarship - The Irish Association of Law Teachers* (Round Hall 2011) 19.

[36] (Dublin 1919). See also, M Griffith, 'A Short Guide to the Public Record Office of Ireland' (1952-1953) 8 Irish Historical Studies 45.

[37] Wood (n 16) 49.

Dr DA Chart, who had previously worked at the destroyed Public Record Office at Dublin's Four Courts. His knowledge of the lost material allowed him to collect substitute documents, when possible, from private sources within Northern Ireland and beyond. The location of PRONI has moved a number of times throughout its history. It has recently settled down in a purpose built facility in Belfast's Titanic Quarter. Legal material of interest to historians in all parts of the island of Ireland can also be accessed at the National Archives of the United Kingdom at Kew, London.

Only government departmental records older than 30 years can be accessed in Ireland and the United Kingdom.[38] Both jurisdictions are gradually moving towards a "20-year rule".[39] Freedom of information legislation also allows government departmental records to be accessed before the expiry of 30 years, subject to certain restrictions.[40]

Many archives have placed some of their more important items online. There are obvious advantages to doing so, including reducing the need to handle the original documents and making material accessible to a far wider range of researchers. Nevertheless, at the time of writing, the number of archive documents online still constitutes a very small portion of sources available. The need to travel to visit an archive still remains the norm. The traditional tools of archive research are a pencil (never a pen) and paper, but this has changed with the advent of laptops and digital cameras. While laptops have proved unproblematic for archives, apart from the difficulty of providing enough power sockets, the advent of digital cameras has created particular challenges for researchers. The most pressing is maintaining discipline and avoiding the temptation to simply photograph every document accessed without any analysis of its relevance or utility. This approach is little more than a form of procrastination and may also cause unnecessary inconvenience to archivists and other researchers.

Few archives allow completely unregulated use of digital cameras and some form of application for permission to photograph documents may be required. Most archives forbid the use of flashes when photographing documents. Otherwise, the rules differ widely between different institutions and it is imperative to check them before producing your camera. At the time of writing, the National Archives of Ireland has recently altered its rules to

---

[38] National Archives Act 1986 in Ireland and Public Records Act 1967 in the United Kingdom.
[39] Constitutional Reform and Governance Act 2010.
[40] Freedom of Information Act 2014 in Ireland and Freedom of Information Act 2000 in the United Kingdom.

allow greater use of digital cameras. Digital cameras allow researchers to make greater use of limited time in the archives, particularly those who have travelled long distances. Photography may also assist in the preservation of paper documents, as it results in less physical touching of the document and much less chance of damage than photocopying. Nevertheless, some archives continue to forbid digital photography under any circumstances.

Many of the private papers stored at University College Dublin Archives contain a wealth of material awaiting scrutiny by legal scholars. These include the voluminous personal papers collected by such notable figures as Eamon de Valera (1882-1975), John A Costello (1891-1976), Cearbhall Ó Dálaigh (1911-1978), Hugh Kennedy (1879-1936) and Patrick McGilligan (1889-1979). The policy of this archive is to place as much material as possible on microfilm, in order to preserve the original documents. At the time of writing, this archive does not permit digital photography.

III – SECONDARY SOURCES

Textbooks and Other Publications

Those interested in examining the legal history of England are served by a number of textbooks that offer a general overview of this topic. Sir John Baker's *Introduction to English Legal History* provides a scholarly introduction to this area.[41] The same author has also helped to produce an essential guide to sources of private law up to 1750.[42] Older general sources such as Maitland and Pollock's *History of English Law before the time of Edward I*[43] and Holdsworth's *History of English Law* may still prove useful.[44] Unfortunately, Holdsworth's ambitious text is often criticised because the depth of research does not come up to standards of scholarship deemed acceptable to modern scholars.[45]

No equivalent introductory text exists for scholars of Irish legal history. One of the earliest efforts to provide a short chronological introduction to Irish legal history was attempted by FH Newark in the 1940s, followed by

---

[41] (4th edn, Oxford University Press 2002).
[42] JH Baker and SFC Milsom (eds), *Sources of English Legal History – Private Law to 1750* (2nd edn, Oxford University Press 2010).
[43] 2 volumes (Cambridge University Press 1895).
[44] 17 volumes (Sweet and Maxwell 1923-1966).
[45] RA Cosgrove, 'The Culture of Academic Legal History: Lawyers' History and Historians' Law 1870-1930' (2002) 33 Cambrian Law Review 23, 29-30.

AG Donaldson in the 1950s.[46] A more recent introduction and bibliographical guide is provided by J Sinder, who offers a useful starting point for those new to the field.[47]

Old textbooks may be useful sources in examining the state of Irish law at a particular point in the past. Unfortunately, the number of Irish law textbooks produced in the 19th and 20th centuries is disappointingly small. The small size of the Irish market was, and remains, the greatest challenge faced by law publishers. Hugh Kennedy, writing in the early 1930s, lamented the continuing dependence of Irish law schools on foreign textbooks. He hoped that the foundation of the Irish Free State would witness a flowering of Irish legal scholarship that would inject a spirit of intellectual vitality into Irish schools of law.[48] These ambitions had to wait until the 1970s, which saw the beginning of the publication of many new textbooks on Irish law, for fulfilment.[49] The assistance offered by the Law Society and funds generously donated by the Arthur Cox Foundation were important contributors to this expansion in Irish legal textbooks.[50]

The challenges faced by researchers in this area are offset by a considerable expansion in secondary sources in the field of Irish legal history in recent decades. WN Osborough has described the period following 1970 as 'the breakthrough years'.[51] There are a number of reasons for this expansion, but two stand out for particular attention. The first was a policy adopted by the *Irish Jurist*, since 1966, of providing particular encouragement for the submission of articles on subjects concerning legal history. The second was the foundation of the Irish Legal History Society, which has come close to publishing a book for every year since its foundation in 1988.

WN Osborough's *An Island's Law – A Bibliographical Guide to Ireland's Legal Past* (Four Courts Press 2013) goes some way towards compensating for the absence of a general textbook by creating a bibliography of Irish legal

---

[46] FH Newark, 'Notes on Irish Legal History' (1947) 7 NILQ 121. This was reprinted in 1960 as a pamphlet published by Queen's University Belfast. See also, AG Donaldson, *Some Comparative Aspects of Irish Law* (Cambridge University Press 1957).

[47] J Sinder, 'Irish Legal History: An Overview and Guide to the Sources' (2001) 93(2) Law Library Journal 231.

[48] T Mohr and J Schweppe, 'Irish Scholarship, Irish Law and the Irish Association of Law Teachers' in Mohr and Schweppe (eds) (n 35) 3.

[49] R Ní Uigín and C Dolan, 'Thirty Years of Irish Legal Publishing' in Mohr and Schweppe (eds) (n 35) 71.

[50] JF Buckley 'Legal Publishing' in EG Hall and D Hogan, *The Law Society of Ireland 1852-2002: Portrait of a Profession* (Four Courts 2002).

[51] WN Osborough, 'Legal History: Confronting the Challenge' in Mohr and Schweppe (eds) (n 35) 144.

historical works. The volume brings together two bibliographical guides published in the German journal *Zeitschrift für Neuere Rechtsgeschichte* in 1986 and 2008, and adds new material that brings the survey up to 2012. The resulting volume, published by the Irish Legal History Society, provides an extremely useful guide to secondary sources on Ireland's legal past.

Osborough's guide divides Irish legal history into key subject areas, for example works on the Irish courts, legislation and local government. The guide also covers historical works on areas of substantive law, such as the law of property, constitutional law, criminal law and ecclesiastical law. The important works in each division are examined in order of the chronology of the subject matter concerned. The obvious advantage of this approach is that it ensures that the book is a useful resource to scholars with broad and narrow interests in the field of Irish legal history. The usefulness of this bibliographical guide is enhanced by the inclusion of an index of authors in addition to a general index dealing with subject matter.[52] This guide, along with the article produced by Sinder, offers the best place for scholars who are completely unfamiliar with sources of Irish legal history to start their research.[53]

A key secondary source that deserves a special mention is EH Ball's *The Judges of Ireland, 1221-1921*.[54] This work, published in two volumes in 1926, is of obvious utility for any legal research involving analysis of case law, the judiciary and legal institutions at a particular point in history.[55] Nevertheless, the field of legal biography is relatively undeveloped in Ireland. This situation has been somewhat ameliorated by the publication of the *Dictionary of Irish Biography* or *'DIB'*.[56] James McGuire, one of the editors responsible for the launch of this important scholarly resource, provides an overview of legal biography in the *DIB* from the time of Dubthach of the moccu Lugair, an early medieval poet and judge, to Mella Carroll (1934-2006), the first woman to be appointed as a judge of the Irish High Court.[57] The British equivalent to the *DIB*, the *Oxford Dictionary of National*

---

[52] See also, P O'Higgins, A *Bibliography of Periodical Literature Relating to Irish Law* (Northern Ireland Legal Quarterly 1966, with supplements 1973 and 1983).

[53] Sinder (n 47).

[54] (J Murray 1926).

[55] For additional details on medieval judges and legal officials, see HG Richardson and GO Sayles, *The Administration of Ireland, 1172-1377* (Irish Manuscripts Commission 1963).

[56] J McGuire and J Quinn, *Dictionary of Irish Biography* (Cambridge University Press 2009). An internet database is also available on a subscription basis.

[57] J McGuire, 'Law as a "Field of Interest" in the Royal Irish Academy's *Dictionary of Irish Biography*' in Larkin and Dawson (eds) (n 15) 3-4.

Biography or *'ODNB'*, also contains useful biographical material for many persons who contributed to the development of Irish law over the centuries.[58]

The *DIB* has been criticised for its focus on judicial biography at the expense of attention to barristers and solicitors. James McGuire points out that solicitors and barristers do not leave behind written judgments, tangible records for the historian.[59] Nevertheless, there are now a large number of general works that deal with the development of the legal professions in Ireland.[60]

Law Journals

The oldest law journal in Ireland is the *Irish Jurist*. A journal bearing this name has been in existence since 1848. This history of over one and a half centuries has seen many changes of identity and structure.[61] Since 1966 this journal has been associated with the School of Law, University College Dublin. The decades that followed have seen 'the Jurist' consolidate its position as a leading law journal.

Recent decades have witnessed an explosion of new Irish law journals. For example, the *Dublin University Law Journal* began in 1976 and many student journals and journals dedicated to specialised areas of Irish law followed.[62] The range of law journals was far more restricted in the early 20th century. The 20th century witnessed a break in the long existence of the *Irish Jurist* between 1905 and 1935.[63] The Law Society of Ireland, responsible for regulating the solicitors' profession, did establish a gazette in 1907.[64] However, this publication could not really be described as a journal, as its contents focused on the discussions of the governing council, reports of court

---

[58] HCG Matthew and B Harrison (eds), *Oxford Dictionary of National Biography* (Oxford University Press 2004). An internet database is also available on a subscription basis.

[59] McGuire (n 57).

[60] For example, see E Keane et al, *King's Inns Admission Papers, 1607-1867* (Irish Manuscripts Commission 1982); D Hogan, *The Legal Profession in Ireland, 1789-1922* (Incorporated Law Society of Ireland 1986); C Kenny, *King's Inns and the Kingdom of Ireland: The Irish 'Inn of Court', 1541-1800* (Irish Academic Press 1986); D Hogan and WN Osborough, *Brehons, Serjeants and Attorneys: Studies in the History of the Irish Legal Profession*, (Irish Academic Press 1990); K Ferguson (ed), *King's Inns Barristers, 1868-2004* (King's Inns 2005); A Hewitt, *The Law Society of Northern Ireland: A History* (Law Society of Northern Ireland 2010) and A Hart, *A History of the Bar and Inn of Court of Northern Ireland*, (Nicholson and Bass 2013).

[61] 'History of the Irish Jurist' <http://irishjurist.com/history.htm≥ accessed 30 March 2015.

[62] The *Dublin University Law Journal* was preceded by the *Dublin University Law Review* in the late 1960s and early 1970s.

[63] 'History of the Irish Jurist' (n 61).

[64] 1:1 (1907) Irish Law Society Gazette.

decisions, and other news relevant to solicitors. Nevertheless, the contents of the *Gazette of the Incorporated Law Society of Ireland,* popularly known as the 'Irish Law Society Gazette', do provide some interesting insights into historical developments. A British publication, known as simply *The Law Journal*, did publish a special Irish section, but this only lasted for a few years in the early 1930s. Otherwise, legal historians are largely reliant on the *Irish Law Times and Solicitors' Journal* for much of the 20th century.

Law journals are not just useful for finding articles and case reports relevant to the history of Irish law. They are, in themselves, useful historical sources that are seldom utilised by political historians. For example, Irish law journals illustrate the strong support offered by Irish unionists and constitutional nationalists for the war against Germany after 1914.[65] Contributors to Irish law journals certainly displayed little sympathy for the Easter rising of 1916.[66] Law journals also reflect the grim progress of the Anglo Irish War, also known as the Irish War of Independence, that began in 1919. The news section of the *Irish Law Times* and *Solicitors' Journal* provides accounts of courthouse after courthouse going up in flames in the smaller Irish towns.[67] Law journals also recorded the events that led to the signing of the 1921 Treaty that heralded the final secession of the 26 counties from the United Kingdom and the birth of the Irish Free State.[68]

Law journals also reflect the impact of the inevitable divergence between the law of the Irish Free State and that of the six counties of Northern Ireland that remained part of the United Kingdom after 1922. This reality ensured that law journals published in Dublin paid less and less attention to the North with the advance of time. In the 1920s, the editorial policy of the *Irish Law Times* and *Solicitors' Journal* made a valiant effort to give substantial attention to both jurisdictions on the island of Ireland. Nevertheless, the challenge of covering legal developments in two rapidly diverging jurisdictions increased with the passage of time. The *Irish Law Times* and *Solicitors' Journal* took the obvious course of paying greater attention to the southern jurisdiction, where most of its readership resided. After 1935, a revived *Irish Jurist* also claimed to cover both jurisdictions, but the bulk of its attention was firmly

---

[65] Special war supplements of the Irish Law Times contain recruitment appeals from the British army and lists of the names of members of the legal professions fighting in the war. For example, see (1916) 50 ILTSJ.
[66] For example, see (1916) 10(1) Irish Law Society Gazette 4 and (1916) 50 ILTSJ 120.
[67] For example, see (1920) 54 ILTSJ 130, 135, 206, 223, 236, 241, 247, and 255.
[68] For example, see (1922) 56 ILTSJ 295.

fixed on the Irish Free State.[69] These developments paved the way for the creation, in 1936, of a separate law journal for Northern Ireland called the *Northern Ireland Legal Quarterly* (NILQ). Nevertheless, law journals south of the border continued to claim that they were all-Ireland publications. The *Irish Law Times and Solicitors' Journal* continued to declare its intention to cover legal developments in Northern Ireland in addition to those in the South throughout the 1930s and 1940s, even though this position became a fiction with the passage of time. The intention to continue reporting cases from Northern Ireland continued to appear on the cover of every issue of the *Irish Law Times* until 1973, when political realities within Northern Ireland reasserted themselves onto the consciousness of the population south of the border.[70]

There are a number of challenges that face researchers in making use of older Irish law journals. These publications are seldom available online and most libraries have incomplete hardcopy collections. The articles in the older journals tend to be quite brief and their authorship is seldom disclosed. It is not always possible to identify the editors of a particular law journal at a particular time, and more research in this area would be very welcome.

IV – Conclusion

No honest guide can deny that there are many challenges facing researchers in the field of legal history. Yet, it is important to emphasise that these challenges are not insuperable. This chapter has tried to offer encouragement for more researchers to enter this field, despite the challenges entailed. The necessity for doing so is highlighted by the story of the destruction of much of the relevant source material. Although pictures of the burning Public Records Office in 1922 have become iconic images, the unfortunate reality is that the great majority of Irish state documents were destroyed in the years *before* 1922. These were not obliterated by explosion or fire, but by poor storage conditions. For example, in 1758 a serious fire at Dublin Castle resulted in the destruction of five out of the ten presses in which records were kept. However, the dampness of the Irish climate was just as destructive as fire. The damage in the 1758 fire would have been worse if one of the keepers had not removed the records from two of the presses that were later burnt. He had done this to protect the records from rainwater,

---

[69] For example, in 1935, the Irish Jurist reported 20 cases from the Irish Free State and just 4 from Northern Ireland. In 1936, the ratio was 26 cases from the Irish Free State and 5 from Northern Ireland. In 1937, the ratio was 33 cases from the Irish Free State and 5 from Northern Ireland.
[70] (1972) 106 ILTSJ i and (1973) 107 ILTSJ i.

found to be leaking through the roof.[71] Complaints of records being destroyed by rain and leaks were a continuous feature of the administration of Dublin Castle from the 14th century onwards. Yet, the most destructive force of all is that of human neglect. For example, in the 1850s, the archivist James F. Ferguson stubbed his toe while visiting a government office in Dublin and discovered that the offending item was a patent roll of Edward II that was lying 'amongst a heap of dirty parchments which had been thrown upon the floor'.[72]

The story of the destruction of so many primary sources relevant to the history of Irish law highlights the need to encourage more scholars to seek out historical sources relevant to the field of Irish law. Indifference and neglect have proved far more destructive to Ireland's legal past than fire, war or even the Irish climate. This highlights the need to widen interest in Ireland's legal past beyond a handful of specialist legal historians.

---

[71] P Connolly, 'The Medieval Irish Plea Rolls – An Introduction' (1995) (Spring) Journal of the Irish Society for Archives 3, 4.
[72] Crooks (n 15) 294.

CHAPTER 6

Community-Based Research

Mary ROGAN*

The idea of the 'engaged university' is one which has become very attractive to policymakers and senior administrators in the world of higher education. While there is a definite push at the level of policy towards more engagement between universities and the community, very practical barriers to this work exist within the academy. Not least of these is the difficulty in capturing this work for the purposes of measuring impact, for progression and for promotion. Community-based learning and research, however, has particularly great potential in the area of law.

Community-based research has given rise to a variety of definitions, but the central feature of such work is the concept of collaboration. Strand *et al* emphasise the key characteristic of community-based research as proactive collaboration amongst students and members of the community.[1] It is important to note that community-based research may involve a wide variety of research methodologies. A project could use the doctrinal method, qualitative work, quantitative analysis, policy analysis, or, indeed, any method suitable to carry out the work. Community-based research is an *approach* to research design and methodology. It also requires a particular focus on dissemination.

At its core, community-based research involves a researcher designing a project in collaboration with a community partner, such as an NGO, and thereby responding to the partner's particular research needs.

Collaboration between researchers and community partners can provide unique opportunities for access to data, to novel dissemination methods, and to forms of learning which are not possible to achieve in the traditional forms of research. Close working with a community partner can support the creation

---

* School of Law, Trinity College Dublin. I wish to thank my community partners and fellow researchers, Kate O'Hara, Deirdre Malone, and all at the Irish Penal Reform Trust (www.iprt.ie), as well as the reviewers for their helpful comments.
[1] K Strand, S Marullo, N Cutforth, R Stoecker and P Donohue, 'Principles of Best Practice for Community-Based Research' (2013) 9(3) Michigan Journal of Community Service Learning 5.

of a research project with a real prospect of impacting on policy, or changing practice. There are also many challenges involved for both researchers and community partners conducting such studies, both practical and more symbolic.

This chapter will place community-based research in the context of wider debates about the role of higher education and research in society. It will then describe the key elements of community-based research, before moving to a series of reflections on carrying out this kind of research. The chapter will conclude by exploring some questions regarding how community-based work may be used in legal contexts.

I – COMMUNITY ENGAGEMENT

Civic engagement has emerged in many jurisdictions, particularly the United States, as a goal of higher education. As Kezar has shown, a burgeoning number of university mission statements emphasise the importance of developing good and close relationships with local, national and global communities.[2] This movement was driven initially by the growth of service-learning or community-based learning, whereby students engaged in some kind of service activity, for credit, as a formal and embedded part of the curriculum. This, in turn, emerged from a push towards volunteering within the university environment.

Community-based learning as currently understood is now over 30 years old in the US, but is emerging as a form of pedagogy in its own right on this side of the Atlantic only more recently. This work seeks to integrate meaningful community service with teaching and learning. Definitions are contested and vary, but usually also involve concepts such as a desire to enrich the learning experience, teach civic responsibility and strengthen communities. Its key difference from volunteering is that the work is done for credit.

A working definition of community-based learning (CBL) is that of a form of learning which, at its core:

1. Seeks to facilitate students in the active practise of the skills acquired during Higher Education;

---

[2] A Kezar, 'Redesigning for Collaboration in Learning Initiatives: An Examination of Four Highly Collaborative Campuses' (2006) 77(5) The Journal of Higher Education 804.

2. By means of engagement with the community (e.g. a community-based group) on a 'real-world' issue or problem in a way which meets actual community needs.[3]

Other definitions include an element of reflection on the part of the students involved and a degree of integration into the curriculum.[4] Yet other approaches emphasise the potential of CBL to expand the purposes of higher education institutions to include wider engagement with society.[5] Usually, CBL involves students working with a community group or project, carrying out activities which are useful to that group but which are also desirable learning outcomes as approved by the higher education institute involved.

Much has been written about the positive benefits of community-based learning in terms of encouraging students to become more caring and responsible, and on CBL as a vehicle for fulfilling higher education institutions' obligations to wider society.[6] A lot of CBL work seeks to facilitate students in developing their understanding of their civic responsibilities and the ethical dimensions of their work. However, as well as working on the affective domain of learning, CBL promises to act across a variety of objectives for student learning. CBL often involves group work, usually working on a problem, incorporating some kind of reflective activity, and always in collaboration with a community partner.

There is now a good deal of literature which shows that engaging in such activity improves wider academic outcomes, encourages more awareness of civic responsibility and creates a greater likelihood of the participants going on to do further community-based work.[7] The various types of learning

---

[3] R Bringle and J Hatcher, 'Implementing Service Learning in Higher Education' (1996) 67 Journal of Higher Education 67(2) 221-239. See also, J Schine, *Service Learning* (University of Chicago Press 1997).

[4] F Pritchard and G Whitehead, *Serve and Learn: Implementing and Evaluating Service Learning in Middle and High School* (Lawrence Erlbaum Association 2007).

[5] R Rhoads and J Howard J (eds), *Academic Service Learning: A Pedagogy of Action and Reflection* (Jossey Bass 1998).

[6] J Eyler and D Giles, *Where's the learning in service-learning?* (Jossey-Bass 1999); B Jacoby, 'Fundamentals of Service-Learning Partnerships' in B Jacoby (ed), *Building Partnerships for service-learning* (John Wiley and Sons 1996).

[7] JS Eyler, DE Giles, CJ Gray and CM Stenson, *At a Glance: What we Know About the Effects of Service-Learning on College Students, Faculty, Institutions and Communities, 1993-2000* (3rd edn, Vanderbilt University 2001).

outcomes have been described as a 'kaleidoscope'.[8] It is important to note, however, that there remains a dearth of research on the Irish context, or, indeed, any research that occurs outside the United States.

It is also important to note that, as well as a genuine and sincerely held desire on the part of many service-learning practitioners to support student learning in innovative ways and to encourage active citizenship, the drive towards engagement can also be linked to concerns about the role and purpose of universities, following increasing costs of tuition, public distrust, and a broader questioning of the use of public funds. Along with this move to increase student participation in community service, there has also been a drive towards a more engaged faculty. There is, however, often a lack of clarity about what this means or what it should look like, with engagement being held to encompass everything from Erasmus-style partnerships, to sitting on boards, to media work.

II – COMMUNITY-BASED RESEARCH

Community-based research (CBR) is often cited as the form of scholarly work that meets the needs of society, while also fulfilling the research function which is at the heart of the academic position.[9] Emerging from service or community-based learning, CBR is a collaborative process, and an approach to research, which can employ a variety of methods. It is often associated with participatory research, though not exclusively so, and in the context of legal research, its usual method is the socio-legal one, whereby the research seeks to examine the impact of law in practice, for example, but it is important to stress that it is not restricted to such a method.[10]

CBR takes many forms, and precise definitions are difficult. Stringer[11] laid out five criteria for community-based research as follows:

1. Research which brings academic researchers into collaborative efforts with community residents and leaders to produce knowledge;

---

[8] S Mintz and G Hesser, 'Principles of Good Practice in Service Learning' in B Jacoby (ed), *Service Learning in Higher Education: Concepts and Practices* (Jossey Bass 1996).

[9] M Beckman, N Penney, and B Cockburn, 'Maximizing the Impact of Community-Based Research' (2011) 15(2) Journal of Higher Education Outreach and Engagement 83; S Eckerle Curwood, F Munger, T Mitchell, M Mackeigan, and A Farrar, 'Building Community-University Partnerships: Are Universities Truly Ready?' (2011) Michigan Journal of Community Service Learning 15.

[10] K T Brown, 'A Pedagogy of Blending Theory with Community-Based Research' (2011) 23(1) Journal of Teaching and Learning in Higher Education 119.

[11] E Stringer, *Action Research* (2nd edn, Sage Publications 1999).

2. Research which engages all involved in a co-learning process;

3. Research which takes a systemic perspective;

4. Research which builds community groups' capacity to conduct needed changes; challenges the existing canons of disciplinary research and pedagogical practice; and

5. Which balances research and action.

Strand et al view CBR as 'a collaborative enterprise between academic researchers (professors and students) and community members. CBR validates multiple sources of knowledge and promotes the use of multiple methods of discovery and dissemination of knowledge produced. CBR has as its goal social action and social change for the purpose of achieving social justice'.[12] O'Reilly and Bates have also identified the central elements of CBR as those which involve collaboration for mutual benefit between community partners, who may propose the research idea, and student researchers and supervisors, who complete the work.[13]

This particular dynamic has most impact on dissemination, usually requiring researchers to present their findings in the usual academic formats, but also in ways which can best assist the community partner. As CBR usually seeks to give rise to reform, those mechanisms of dissemination are usually in the form of policy briefings, proposals for amendments to the law, or draft laws, and recommendations for change.

It is critical that community-based activity is collaborative, a two-way street, and not simply a piece of research commissioned by a community partner and carried out by an academic, and presented to the partner at the end. Community-based researchers often describe their work in terms of the need to base their actions on values, particularly a desire to combat social injustice, to recognise power dynamics, and to promote mutually beneficial relationships.

---

[12] K Strand, S Marullo, N Cutforth, R Stoecker and P Donohue, 'Principles of Best Practice for Community-Based Research' (2003) 9(3) Michigan Journal of Community Service Learning 5, 8.
[13] N O'Reilly and C Bates, 'A Reflective Conversation: Community and HEI Perspectives on Community-Based Research' (2014) 6(1) AISHE 1.

III – COMMUNITY-BASED RESEARCH IN LAW: PROS AND CONS

Within law, CBR has enormous potential. The potential audience for, or beneficiaries of, such work include those who struggle to vindicate the theoretical right of access to justice. Community organisations are often in considerable need of support, particularly for accessible, useful and practical information about an area of law, or an area affected by the law. As student-run law clinics have demonstrated, the level of unmet legal need within the community can be significant. Amongst vulnerable groups and marginalised communities, legal services can be difficult to access, and such communities are forced to rely on unpaid and *pro bono* legal activities. Legal professionals who work with such groups are themselves under-resourced and overstretched.

Unmet Legal Need

Though they cannot, and should never be, substitutes for properly funded systems of ensuring access to justice, CBR projects can help to support organisations in very practical ways, while providing opportunities for students to develop their research skills, and for experienced researchers to develop their research careers in ways which directly benefit society.

While this is a practical and direct benefit of CBR in many situations, there are clear dangers where people with legal needs are obliged to rely on voluntary or *pro bono* initiatives, rather than on systemic mechanisms of achieving access to justice. *Pro bono* activity can be viewed as a way of propping up creaking and unfair legal systems, which deny people access to properly funded legal assistance, and which deny legal professionals appropriate remuneration and recognition for their work. However, in the absence of such systems, unmet legal needs must be of concern to legal practitioners and researchers. CBR approaches provide an opportunity to support the meeting of legal needs in structured and better-resourced ways.

Civil Society And The Bridge From Academia To Policy

From experience, it seems that an important driver for engaging in CBR is the ability to bring findings to a willing audience, and to support proposals for reform. Non-governmental organisations (NGOs) have a unique role to play in supporting social progress. When the United Nations was established in 1945, the UN Charter provided for NGO participation.[14] The important role played by NGOs in shaping decision-making processes and supporting

---

[14] UN Charter, Article 71, Chapter 10.

policy reform has been documented.[15] The UN Secretary General, Ban Ki-moon, has described civil society as 'the oxygen of democracy'.[16]

Civil society organisations also have unparalleled potential to act as bridges between academic research and policy reform. Many are highly experienced in the practice of advocacy, lobbying, raising awareness of issues, and providing technical expertise when reforming practice. Academics may find such organisations to be very useful conduits for locating policy audiences for their work.

A unique feature of CBR concerns this opportunity to have influence. Particularly in organisations working in the legal sector, and especially in public interest law, research can have a very direct impact on policy. If researchers prize the possibility of having influence in reform processes, and of improving whatever situation their research relates to, CBR can provide a very fruitful mechanism. Most NGOs have well-developed strategies for policy engagement and communications. Researchers working with such partners have a ready-made format by which their work can feed in to policy and practice. An NGO partner is likely to be very experienced in media work, creating briefing papers for policymakers, and shaping their arguments for a policymaking audience. That expertise can be invaluable for a researcher, who may find that the academic environment is less likely to provide such training. Having support to craft findings in a way that is useful for policymakers, or to explain complex issues in public settings, can be a distinctive benefit for the researcher.

The Question Of Impact

The question of impact is one which has become increasing prominent in debates about the role and value of academic research in the United Kingdom. Partly, this arises out of broader debates about the role of higher education institutions in society. Within Ireland, the Hunt Report[17] has highlighted the way in which higher education institutions engage with society as an important future strategic direction. The service mission of higher education has given rise to a great deal of discussion about 'engagement', with McLennan describing this term as an 'insistent discourse'.[18] CBR is an

---

[15] A Zettler, *NGO Participation at the United Nations, Barriers and Solutions* (United Nations 2003).

[16] United Nations News Centre, 'UN marks International Day by stressing vital role of civil society for true democracy' (15 September 2015) <www.un.org/apps/news/story.asp?NewsID=51873#.Vgv65kuC34I> accessed 30 September 2015.

[17] C Hunt, *National Strategy for Higher Education to 2030* (Government Publications Office 2011).

[18] G McLennan, 'Disinterested, Disengaged, Useless: Conservative or Progressive Idea of the University?' (2008) 6(2) Globalisation, Societies and Education 195.

obvious mechanism for those pursuing the impact agenda. As Wynne demonstrates, however, the questions of what constitutes engagement and whether and why it should be prized, are fraught with difficulty.[19] Civic engagement activities, in Wynne's view, must not be viewed by institutions as 'add-ons' to their core activity, but rather should be moved from the periphery into the core of institutional life.

There are many barriers to CBR, and the question of what is valued within academia is chief amongst them. This is particularly acute in the UK context, with its Research Excellence Framework (REF) system, but also arises in Ireland with respect to progression and promotion. As the most important indicator by which academic departments are measured, the types of work which can be submitted for the REF clearly take on critical importance. Materials produced for community partners, such as briefing papers and end of project reports, are generally not valued within this constricting framework. As Garland[20] has written insightfully from practical experience in the arena of criminal justice policy, there is a clear tension here between the types of work which are valued in the academic world and those valued by practitioners. Practitioners may not wish to wade through journal articles, while there is little benefit in career terms for the researcher to create a briefing which may, in fact, be read by a practitioner. Similarly, practitioners may expect answers to their questions in a matter of weeks, days, or sometimes even minutes. Complex areas under research militate against such expedition.

A related and broader point arises from such debates, which is most peculiarly appropriate for scholarship in law. Systems of measuring academic performance solely in terms of academic 'outputs' overlook what remains the foundation for legal scholarship: practice. It is striking that the discipline of medicine has maintained links between clinical practice and academia, yet the divide in law seems to be growing wider. The pressures created by existing systems for the measurement of impact are likely to ensure that the gap continues to grow. At the same time, the rarefied notion of 'impact' must not be used to instrumentalise community-based work. Civic engagement is not meaningful when done to satisfy administrative metrics.

The community-based researcher faces a difficult time in resolving these tensions. Truly equal partnerships, critical for successful community-based

---

[19] R Wynne, 'Higher Education Civic Engagement: Project or Orientation' (2014) 6(1) AISHE 1471.
[20] J Garland, 'One Step Forward, Two Steps Backward? Difficulties and Dilemmas with Connecting Hate Crime Policy and Research' (2015) Criminal Justice Policy Review 1.

research,[21] are not created when either side is seeking to fulfil some objective other than creating good research to impact on practice. Both sides must be assisted to become ready for collaboration.[22] Wade and Demb have argued for a process of self-evaluation prior to the interaction and the use of reflection at each stage of the process, to support partners to determine if their vision and values for the work align.[23]

The Importance Of Reflection

Reflection is considered to be a critical element of community-based learning. Though less well-developed as a concept within community-based research, reflection is also an important part of that process.

Reflection involves subjecting one's learning experiences to critical self-appraisal, describing one's activities and then asking questions such as 'what might I have done differently', 'why did I react in that particular way', or 'why was that difficult or effective'. Researchers might keep an ongoing diary or reflective journal, or reflect on their learning at particular points throughout a module or activity.

Reflective writing is well established within nursing education and teacher education, but experience suggests that it is has not been incorporated in a systematic way across legal education. This is partly a product of the nature of the discipline and the traditional manner in which it has been taught. As many socio-legal scholars in particular report,[24] thinking about the context or questioning 'the rules' is positively discouraged within some law schools. The focus of training in this area is explicitly in order to embed existing principles within students' thinking. Challenging them is generally reserved for modules with a more explicitly 'critical' or normative focus, though such modules are often themselves considered to be 'add-ons' to the black-letter subjects. As a result, reflective writing will be rather novel and potentially challenging for many students. It is likely that some will not see the point of such an activity, having been so used to finding out and stating the law, and

---

[21] R Stoecker, 'Challenging Institutional Barriers to Community-Based Research' (2008) 6(1) Action Research 49.

[22] S Curwood, F Munger, T Mitchell, M Mackeigan, A Farrar, 'Building Effective Community-University Partnerships: Are Universities Truly Ready?' (2011) (Spring) Michigan Journal of Community Service Learning 15.

[23] A Wade and A Demb, 'A Conceptual Model to Explore Faculty Community Engagement' (2009) (Spring) Michigan Journal of Community Service Learning 5.

[24] H Genn, M Partington, and S Wheeler, *Law in the Real World: Improving our Understanding of how Law Works* (Nuffield Foundation 2003).

also being assessed on this basis. Shifting assumptions, so crucial to the reflective process, may not come naturally.

Another reason why self-analysis of the 'process' of learning law may be somewhat underdeveloped relates to the fact that legal research methodology has often not been a particularly important part of a legal education. Though this is changing for the better in many institutions, legal research skills are often implicit and developed through personal trial and error, without a theoretical framework in which they can be grounded or to which they can be compared. Legal research methodology is the topic of few texts when compared with the methods of, for example, the social sciences.

The Centre for Legal Education in the United Kingdom has advocated the use of reflection for law students.[25] Its report takes as its premise that:

> reflection on what they know and don't know helps students to appreciate that law is a *social* science open to interpretation. It also helps students to understand that learning is individual, and that only they can make the connections to existing knowledge such that they make sense of law for themselves.[26]

Maughan and Webb[27] also suggest that reflective narratives are a suitable means of assisting students to document their learning, both in relation to specific legal skills, but also the application of legal knowledge in practice and theories about the legal process.

Another insight from Hinett relates to the importance of reminding law students that their emotions, values, and judgment are suitable topics for exploration, and that their intuition is an important skill to develop. More than this, researchers in law can benefit from a realisation that the basis for their work is, essentially, human activity, involving social relationships as well as responsibilities. It is far more than a paper or advocacy based 'game' between a number of highly skilled individuals, with no consequences beyond the parameters of those interchanges. The effect on the lives of clients and on communities and societies is often unstated, but crucially important. Community-based learning and research, and particularly reflection thereon,

---

[25] K Hinett, *Developing Reflective Practice in Legal Education* (UK Centre for Legal Education 2002).
[26] ibid 5 emphasis in original.
[27] C Maughan and J Webb, *Lawyering skills and the legal process* (Cambridge University Press 2005).

'means that students have an opportunity to understand for themselves the complexity of human problems',[28] an insight most particularly developed in the area of human rights training.

Reflection can be used quite simply as a mechanism to support the learning journey of the researcher, to think about challenges, and to develop strategies for future work. It can support the development of resilience in what is often an arduous and frequently intimidating process. Reflective accounts created by research participants can also be a source of data.[29] Within ethnographic research in particular, the researcher's field notes and reflections may be used as another source of information.

In the community-based context, sharing reflections between researcher and community partner could be a powerful source of learning, as well as providing some intriguing possibilities for discussing methodology.

IV – Practical Reflections on Community-Based Research

CBR does not follow the traditional methods or paths of legal research. As such, and with any innovation, charting a new path can pose a series of practical difficulties. Community-based researchers must negotiate with a wider range of partners than would otherwise be the case. The community organisation brings a very exciting new dimension to such work, but these relationships must also be carefully managed.

In the spirit of promoting reflection, which is at the heart of community-based activity, I wish to explore some of my own experiences in this area.

First Steps: Community-Based Learning

My first steps into this world commenced, similarly to many others, when I established a CBL module, in my role as a Lecturer at Dublin Institute of Technology. This, called 'Law and Society', which has been running for six years in Dublin Institute of Technology, seeks to facilitate students in carrying out a piece of small-scale research for a community partner. Students have worked with the Irish Penal Reform Trust (IPRT) and also partnered with the Public Interest Law Alliance on one project. IPRT is a non-governmental organisation which campaigns for progressive penal reform. One of its objectives is for penal policy to be evidence-based. IPRT uses

---

[28] Hinett (n 25) 18.
[29] For example, J Fook and F Gardner, *Practising Critical Reflection: A Resource Handbook* (Open University Press 2007).

research as the basis for its policy and advocacy work. Research is therefore critical to the activities of the organisation. However, as with many NGOs, it is difficult for the organisation to carry out research itself, or to commission research on the scale necessary to keep up with its needs. Partnering with academic institutions therefore provides a useful mechanism to increase IPRT's research capacity.

'Law and Society' is a research-based module, run over two semesters. It is a module for which students receive credit which goes towards their final awards. The module is worth 10 ECTS credits. The students are tasked with producing a report of their research for IPRT. The topic is selected by the community partner, in conjunction with the academic. Following a good deal of trial and error, this research brief has evolved into a request for students to examine the international human rights standards on a particular topic, such as older people in prison, along with examples of best practice in the area.

A key feature of the module is the use of group work. The report produced by the students is marked, and, in most instances, this mark is applied across the whole group, with each student receiving the same mark. At the beginning of the year, students elect office holders, including a project manager and a secretary, and divide out various production tasks, such as the creation of the final presentation, formatting and editing. Students also decide on how the research tasks will be carried out. Most of the research is conducted outside the classroom.

Students meet together with their facilitator on a weekly basis. For the first few weeks, the emphasis is on research methods, with a particular focus on database searching. Later on, each workshop starts with a short debrief on how the previous week has been, a review of the agreed timeline, discussion of any issues arising, followed by in-workshop research. The facilitator's role is to bring out any emerging difficulties, to answer any questions, and to support the research process. Regular contact with the NGO is required. This aspect is designed to blend some of the experiences characteristic of clinical legal education, with those of community-based learning and research. Students have a responsibility to a real organisation, and real people, with a deadline, and they experience the changing requirements of a 'client'.

At the end of the project, the students produce a report on the information they have gathered, and make a presentation of the key findings to IPRT in the IPRT offices. Research reports have been used by IPRT to support its policy work, and to assist in the development of larger projects. For example, the 2011/12 group worked on barriers to prisoners accessing justice.

This report supported the development of a briefing paper. The 2013/14 group worked on the position of older people in the prison system, an issue upon which IPRT has commissioned a larger research project.

This form of community-based learning and research has a number of advantages. One of the main advantages is that the project has many of the benefits of clinical legal education — development of the skills of legal research, group work, developing an awareness of deadlines and the responsibility to provide accurate and timely information to a client - without many of the administrative burdens associated with that activity. It is particularly useful for those starting off and feeling their way in the area of clinical legal education. Students are not going out on placement and are working with a single client. This is of benefit to those who do not have extensive administrative support for a wider clinical legal education programme. The approach is suitable across a wide range of community partners and NGOs.

Small Beginnings: Starting Off In Community-Based Research

The possibilities of other research collaborations with community partners emerged from this work. A very important feature of community-based learning and research is the importance of a good relationship with the community partner. The development of trust is critical for the success of such projects.

Arising out of our earlier work, IPRT and I made an application for funding under what was then the Irish Research Council for the Humanities and Social Sciences' 'Knowledge Exchange' strand of its 2010-2012 Research Development Initiative. The project was called 'Talking about punishment: understanding prisoners' rights and how they might be vindicated'. This project arose from our common experiences that awareness of the rights of prisoners was underdeveloped, amongst prisoners, prison administrators, and the community at large.

One of the critical issues within CBR is the format taken by the outputs of such work. As discussed above, there can often be a tension here between writing in the traditional academic forms of journals, books and book chapters, and the formats which may be most useful to the community partner, often briefing papers, reports, and press releases. It is submitted that the academy must question the measures it uses for success. We must place greater value on policy briefings and involvement in the policy process in order to encourage further such activity, and to recognise the contribution which researchers are making to policy. The best CBR will have peer-reviewed publications at its core, but will equally promote and celebrate those outputs which are of greatest assistance to the community partner.

'Talking about Punishment' was based, and stimulated further work, on legal research into prison law and prisoners' rights. Drawing on that scholarship, the project produced an information booklet for prisoners on rights, which was given 'Plain English' certification, and was also produced in an audio format. It was translated into Arabic, Polish, and Lithuanian. The project also created an information booklet aimed at prisoners' families on the issue of deaths in prison. Research reports for legal professionals on aspects of prison law were also created. These sought to create greater awareness of prison law amongst practitioners, and to support their capacity for research ad practice in this field. The project also supported seminars in prison, with politicians, and with community organisations.

The value of this project was the joining together of the skills of the academic and the community partner. The community partner draws on its experience of practical issues and concerns, to design outputs which would have the greatest impact. The skills of academia in research design, and writing in particular, can be brought to bear to ensure that the materials created are authoritative and credible.

Community-Based Research And The PhD Project

'Talking about Punishment' was the springboard for a PhD project, which I jointly supervise with IPRT. The Irish Research Council, again reflecting a renewed focus on impact, administers a programme called the 'Employment-based' PhD scheme. This scheme involves PhD students being employed in a variety of settings, including in industry and in the community and voluntary sectors, to carry out their PhD research. Under the terms of the award, the PhD scholars must spend at least 30% of their time with the employment partner. The funding for the scholar comes from the employer and the Irish Research Council.

IPRT is an employer under this scheme. We jointly supervise a project examining community service orders in comparison to short term prison sentences. The scheme allows small organisations to gain PhD-level research, of which it might not otherwise be in a position to receive the benefit. The student also receives the opportunity to learn skills which are rarely possible to develop in a systematic way in a traditional PhD project. Researchers can see how organisations use research, how to engage with policymakers, how to present research findings to a variety of audiences, how to deal with the pressures of such demands, and how to engage in team-work effectively.

V – PRACTICAL MATTERS AND COMMUNITY-BASED RESEARCH

All research requires a good deal of negotiation and patience, but CBR, while affording many opportunities, also poses some unique challenges. In this section, I wish to provide some reflections on those challenges and to offer some ways of dealing with them.

The first essential element in CBR is upholding the principle that the relationship is mutually beneficial. Organisations, often struggling with resources, cannot be the vehicle by which a research career is made, and similarly, impossible expectations cannot be placed upon the researcher. At the outset, the design of any CBR project must be collaborative.

It is a critical element of true CBR that the relationship is mutually beneficial. Researchers must not take the approach that they are bringing their expertise to the community partner. Rather, they must see the ways in which the community partner brings both practical expertise and the opportunity to have influence. This must be established as the ethos of the partnership. Such research projects must arise out of a mutual desire on the part of the partners to engage in this work, not simply because it is in 'vogue' or because of funding pressures. A great deal of discussion is necessary long before any projects are conceived of. The partners must establish whether they share similar views and values concerning the process and goals for such work. The project should arise from these discussions, being proposed as something of central importance to the community partner.

The community partner must be clear on its strategic objectives in entering the research relationship. The topic must align closely with the areas of interest of the organisation. From the very beginning, all parties must be very clear on 'ownership' of the project. Formal agreements should be signed concerning intellectual property rights. Most third level institutions have supports for community-based learning and research, and can assist in the drafting of these documents. Protocols should also be developed concerning the authorship of publications, ideally at the very outset. Different protocols may be required depending on the nature of the publication. Briefing papers and policy documents may be of most interest to the community partner. The number, type, and authorship expected concerning these publications should be clear to all concerned. Similar considerations should apply for any presentations made concerning the research. All these protocols should cover the situation of when the formal research relationship ends e.g. at the end of the PhD project.

As described above, there are much broader debates within academia concerning the role of the academic: should researchers diagnose and observe? Should they get involved in reform? Very practical consequences of this tension can arise in community settings. A situation may well arise where the findings of the research do not advance, or flatly contradict, the policy positions adopted by the community partner. Again, such scenarios must be discussed and planned for in advance. There must be no restriction on researchers to publish whatever they find. Concomitantly, community organisations must not be obliged to ascribe their name and professional reputation to research with which they do not agree, and must have the opportunity to see such work in advance, and comment upon it, if the organisation so wishes.

When the researcher is working in-house, there must be careful protocols concerning the expectations of the employer regarding any additional duties over and above the research project. Most pertinently in organisations working in the area of law, there may be an expectation that the research or researcher may operate as a substitute for formal legal advice. Such a misconception must be addressed before the project commences.

Once the project is underway, formally scheduled and regular communication must be maintained. All research projects change shape as they get underway and these changes must be discussed. If the project involves a student, then there must also be formal opportunities for the student, academic supervisor and community partner to meet and discuss the project. It is the responsibility of the academic supervisor or academic to set the parameters of the project and to give a realistic assessment of what is possible to achieve.

VI – CONCLUSION: THE POTENTIAL OF COMMUNITY-BASED RESEARCH

CBR can be energising and transformative, for the community partner and for the researcher. The opportunity to bring the highest quality research to bear on policy and practice is rare. Conducting research on an area identified as one of real need and with the potential for real impact is a privilege.

CBR, however, requires careful preparation and planning by all the partners. It can be more constraining than other forms of research, in light of the expectations of the partner, and, indeed, the researcher. Community partners could simply commission research, which is quite different to the collaborative approach examined in this chapter.

A very good guide to successful CBR is to keep a single question in mind: what is it all for? CBR must not be a vehicle purely to launch a research career, nor can it be a formulaic or tokenistic exercise designed to fulfil some externally imposed criteria or metrics about 'impact'.[30] The project cannot be only a cost-effective way of getting research support, or a roundabout way of funding an extra post. When CBR is collaborative, has regular channels for frank communication, and is carefully planned, it can have a transformative effect on community partners, researchers, policy and practice.

---

[30] L Wenger, L Hawkins, and S Seifer, 'Community-Engaged Scholarship: Critical Junctures in Research, Practice, and Policy' (2012) 16 Journal of Higher Education Outreach and Engagement 171.

CHAPTER 7

Socio-Legal Methodology: Conceptual Underpinnings, Justifications and Practical Pitfalls

Darren O'Donovan[*]

This chapter will focus upon conceptually mapping the place of socio-legal methodology within legal research. Questions to be addressed include: what are the underlying theories regarding the nature of law and legal argument underpinning this form of scholarship? How do we understand the position of law in relation to the general social sciences? Having located this methodological school, I will then proceed to consider what reasons students or researchers might have for engaging in socio-legal research. This will be achieved by discussing five major strands of socio-legal research and how they seek to make distinctive contributions to knowledge. It will be shown that socio-legal scholarship has challenged doctrinal legal research culture by questioning the assumed centrality of law and legal institutions to many social problems. It has sought to present a more complex understanding of 'how legal rules, doctrines, legal decisions, institutionalised cultural and legal practices work together to create the reality of law in action'.[1] As a result, the proponents of the methodology have successfully challenged legal scholars to display greater policy imagination, by acknowledging law's status as just one form of regulation, and cautioning against overly doctrinal understandings of the discipline.

The chapter is also intended as a practical guide; assisting the reader in negotiating the central pitfalls of adopting a socio-legal approach. Thomson has identified some of the main reasons given by PhD examiners for requiring re-writes of methodology chapters as follows:

– The researcher does not know the difference between methodology and methods.

---

[*] Dr Darren O'Donovan is a Senior Lecturer at School of Law, La Trobe University, Australia.
[1] R Banakar, 'Studying Cases Empirically: A Sociological Method for Studying Discrimination Cases in Sweden' in R Banakar and M Travers (eds), *Theory and Method in Socio-Legal Research* (Hart Publishing 2005) 139.

- There is very little or no explanation of why this methodology has been chosen. The fit with the research questions is not made clear.

- There is no fit between the data that will be produced through the use of these methods and the data that is needed to answer the research questions.

- The blank and blind spots, that is, the limits of the methodology, and/or the research design, are not considered.[2]

Whilst lawyers might not be comfortable with the social sciences language of 'data', this list remains helpful in considering the fundamentals of justifying one's choice of methodology. This chapter will illustrate how to overcome these hurdles in the relation to socio-legal methodology.

Finally, we will also engage with an overarching question which often troubles the legal researcher confronted by socio-legal techniques: 'Am I still a lawyer?' The author will argue that, rather than reductively placing law within the social sciences, socio-legal methodology allows the researcher to chart more complex answers to what can still remain distinctly legal problems. Rather than artificially detaching the 'legal aspects' of problems, what emerges is research with a more holistic understanding of what problems the law can solve and what social, economic and cultural factors it remains dependent upon.

I – DEFINING SOCIO-LEGAL METHODOLOGY

Thomson's list above helpfully underlines the critical importance of disentangling the concept of methodology from that of research methods. In their critique of the poor standard of methodology in human rights law research, Coomans, Grunfeld and Lamminga provide an excellent definition of the concept:

> A work's methodology is essentially its 'approach'. It addresses the question of how to find relevant information, how to organise it, and how to interpret the results. Reflection on methodology is not a luxury and does not detract from one's substantive research efforts. There is no contradiction between method and substance. Method *is* the substance. Arguably, the description of a work's methodology is the

---

[2] P Thomson, 'Thirteen Reasons Researchers get Asked to Write Their Methods Chapter Again' (2013) <http://patthomson.net/2013/01/31/thirteen-reasons-researchers-get-asked-to-write-their-methods-chapter-again/> accessed 5 August 2015.

most interesting and revealing part of any academic paper (or research proposal).[3]

This quote underlines an important point: that all legal writing has an underlying conceptual framework, with its emphasis or omissions reflecting an immanent statement about the nature of law. This is, crucially, distinct from the methods or techniques which are applied in the research. Method refers simply to a research tool, for example, a qualitative method such as interviews. Methodology is the justification for using a particular research method in answering a specific research question. For socio-legal methodology, it is particularly important that the legal researcher not simply instrumentalise techniques such as surveys, but rather understands the underlying methodological justification underpinning their decision to use the method.

So what is the 'approach' which socio-legal scholars take to legal research? The author would adopt a broad tent definition, which views socio-legal scholarship as driven by an underlying jurisprudential commitment to study law in its context. As Thomas notes, this reflects the common position that:

> Empirically, law is a component part of the wider social and political structure, is inextricably related to it in an infinite variety of ways, and can therefore only be properly understood if studied in that context.[4]

Thus, law is not viewed as an autonomous force to which society is subjected, but rather shapes and is shaped by broader social, political and economic logics, contexts and relations. As the Socio Legal Studies Association defined the field in 2009:

> Socio-legal studies embraces disciplines and subjects concerned with law as a social institution, with the social effects of law, legal processes, institutions and services and with the influence of social, political and economic factors on the law and legal institutions.[5]

---

[3] F Coomans, F Grunfeld, M Kamminga, 'Methods of Human Rights Research' (2010) 32 Human Rights Quarterly 179, 183-84 (emphasis in original).

[4] P Thomas, 'Curriculum Development in Legal Studies' (1986) 20 Law Teacher 112.

[5] Socio Legal Studies Association, *SLSA Statement of Principles of Ethical Research Practice* (January 2009) 1.2.1. <www.slsa.ac.uk/index.php/8-general-information/4-slsa-statement-of-principles-of-ethical-research-practice > accessed 5 August 2015.

Two core planks of socio-legal research may thus be identified:

- *Law in action scholarship*: how legal norms actually function in reality and what actors shape their implementation.

- *Theoretical perspectives* on the relationship between law and society, which are informed by sociology, history, philosophy, economics, anthropology, political science and psychology.

As is reflected by the 'interpretive turn' in sociology, these two categories are not exclusive: the reality is that theory is informed by empirical scholarship and vice versa.[6] Work should be theoretically informed and empirically grounded, and therefore socio-legal scholars often work in the middle ground between these two approaches. The reader will be struck by the sheer breadth of the definition of 'socio-legal' work. Indeed, it could be alleged that socio-legal research refers to anything which goes outside the 'internal perspective' of doctrinal methodology.[7]

II – FRAMING SOCIO-LEGAL RESEARCH QUESTIONS

Two of the criticisms highlighted earlier by Thomson focus upon how research questions are framed. A first step for the researcher in addressing methodology is to consider the research question that has been posed, and whether it implicitly adopts socio-legal premises. In past doctoral workshops in which the author has participated, two introductory questions have been used for such reflection:

- Have you used the words 'inadequate', 'effective' or 'reform' in your research proposal or discussion and in what sense was it used?

- Does your analysis draw upon certain open-textured and interdisciplinary concepts, such as rights, economic efficiency or deterrence?

Asking these questions permits us to identify possible 'windows' for the entry of social scientific knowledge and methods. The researcher, in answering these types of questions, will have to respond with a values statement, or by attempting to separate legal considerations from the

---

[6] The interpretive turn rejects the idea of the neutral observer producing neutral knowledge, arguing that the social world should not be understood as a collection of external 'facts,' but a product of socio-historically situated practices and interactions.

[7] See generally, C McCrudden 'Legal Research and the Social Sciences' (2006) 122 Law Q Rev 632.

political or economic. For instance, in relation to the second question, the researcher may answer that 'while any study on competition law could be viewed as being concerned with economic efficiency, I'm more concerned about the failure of the courts to properly define what anti-competitive practices are'. The exercise therefore also causes us to ask: what are the yardsticks which doctrinal methodology uses to assess the law? Furthermore, how does the doctrinal lawyer effect closure and defend adopting an 'internal perspective'?

Socio-legal methodology is often stumbled into at the proposal stage of any legal research, as the student or researcher discusses 'the need for reform' or alleges the existence of 'ineffective' legislation. It is at this stage that the student needs to reflect upon the fundamental yardstick they are using. In criticising the law, are they relying upon purely doctrinal values such as clarity, internal logic and consistency? Or is the focus upon *policy*, namely the effects which law has on society? The researcher could also reflect upon the challenge of shaping effective reform, by considering factors such as:

- In calling for law reform, what are you asking law (e.g. legislation) to achieve?

- Are you asking it to do too much?

- Do legal interventions need to be supported by or to support a process of broader social change?

- Are there other policy innovations necessary to support your reform?

The research question posed by the researcher will always carry a methodological undertow within it, which must be accounted for and in the pursuit of which appropriate methods must be adopted. Of course, the research question can be reframed to suit the researcher's preferred methodology, but the implications of this must be fully justified. Researchers must be prepared to defend their *rejection* of a particular methodology. This is a key part of describing how the author settled upon their methodology – without it the research project may struggle to avoid the following pitfalls:

• Leaving an unpacked/unaddressed concept/alternative. (*Exhaustiveness*);

- Leaving out something without justifying it. (*Parameters of your study*);

- Failing readability: explaining how your argument builds and how you have proved it. (*Structure*)

The remainder of this chapter should therefore not be viewed as merely directed at socio-legal researchers, but rather researchers in law generally. A doctrinal researcher who does not reflect upon the possibility of socio-legal approaches may, for instance, be unprepared for queries under the exhaustiveness and parameters headings.

Having introduced the methodology, this chapter will now map five major themes in socio-legal research. These sections will illustrate how socio-legal research analyses the interaction of law and society, making unique contributions to knowledge over and beyond a solely doctrinal approach.

III – Theme 1: Critiquing Closure — Doctrinal and Socio-Legal Scholarship

The first challenge in justifying the use of socio-legal methodology is to describe the understanding of law which underpins it. For the early career researcher, it is important to query the interaction of, and divisions between, doctrinal and socio legal scholarship. Is law a product of internally constructed rules, procedures and reasoning, or is it influenced by external social forces and interests? Socio-legal methodology seems to draw upon a view that law is an inevitably social phenomenon — representing the product of collective thought and action. As Allott notes:

> Law seems to have a special status among social phenomena by reason of its forms, its rituals, its specialized language, its special rationality even, and its specific social effects. But on the other hand, law is clearly embedded in the totality of the social process which is its cause, and on which it has a substantial determinative effect, not least in providing the continuing structure of society, its hard programme.[8]

Thus, the law is not 'something apart' from the rest of society, neither is it merely a reflection or reproduction of other non-legal spheres. In adopting a socio-legal approach therefore, the researcher often faces a burden of

---

[8] P Allot, *The Health of Nations: Society and Law Beyond the State* (Cambridge University Press 2002) 36.

justification: how would they map the relative or partial autonomy of law and legal reasoning from broader society?

Thus a major contribution of socio-legal methodology is to unravel the false closure which may shape the law, and to show the role which extra-legal factors or assumptions may play in putatively 'neutral' legal reasoning. As a core debate within jurisprudence, many possible instances of this could be shown, from postmodernism to critical legal studies. All of these represent distinct research traditions, rebutting the separation of law from politics, religion or other social norms.

Feminist legal theories contribute perhaps the most developed discussion of how socio-legal research can expose the exclusionary patterns of the existing legal tradition. In a classic article, Bartlett attempted to provide a typology of 'feminist' research methods. The first of these - 'asking the woman question' - may be defined as 'how the substance of law may silently and without justification submerge the perspectives of women and other excluded groups.'[9] This represents part of a broader methodology of *positionality*, which asks: 'What assumptions are made by law (or practice or analysis) about those whom it affects? Whose point of view do these assumptions reflect? Whose interests are invisible or peripheral? How might excluded viewpoints be identified and taken into account?'[10]

Recent examples of feminist legal methods provide examples of innovative methods which fulfil this underlying methodological commitment. Initiatives such as the Women's Court of Canada and feminist judgment projects have sought to subvert and reimagine existing legal norms by showing the possibilities for very different legal rulings and systems. As the editors of the United Kingdom Feminist Judgments Project note:

> The [project] represents a form of academic activism, an attempt to tackle power and authority not from the distance of critique but on their own ground. By appropriating judgment-writing for feminist purposes, the judgment writers engage in a form of parodic — and hence subversive — performance. In much the same way as Judith Butler describes 'drag' as performance that subverts gender norms, these feminist academics dressed up as judges powerfully denaturalize existing judicial and

---

[9] The others being feminist practical reasoning and consciousness raising. K Bartlett, 'Feminist Legal Methods' (1990) 103(4) Harvard Law Review 829.
[10] ibid 848.

doctrinal norms, exposing them as contingent, and as themselves (the product of) performances.[11]

As Margaret Davies notes, a further aspect of such an approach is its 'equally powerful constructive dimension', which could function 'to alter our perception of the 'normal' and offer 'positive reconstructions of the concept of law'.[12] The forthcoming book publication of Northern/Irish Feminist Judgment Project represents a notably innovative addition to Irish legal scholarship; one in which methodological commitment has been combined with a distinctive method (writing the alternative judgment).[13]

IV – THEME 2: WORKING INSIDE OUT — INTERACTIONS BETWEEN SOCIO-LEGAL SCHOLARSHIP AND THE DOCTRINAL METHOD

While socio-legal methodology is most often used to confront doctrine, could it also play some role within its confines? Can socio-legal research be applied to *improve* doctrine? Doctrinal research is obviously shaped by a core 'authority paradigm' i.e. a focus upon authoritative sources which focuses upon the pedigree rather than merits.[14] It takes an internal participant-oriented epistemological approach to its object of subject. Yet is this internal logic entirely sealed off? In evaluating the possible impact of socio-legal methodology, the researcher should consider whether law and legal institutions are, in fact, open to the application of other knowledges. An early advocate of the interdisciplinarity of *traditional* legal scholarship was Richard Posner, who, in 1987, spoke of the decline of law as an autonomous discipline.[15] This, he argued, was rooted in the increasing contributions made by law's 'complementary disciplines', such as economics, which were supplying streams of knowledge underpinning legal doctrine. This position can actually be taken further if one argues that even the core elements of doctrinal reasoning have their roots in logic (deduction, induction and analogy) or in subjective argument-based methodologies of the humanities.

---

[11] R Hunter, C McGlynn and E Rackley, 'Feminist Judgments: An Introduction' in R Hunter, C McGlynn and E Rackley (eds), *Feminist Judgments: From Theory to Practice* (Hart Publishing 2010) 8.
[12] M Davies, 'Feminism and the Idea of Law' (2011) 1(1) Feminists@law 2.
[13] M Enright, J McCandless and A O'Donoghue, *Northern/Irish Feminist Judgments: Judges' Troubles and the Gendered Politics of Identity* (Hart Publishing forthcoming 2016).
[14] G Samuel, 'Interdisciplinarity and the Authority Paradigm: Should Law Be Taken Seriously by Scientists and Social Scientists?' (2009) 36(4) Journal of Law and Society 431.
[15] R Posner, 'The Decline of Law as an Autonomous Discipline: 1962-1987' (1987) 100 Harvard Law Review 761.

While the requirements of formal legal doctrine represent an unavoidable normative constraint upon what is deemed a conventionally 'acceptable' legal argument, legal theorists have long debated the extent to which policy plays a role in cases. Even legal positivist accounts, such as that of HLA Hart, accepted the existence of hard cases, in which discretion was to be exercised.[16] Judicial reasoning is often consequentialist in nature, where the answer to the question before the court depends, not upon the exact linguistic content or scope of a statute, but upon which of the options before the court would best serve the legislation's underlying purpose.[17] In considering the contribution which socio-legal methodology can make to doctrine, one should consider the extent to which judges make normative arguments, especially:

- *Economic arguments* regarding the efficiency of imposing particular legal duties;

- *Institutional competence arguments* regarding the division of labour between public institutions in pursuing social goals;

- *Judicial administration arguments* regarding the impact of certain requirements (e.g. procedural fairness or evidential requirements) upon the administration of justice.

In addition to policy underpinnings, judicial decisions may also draw upon 'social facts', which Burns has defined as:

> ...general 'background' judicial understandings of the world, institutions and human behaviour [which] provide context and inform the judicial development and application of law, or are used as 'social framework' to assess or interpret the adjudicative facts of the particular case.[18]

Surveying negligence cases, Burns shows that judicial reliance upon such facts often occurs without proper empirical support.[19] Malbon has referred to

---

[16] It is important to note that Hart believed such discretion was based on recognised patterns of reasoning, with lawyers and legal scholars remaining able to predict the outcomes.

[17] T Roux, 'Judging the Quality of Legal Research: A Qualified Response to the Demand for Greater Methodological Rigour' (2014) 24(1) Legal Education Review 173, 176-77.

[18] K Burns, 'It's Not Just Policy: The Role of Social Facts in Judicial Reasoning in Negligence Cases' (2013) 21 Torts Law Journal 80.

[19] ibid.

judicial use of unexpressed extra-legal matters and values in judicial reasoning as the 'dark matter' of judicial reasoning.[20]

This section represents a quick sketch of the trend towards viewing legal doctrine as open to the application of knowledge from other disciplines. What is crucial for the researcher is to properly explore their own understanding of how much space there is *within* doctrinal reasoning for the application of other knowledges.

V – Theme 3: Closing the Gap — Law in the Books versus Law in Action

Socio-legal methodology also draws upon legal realism in its focus upon how law actually functions in society. Doctrinal legal research directs itself solely towards the normative function of rules: identifying their prescriptive *content* rather than their actual effect. Socio-legal methodology tackles certain key silences in doctrinal legal scholarship and adopts a more realistic approach to law as merely one form of regulation.

At its most narrow, doctrinal scholarship can sponsor an unduly instrumental perception of law. Three assumptions often shape this instrumental understanding:

1. The assumption of perfect legal knowledge. This holds that law is communicated in a uniform, undistorted way to those subject to it;

2. The assumption of legal monism. This holds, due to the fact it emanates from the State, law inherently supersedes other sources of regulation (such as business, culture and peer pressure);

3. Law may be projected as an autonomous instrument of social intervention not dependent on other forms of regulation.

Against this, Griffiths argues for a sociologically rooted approach to law as regulation, which removes these assumptions, and focuses upon:

1. *The 'socially contingent character of legal communication'*, which looks at how legal rules are translated into concrete contexts. This is seen, for example, in the idea that negligence litigation has produced

---

[20] J Malbon, 'Judicial Values' in I Freckleton and H Selby (eds), *Appealing to the Future: Michael Kirby and his Legacy* (Lawbook Co 2009) 581.

disproportionately defensive medicine amongst doctors or that corporate regulation is crowded out by the realities of business life;

2. *Legal pluralism*, which focuses upon the idea that there are many other forms of regulation. For example, in a medical law context there may be the employer-employee relationship, peer norms etc., which are viewed as more significant;

3. *Law as inseparable from the social context which produces it.* Ultimately, though we may contest the degree, the fact remains that most legal rules are executed by specialised agents within broader society. Thus the efficacy or enforcement of a piece of legislation is ultimately conditioned upon broader social and human factors.[21]

The key question here is not whether focusing upon legal rules is an invalid form of scholarship, but rather that such a focus must be recognised and set in the context. In effect, any form of legal scholarship emphasising legal rules over other interventions has an underlying doctrinal framework which must be unpacked. The socio-legal researcher moves beyond such strictures and attempts to chart the collision of law with real world actors and institutions.

At this point, it must be stressed that the blanket association of socio-legal methodology with public law is incorrect — indeed many areas of company law have deeply engrained socio-legal traditions. It is, for example, rare to find a company lawyer who does not regard themselves as a scholar of corporate governance. The latter field analyses the many factors, of which law is one, which determine how a company is governed. The move from discrete topics of company law to the overarching rubric of governance has facilitated a more holistic research methodology. The term 'corporate governance' has thus been described as a conceptual 'meeting point' for disciplines such as law, economics, behavioural sciences and sociology.[22] Reflecting the success of this methodological innovation, Reisenhuber has called for 'contract governance' to receive similar prominence within contract law — a subject often associated with doctrinal dominance.[23]

---

[21] This is a summary of Griffiths' complex paradigm for measuring 'the social working of legal rules'. See generally, J Griffiths, 'The Social Working of Legal Rules' (2003) 8 Journal of Legal Pluralism and Unofficial Law 1.

[22] A Dixit, 'Governance Institutions and Economic Activity' (2009) 99(1) American Economic Review 6.

[23] K Riesenhuber, 'A Need for Contract Governance?' in Y Atamer and S Grundmann (eds), *Financial Services, Financial Crisis and General European Contract Law* 61-84.

VI – THEME 4: LEGAL PLURALISM AND OVERLAPPING NORMATIVE ORDERS

Legal pluralism, as Merry argues, is 'a central theme in the re-conceptualisation of the law/society relation', and deserves direct treatment in any chapter introducing socio-legal methodology. It was referenced in the last section, which discussed how socio-legal researchers often look at law as one form of regulation. Legal pluralism has been defined by Griffiths as 'that state of affairs for which behaviour pursuant to more than one legal order occurs'.[24] Clearly, in the globalised era, it is becoming standard to account for competing domestic and international legal norms governing particular disputes or subject matter. Here however, I wish to introduce a broader concept of legal pluralism that argues that the law is not limited to official state legal institutions. Instead, law can also be found in the ordering of social groups across society. Moore argues that such scholarship attempts to understand the impact of semi-autonomous social fields, which:

> ... can generate rules and customs and symbols internally, but that [are] also vulnerable to rules and decisions and other forces emanating from the larger world…The semi- autonomous social field has rule-making capacities and the means to induce or coerce compliance; but it is simultaneously set in a larger social matrix which can and does, affect and invade it.[25]

Thus, for instance, attempts to evaluate the role of law in internet regulation would need to include the internal ordering of hackers or internet standardisation bodies.[26]

Legal pluralists, unsurprisingly, conflict over the fundamental question, 'what is law?' and how to distinguish legal from general social interaction.[27] Tamanaha describes these questions as intractable, and argues that rather than fragmenting legal pluralism, one should focus upon 'framing situations in ways that facilitate the observation and analysis' of the interlinkage of law and society.[28] Attempting to bring some unity to legal pluralist scholarship,

---

[24] J Griffiths, 'What is Legal Pluralism' (1986) 24 Journal of *Legal Pluralism* 2.
[25] S Moore, 'Law and Social Change: The Semi-Autonomous Social Field as an Appropriate Subject of Study' (1973) 7(4) Law and Society Review 720.
[26] An excellent example of a legal analysis of the impact of such informal, non-state actors is K Bowrey, *Law and Internet Cultures* (Cambridge University Press 2005).
[27] Indeed, many lawyers would prefer terms such as regulatory pluralism or normative pluralism to *legal* pluralism.
[28] B Tamanaha, 'Understanding Legal Pluralism: Past to Present, Local to Global' (2008) 30 Sydney Law Review 411.

he proposes the following typology of normative orders, which can overlap and interact with official law:

- *customary/cultural*. This refers to shared social rules and customs, as well a social institutions and mechanisms evident for example in indigenous or local laws;

- *religious/cultural*. Religious normative ordering extends from the theocratic form of government to more informal cultural adherence;

- *economic/capitalist*. This is a particularly significant normative order in the era of neoliberalism and globalization. Tamanaha notes that it can range from:

Informal norms that govern continuing relations in business communities (including reciprocity, and norms that discourage resort to official legal institutions in situations of dispute), to norms governing instrumental relations, to standard contractual norms and practices, to private law-making in the form of codes of conduct, shared transnational commercial norms, arbitration institutions, and so forth, including shared beliefs about capitalism (like 'market imperatives').'[29]

- *functional* normative systems. These are grounded in institutions founded for the pursuit of particular functions such as universities or hospitals. While interacting with official law, each enjoys some autonomous internal ordering;

- *community/cultural normative systems*. This is a diffuse category capturing the internal cultures of communities howsoever formed (I have already instanced the example of hackers above). [30]

I have foregrounded this typology here as it has proved useful as an introductory gateway in methodology workshops the author has undertaken. It must be stressed that there is nothing natural or essentialist about these categories, rather Tamanaha describes them as rough labels used to mark off subjects and situations that repeatedly arise in legal pluralist writings.[31] With this rough map, participants can be invited to consider what a legally pluralist approach to their area of study could look like. Accounting for these

---

[29] ibid.
[30] ibid 397-400.
[31] ibid 397.

normative sites prevents the overvaluation of law and legal institutions, allowing a deeper concept of the relationship between law and society to take root. As Tamanaha concludes, 'the longstanding vision of a uniform and monopolistic law that governs a community is plainly obsolete' and coexisting normative systems should be accounted for when considering compliance with, or even the design of, legal norms.[32] Clearly the methodology is often best teamed with empirical methods, whether qualitative or quantitative, which seek to map the impact of the relevant competing normative system.

Finally, it should be noted that international law has a distinctive scholarship of legal pluralism based around the interaction of 'hard' and 'soft' law. The former refers to the international legal norms, such as treaties, custom and other sources relied upon and applied in binding international legal fora. Soft law refers to legal norms that, while not formally binding, nevertheless exert some quasi-legal force, by shaping behavioural change and inducing compliance. It often describes goals to be achieved rather than grounding actual duties, programmatic actions rather than detailed prescriptions, guidelines rather than obligations. Some commentators have argued that a 'quest for softness' is increasingly marking regulation, with flexibility being prized over 'hard' legal norms.[33] The reality of increased normative choice in regulating a state of affairs often requires legal scholars to critically account for the additional value of 'hard' legal norms versus soft law interventions. In effect, even a doctrinal researcher is increasingly called upon to answer the question: 'why law?'

VII – THEME 5: LEGAL CONSCIOUSNESS AND PERSON-CENTRED RESEARCH

In charting the dominant strands of socio-legal research and their benefits, this chapter has shown how researchers move beyond rule-centric research. We now arrive at the strongest example of this: the study of legal consciousness, which is marked by its focus upon everyday, individual lives. Marc Galanter offers an open definition of the field:

> Legal consciousness scholarship seeks to decentralize the study of law, emphasizing the role of law in everyday life rather than the behavior of distinctively legal institutions and actors. Scholars seek to show how legal

---

[32] ibid 409-10.
[33] H Hillgenberg, 'A Fresh Look at Soft Law' (1999) 10 European Journal of International Law 499.

constructs acquire meaning through everyday social interaction, contest, and routine.[34]

Legal consciousness was traditionally more popular in the United States law and society tradition than in the United Kingdom and Ireland. More recently, however, a number of commentators have argued that it should be given greater prominence, and there is evidence of its increased application.[35]

Legal consciousness is, in many ways, a 'law last' approach — as it focuses upon individual lives, very often allowing it to focus upon the absence of law where we would expect it to be. Ewick and Sibley's landmark text in the field, for example, is shaped by a distinctive approach to qualitative interviewing. In interviewing 430 individuals for the study, the authors made the methodological decision not to start with the individual's experience of formal legal proceedings but rather asked 'open questions about neighbourhoods, friends and family', progressing to explore things which troubled or bothered people in their ordinary lives.[36] This question structure allowed for the charting of law's absence or marginality as well as its presence.

Legal consciousness research often centres upon those who resist the law, experiencing it as arbitrary and capricious. Austin Sarat's early study of welfare recipients found that law was 'a shadowy presence' for many within the system, and that complex forms of resistance shaped their responses to it, with individuals displaying the ability 'to respond strategically, to manoeuvre and to resist the "they say(s)" and "supposed to(s)" of the welfare bureaucracy'.[37] There is an inevitable tension between the methodology's critical tradition and those who would instrumentalise legal consciousness research by linking it to policy priorities, such as access to justice. Nevertheless, legal consciousness methodology has been employed to discover reasons why those subjected to discrimination do not pursue formal complaints, with studies identifying an 'ethic of survival', as well as various

---

[34] Galanter stresses that the lack of consensus around the concept in M Galanter, 'Law: Overview' in N Smelser and P Baltes (eds), *International Encyclopedia of the Social and Behavioural Sciences, Volume 12* (Elsevier 2002) 8539-540.

[35] D Cowan, 'Legal Consciousness: Some Observations' (2004) 67(6) *Modern Law Review* 928.

[36] P Ewick and S Sibley, *The Common Place of Law: Stories from Everyday Life* (Univ of Chicago Press 1998). The interviews would eventually progress to discuss encounters with the law.

[37] A Sarat, 'The Law is All Over: Power, Resistance, and the Legal Consciousness of the Welfare Poor' (1990) 2 Yale Journal of Law and the Humanities 343.

'coping' tactics such as deflection through humour.[38] The author's own area of administrative law, often distorted by an overemphasis upon doctrine, has recently seen renewed efforts to chart the attitudes of first instance decision makers to the law.[39]

VIII – THE CHALLENGES OF SOCIO-LEGAL METHODOLOGY

In PhD workshop discussions regarding socio-legal methodology, two key anxieties are often raised by researchers. First, there is the question, 'am I still a lawyer?', which, in a smaller jurisdiction such as Ireland, often reflects a fear of deviating too far from legal professional contexts. Secondly, there is the fear of falling between two stools. This refers to the fear that, in effect, the student is committing to 'two' PhDs – one in 'law' and another in the social sciences, and may end up not satisfying peers in either discipline.

This chapter has already engaged extensively with the first anxiety, but largely at the conceptual level. In introducing key strands of socio-legal research, we have seen how they look to foster a broader identity for lawyers, and for the concept of law. There is no doubt, however, that part of the 'am I still a lawyer' anxiety is rooted in more pragmatic concerns such as credibility and employability. Many early career researchers are emerging from a doctrinally dominated education and practice context. As lawyers, we are imbued with 'internal conventional perspective', where quality is judged predominantly by demonstrating adherence to the accepted norms of an internal discourse. I would argue that students tend to overestimate the pre-eminence of doctrinal approaches in academia and practice, with the result that 'academic' approaches to law attract negative preconceptions.

This is not helped by practitioners who insist that academics have travelled too far from the courtroom or the primary law. Perhaps the most memorable condemnation was delivered by Justice Meagher of the High Court of Australia, who bemoaned the:

> ...multitudes of academic homunculi who scribble and prattle relentlessly about such non-subjects as criminology, bail, poverty, consumerism,

---

[38] See K Bumiller, *The Civil Rights Society: The Social Construction of Victims* (Johns Hopkins UP 1988) and B Quinn 'The Paradox of Complaining: Law, Humor, and Harassment in the Everyday Work World.' (2000) 25 Law Soc Inq 1151.

[39] M Hertogh 'Through the Eyes of Bureaucrats: How Front-Line Officials Understand Administrative Justice' in M Adler (ed), *Administrative Justice in Context* (Hart Publishing 2010) 203-225.

computers and racism. These may be dismissed from calculation: they possess neither practical skills nor legal learning. They are failed sociologists.[40]

The more recent comments of United State Chief Justice Roberts condemning the disconnect between legal scholarship and practice also attracted lively debate. Justice Roberts alleged that law reviews no longer offer much insight to the bar with the articles 'likely to be [about]…the influence of Immanuel Kant on evidentiary approaches in 18th Century Bulgaria'.[41]

Discussing socio-legal methodology in Ireland requires reflection on the roles of, and interaction between, the profession, academia and government. A smaller jurisdiction often creates an inherent doctrinal demand: Ireland has the same amount of law requiring doctrinal exegesis and synthesis as any country, but possesses fewer academics. Nevertheless, the recent rise of the PhD in law qualification has created a fresh academic pathway where once academic qualifications centred on practice backgrounds. The increased availability of research funding in Ireland proves a more solid base for law and society research. Peer discussion of research methodology within academia is also an important element, with other jurisdictions having found that a majority of academics engage in some form of socio-legal scholarship irrespective of their public or private law background.[42]

As much law and society research exists to support the development of evidence-based policy and to resource public debate, it should attract government funding and support. This is particularly the case in Ireland, where a weak regulatory and policy-making infrastructure was a key factor

---

[40] R Meagher, 'Now You Can Learn Practice in Theory' (Seventh Law Conference, Hong Kong, 20 September 1983) 175. This and other academic-judicial exchanges were recently discussed by Australian Chief Justice Robert French in 'Judges and Academics - Dialogue of the Hard of Hearing' (Inaugural Patron's Lecture at the Australian Academy of Law, Sydney, 30 October 2012) <www.hcourt.gov.au/assets/publications/speeches/current-justices/frenchcj/frenchcj30oct12.pdf> accessed 5 August 2015.

[41] Chief Justice of the United States, John G. Roberts Jr., *Interview at Fourth Circuit Court of Appeals Annual Conference* cited by D Wood in 'Legal Scholarship for Judges' (2015) 124 Yale Law Journal 2594.

[42] University of New South Wales Law School, *What Makes You Tick? Report on a Survey of the Factors that Condition High Quality Research* (UNSW Law 2013), 71% of researchers characterised their research as socio-legal. A 2004 study of the United Kingdom academic community found that 50% of legal academics surveyed viewed themselves as primarily engaged in socio-legal or critical legal research. See also, F Cownie, *Legal Academics: Culture and Identities* (Hart Publishing 2004).

in our recent financial crash. Despite being a small country with limited resources, Ireland's civil service culture has been criticised as unduly closed, with a former Director of the Economic and Social Research Institute calling for greater connection with experts.[43] In the legal context, the standing of socio-legal research is also not helped by the recurring tendency in political circles to propose the abolition of the Law Reform Commission. More positively however, the increasing emphasis placed upon the parliamentary committee procedure can help platform the policy contributions of legal academics.

Returning to the individual researcher, a key part of overcoming the 'am I still a lawyer' anxiety is taking ownership of the *legal* aspect of socio-legal methodology, and cultivating a feeling of control over the research. Without this, PhD candidates may wonder whether they will reach a point whereby their viva is better conducted by a social scientist or whether their supervisor will be sidelined, resulting in greater isolation. Students should also be aware that socio-legal methods exist on a continuum, with very few projects ultimately 'crossing' disciplinary lines. The following typology of interdisciplinary research, which Mattias Siems has recently put forward, in my view, underlines how unlikely it is that a law student would engage in a monodisciplinary work of sociology or philosophy. Siems identifies four types of interdisciplinary work:

- *Basic Interdisciplinary Research*: uses the same questions as starting points as traditional legal research, can be framed as the question of whether law and legal sources actually matter;

- *Advanced Interdisciplinary Research Type 1*: refers to research questions that are not about the law as such e.g. which measures are used to tackle climate change. This research attempt to provide a comprehensive view of a topic rather than look at one piece of the jigsaw;

- *Advanced Interdisciplinary Research Type 2*: Attempts to integrate scientific methods into legal thinking;

- *Advanced Interdisciplinary Research Type 3*: This combines the first and second type, by asking an interdisciplinary research question

---

[43] F Ruane, 'Research Evidence and Policy-making in Ireland' (2012) 60(2) Administration 119.

and attempting to integrate scientific methods into the legal analysis elements.[44]

What this typology underlines is that even ambitious socio-legal projects contain a 'return to law' phase, where the academic returns to consider the impact which the research has upon law. Roux, I believe, speaks for a sizeable proportion of legal researchers, when he argues that:

> ...what drives [legal academics] to engage in socio-legal research is an understanding that transforming doctrinal understandings is a powerful form of social intervention, and that the conventional techniques of doctrinal research do not always provide them with sufficient material to influence doctrinal understandings. They thus paradoxically abandon the traditional methods of traditional doctrinal research in order to achieve their primary purpose.[45]

Even the legal researcher with no faith in law is ultimately saying *something* about the phenomenon, for example that it is not worth the attention it is accorded.

This links to the second anxiety, which is that the researcher will fall between two stools, producing a work which is not framed in terms that feed into doctrinal argument, but not valued by other disciplines due to its superficial application of research methods used by these disciplines. As is evident from reading other contributions to this book, the adoption of empirical research methods requires training and protracted engagement. Yet do not sociologists have the same worries about accounting for law in their projects, the same intellectual distance to travel? Ironically, selling legal researchers on socio-legal methodology often requires them to view themselves as, due to their existing knowledge, uniquely positioned to carry it out, in comparison with other disciplines. Thus, if lawyers do not appreciate or defend the depth of doctrinal legal reasoning, they can undervalue their position within the academy, and cede the interdisciplinary field to sociology. As de Burca points out, the methodological conversation should not be one-sided:

> To the political scientist, legal scholarship often appears to be arid, technical, atheoretical ... full of unstated or unproven assumptions,

---

[44] M Siems, 'The Taxomony of Interdisciplinary Legal Research: Finding a Way Out of the Desert' (2009) 7 *Journal of Commonwealth Law and Legal Education* 5.
[45] Roux (n 17) 189-90.

lacking empirical support, and seemingly disinterested in the actual dynamics of political and social change. To the lawyer, political science scholarship often appears to be obsessed with methodology, jargonistic, and — in particular when it engages with law — remarkably banal.[46]

The intellectual quietism regarding methodology in the legal academy has meant that critiques of legal scholars' use of social sciences methods are more prominent than other disciplines' mistreatment of law. Epstein and King, for instance, have condemned much 'empirical legal scholarship' as deeply flawed, with many peer reviewed papers showing 'little awareness of, much less compliance with, the rules of inference that guide empirical research'.[47] While there is not the scope within the confines of this chapter to evaluate these specific claims, I would argue that legal academics do not regularly engage in similar methodological critiques of the social sciences' treatment of law.

IX – THE PITFALLS OF SOCIO-LEGAL RESEARCH

As I conclude this chapter, however, I do wish to frame some observations on the factors which may lead to the misapplication of socio-legal research methods. First, there is the danger of an 'echo chamber' within the legal academy, whereby early career legal researchers seek out examples of *other* lawyers' socio-legal publications and rely upon these in creating their methodologies. This 'second hand' shortcutting effectively exposes the researcher to the possibility of 'downloading' a methodological 'virus', whereby mistakes or simplifications are compounded within the academy.

This also raises the interesting question of whether the legal academy is prone to 'group think' or 'fads' in its treatment of other disciplines. I would instance two examples: first, the undue dominance of the Chicago school over law and economics scholarship, and secondly, the instrumentalising of postmodernist philosophers such as Foucault in legal research. One of the key lessons learned from 'law and economics' scholarship is that we must always ask 'law and whose economics?' As students of jurisprudence will be aware, until quite recently, law and economics as a field was unduly deferential to devices such as Pareto efficiency and the rational actor thesis. The current emphasis upon law and *behavioural* economics is a corrective to this imbalanced treatment of the discipline, but ironically it may suffer from

---

[46] G de Búrca, 'Rethinking Law in Neofunctionalist Theory' (2005) 12(2) Journal of European Public Policy 313.

[47] L Epstein and G King, 'The Rules of Inference' (2002) 69 University of Chicago Law Review 1.

the same excesses.[48] Legal researchers must pay due attention to the internal disciplinary debates which surround many methods and positions.

The use of postmodernists in legal research can, at times, display a similar selective tendency. One interesting debate surrounds the concept, currently in vogue, of 'governmentality'. This refers to Michael Foucault's particular understanding of 'the art of government', which he refers to as an 'ensemble formed by the institutions, procedures, analyses, reflections, calculations and tactics' which combine to produce a complex form of power.'[49] The concept offers much to socio-legal scholars, as it distinctively maps out the multifaceted nature of governmental power. There is however, a key methodological problem with its employment — the contested status of law in Foucault's thought. Some scholars attribute to Foucault the belief that law has 'been expelled from modernity',[50] with Duncan Kennedy arguing that he presents laws and legal institutions 'as elements in power situations without sharply distinguishing them from other elements'.[51] Even amongst those scholars who believe Foucault's understanding of law to be more constructive, the complexity of the role he ascribes to it is strongly underlined.[52] Thus, any application of the concept of 'governmentality' must reflect fully upon Foucault's understanding of law's status as a discourse. Beyond the specific example, it is a methodological imperative that the legal researcher acknowledges and accounts for the ideological situatedness of social sciences concepts.

Finally, I would underline an overarching danger to the methodology: the undervaluing of the internal perspective. There is a danger that socio-legal approaches can provoke the researcher into looking outside of law and legal institutions for a 'but for', utopian model of change, rather than considering what incremental change law and legal actors can promote. In the United States, Justice Harry Edwards captures this fear by arguing that 'while the schools are moving towards pure theory, the (law) firms are moving toward pure commerce, and the middle ground — ethical practice — has been

---

[48] See, for instance, K Yeung, 'Nudge as Fudge' (2012) 75(1) Modern Law Review 122.

[49] The author strongly underlines that this is a very rough definition of an extraordinarily complex concept. See M Foucault, 'Governmentality' in J Faubion (ed), *Power: Volume 3: Essential Works of Foucault 1954-1984* (Penguin 2002) 201-02.

[50] See generally, A Hunt and G Wickham, *Foucault and Law: Towards a Sociology of Law as Governance* (Pluto Press 1994).

[51] D Kennedy, 'The Stakes of Law, or Hale and Foucault!' (1991) 15 Legal Studies Forum 327.

[52] B Golder, 'Foucault and the Incompletion of Law' (2008) 21 Leiden Journal of International Law 747.

deserted by both'.⁵³ The result is that the idea of law may be emptied out, with "everything important is seen as taking place around law, not within it".⁵⁴

X – CONCLUSION

This chapter has sought to focus upon methodology rather than specific methods, many of which will be discussed by other commentators in this book. In linking my contribution to the discussion of methodology as a whole, I would identify the following key themes. First, theory is indispensable to practical research in law. Personal reflection upon the nature of law's interrelationship with society and its place in solving (or exacerbating) problems is crucial for the formation and delivery of any research project. As Cryer et al argue: 'the theoretical basis of a project will inform how law is conceptualised in the project which in turn will determine what kinds of research questions are meaningful or useful, what data is examined and how it is analysed.'⁵⁵

In my past classroom discussions with PhD students, doctrinal research was often projected as a 'safe' methodology. This is fundamentally flawed — while the doctrinal 'method' may be of great familiarity to the researcher, the selection of the doctrinal methodology will be subjected to the same level of justification and unpacking as the socio-legal. The fact that doctrinal research has often not been subjected to this discussion perhaps reflects the failure of law to take ownership of its own methodology. Thus, a second recurring theme in this chapter has been the need for our discipline to discuss what 'state of the art' legal research actually embraces.

Finally, this chapter highlighted how socio-legal methodology attempts to foster connection and holism in solving research problems. Any interdisciplinary research is deeply challenging, and acquiring the knowledge of the relevant methods is an exhaustive process. It may be initially disempowering for the researcher 'go back' to the classroom. Researchers may doubt their ability to critique particular qualitative or quantitative methods, fearing they will possess only a working knowledge. Yet in the author's view, the practicalities of studying qualitative or quantitative methods can be overcome with proper institutional commitment. At the

---

⁵³ HT Edwards, 'The Growing Disjunction between Legal Education and the Legal Profession' (1992-1993) 91 Mich L Rev 34.
⁵⁴ J R Morss, 'Part of the Problem or Part of the Solution? Legal Positivism and Legal Education' (2008) 18 (1/2) Legal Education Review 55, 65.
⁵⁵ R Cryer, T Hervey, B Sokhi-Bulley, A Bohm, *Research Methodologies in EU and International Law* (Hart Publishing 2011) 5.

individual level, the researcher must construct an understanding of how the knowledge of other disciplines can be applied, the benefits of so doing, and the knock on effects for the project's underlying conception of law. Such interdisciplinary exploration can be the bedrock of a positive self-identity as a *legal* researcher. While it is possible to study 'legal aspects of Eurozone governance' or 'legal mechanisms for combating climate change', such projects must address how they define the 'legal' and the extent to which such aspects can be examined in isolation from other social processes. This is not to erase disciplines or specialisations, but to marry them with an awareness of the danger of fostering intellectual silos. In this context, it worth recalling Myrdal's condemnation concerning the narrowness of macroeconomic scholarship in the 1970s: 'the isolation of one part of social reality by demarcating it "economic" is not feasible. In reality there are not "economic", sociological or psychological problems but just problems and they are complex'.[56]

---

[56] G Myrdal, *Against the Stream: Critical Essays on Economics* (Vintage Books New York 1975) 142.

Chapter 8

Getting Down and Dirty: The Case for Empirical Legal Research

*Michael Doherty**

I – Introduction

This chapter considers the role of empirical research in legal scholarship. More than nine years on from the publication of the seminal report, 'Law in the real World: The Nuffield Inquiry on Empirical Research on Law',[1] the chapter analyses why the conduct, and publication, of empirically-grounded legal research remains relatively limited in the UK and Ireland. The chapter argues that the failure by higher education institutes, including, but not limited to, failings on the part of law schools to develop a more significant research capacity in empirical legal research could have very negative impacts on the next generation of legal scholars. In this regard, the chapter considers the increasing centrality of empirical and multi or interdisciplinary research to accessing funding, and to publishing in top-ranked outlets. It also argues for the inherent intellectual and 'employability' benefits to legal academics and aspirant practitioners of expanding their range beyond 'traditional' means of legal inquiry. The chapter does not seek to examine the conceptual underpinnings of empirical legal research, or the theoretical bases for utilising this method of inquiry. Rather, it sets out some (very) personal reflections of the author and illustrates the argument by using practical examples of empirical legal research. As a result, it seeks to be both a 'call to arms' and a practical guide for those interested in pursuing empirical legal research. Before going on to suggest some reasons why the conduct of empirical legal research remains relatively limited, and considering some practical examples of such research, the next section begins by making the case for empirical research in law.

II – Why Empirical Research?

First, the confession. I am a Professor of Law and currently Head of a University Law Department, but I hold a PhD in Sociology. It may not

---

* Professor Michael Doherty is Head of the Department of Law, Maynooth University.
[1] The Nuffield Inquiry on Empirical Legal Research, 'Law in the Real World: The Nuffield Inquiry on Empirical Research on Law' (hereinafter 'the Nuffield Report') (2006) <www.nuffieldfoundation.org/nuffield-inquiry-empirical-legal-research-law-real-world> accessed 13 July 2015.

surprise readers to learn that, until now at least, I have kept this snippet of information relatively quiet. My web profile and CV simply state the institution from which I obtained my PhD and the topic (more on this anon, but it is sufficiently vague to be capable of being the subject of a PhD in Law). I have not hidden my educational history in job interviews (and neither, I hasten to add, have I misled any interview panels!), but if it does not come up, I do not introduce the issue. This, in many ways, is strange, because any success I have achieved in my career as a legal academic is intimately bound up with my doctoral training. This is true of virtually all academics (as, increasingly, a PhD is seen as a pre-requisite for an academic post), but is probably particularly true in my case as I believe, and this is the premise underlying this chapter, that the training I received in empirical research methodology and the empirical research I undertook for my doctoral thesis have made me a better legal academic than otherwise might have been the case.

A Good In Itself: Skills And Employability

So, first, I believe there is an inherent value in law students and legal scholars being schooled in, and applying, empirical social science research techniques.[2] Qualitative research techniques (e.g., structured or semi-structured interviews, focus groups, and ethnographies) require the development of important 'soft' skills; the ability to manage relationships, to interact with others, to empathise, and to listen. They also require the researcher to be extremely well-organised and flexible, to have the ability to think on his/her feet and respond to challenges and setbacks, and to develop extremely good negotiation skills. An appreciation of, and adherence to, high ethical standards is also crucial.[3] Quantitative research methods (I will focus on the use of surveys) require similar attributes, but add a need for numeracy skills (basic statistical knowledge) and an ability to use data analysis software. Put simply, these are important skills that any well-rounded education should provide. They are also the 'transferable skills' that employers in all spheres and sectors increasingly demand. They take the researcher (for a while at least) out of the library and the IT laboratory, and even help mitigate the loneliness that often accompanies the PhD experience. As noted, a PhD is now generally a pre-requisite for getting an academic post. This has resulted, naturally, in more and more legal PhDs coming

---

[2] There is a huge number of texts on social science research methodology; three I find useful are M Quinn Patton, *Qualitative Research and Evaluation Methods* (4th edn, Sage 2014); R K Yin, *Case Study Research: Design and Methods* (5th edn, Sage 2014); D de Vaus, *Surveys in Social Research* (6th edn, 2013 Routledge).

[3] Does all of this sound very much different to what one would expect of a good practising lawyer?

through and, consequently, more of a need to distinguish one's doctoral work. As Fiona de Londras argues elsewhere in this volume, the use of empirical methods can be a means of marking out doctoral research as making truly original contributions to knowledge.

Publication And Funding

In looking to progress in an academic career, we are all focused on publishing our work in top-quality outlets, and on securing research funding.[4] I will focus first on publication in peer-reviewed journals.[5] There are more journals than ever, but equally more competition to publish in, and more of a push to 'rank' and 'evaluate', these. I have no wish to get mired in debates about the ranking of research outlets, but, as someone frequently involved in making recruitment decisions, it would be foolish to pretend that rankings are totally irrelevant. Let's take the Thomson Reuters Journal Citation Reports (JCR) ranking system as an example. At the time of writing, 140 journals are listed in the 2014 'law' category. This is, for a global ranking system, not a huge number. The list is heavily weighted towards journals publishing in English and those from the US (18 of the 'top 20' are US law journals). Excellent doctrinal research will (should?) always find a home, but this bias does pose an extra challenge to those writing about significant developments involving Irish or UK or, even, European legislation or case law.[6] Take out 'specialist' journals — like those focusing on military law, for example — and the range of journals on the list in which one's work could fit narrows quite dramatically.

Empirically-grounded legal research can be of assistance in at least two ways here. First, it seems to me to be easier to 'generalise', and thus interest a non-local audience in, interview or survey data on a legal topic than it is to explain why that audience might be interested in the niceties of legislation or case law that is jurisdictionally bounded. Even if my view on this is disputed, a good empirical research design is *in itself* of interest; a well-designed project should be relatively easy to transplant to another legal setting.[7] Secondly, to take the example of someone with my own research

---

[4] An interesting feature of modern academia, it seems to me, is that it is not always clear whether it is the actual securing of funding *or* the production of work that is truly useful or important once the cash has been handed over that is valued more…but perhaps this is an issue for another volume….

[5] This is not in any way to comment on the appropriateness of publishing monographs, official reports, blogs, etc., etc., but simply by way of illustrating the point.

[6] A frequent answer to this by authors is to strong-arm in a 'comparative' element, which is often artificial and detracts from the scholarship.

[7] This works both ways; we should always be alert to studies done elsewhere that can be replicated in our own jurisdiction.

interests, there is no 'specialist' employment and labour law journal on the JCR list at all. However, in the 'industrial relations & labor' category (that US bias extends to spelling...), there are 26 journals, most of which I read more frequently than the vast majority of those in the law list. If one moves through the categories on the JCR list, there are many more where legal research sometimes features (but infrequently): e.g. ethics; women's studies; hospitality, leisure, sports & tourism. Indeed, a publication strategy I strongly commend is to always consider the possibility of re-working a legal piece for publication in a journal aimed at a 'non-law' audience. It may well be, for example, that a thorough analysis of damages for disappointment or distress arising from a contractual breach, looking at Lord Denning's judgment in *Jarvis v Swan's Tours*,[8] could be written up in a different fashion that might be of considerable interest to readers of the *Journal of Hospitality & Tourism Research*.[9] Moreover, collaborating on such a piece with a colleague in another faculty might be of considerable pragmatic and intellectual benefit to both parties.

Apart from the last point about collaboration, this might all be seen as quite instrumental, bordering on cynical, and there is, of course, the problem of convincing a recruitment panel in a law school that a publication in, say, *Employee Relations*, equates to one in the *Cambridge Law Journal*. However, there is also a fundamental point about academic and intellectual value to be made here. Does not the complexity of contemporary society require governance and policy analysis that derives from a multi-faceted examination of socio-economic and cultural issues? Is it not a huge positive to engage non-legal audiences in the work we are doing? Is it not a good thing that legal academics speak to political scientists, economists, business scholars, and psychologists (and vice versa, of course)? The pigeon-holing of academics into disciplinary boxes is never a positive and, to me, reached a nadir during media coverage of the economic crisis from 2008, where discourse was dominated by economists. Naturally (some) economists had very valuable analysis to offer, but (particularly, for example, in relation to role of the EU), so did the political scientists, sociologists and, yes, legal academics, who were far less represented on the airwaves and in print.

The same mix of pragmatic instrumentalism and intellectual value can be applied to the issue of research funding. Again, funding is increasingly directed towards projects that promise some kind of 'real-world' pay-off

---

[8] [1972] EWCA Civ 8, [1972] 3 WLR 954, [1973] 1 All ER 71, [1973] QB 233.

[9] Ranked 15/39 in the JCR hospitality, leisure, sports & tourism category.

and that involve collaboration between academics from different disciplines. Take the European Commission's Horizon 2020 programme, which calls for, in its 'Societal Challenges' theme, a 'challenge-based approach (that) will bring together resources and knowledge across different fields, technologies and disciplines, including social sciences and the humanities'.[10] The key areas on which funding under this theme will be focused are ones in which legal researchers can make an obvious contribution: for example, health, demographic change and wellbeing; secure societies - protecting freedom and security of Europe and its citizens; and Europe in a changing world - inclusive, innovative and reflective societies. Equally, however, it is clear a traditional legal focus alone would be unlikely to adequately address these themes. Legal academics leading project bids will need to be able to demonstrate expertise in other areas, or, more likely, an ability and willingness to work with colleagues from other disciplines. This works both ways, of course; a valuable way of 'getting in' to established EU funding consortia is for legal researchers to supplement or support bids led by colleagues in other disciplines. This might actually involve 'traditional' legal research, but, again, a willingness and ability to interact with other disciplines is crucial.

Horizon 2020 is a very 'top-down' example of research funding. However, if one looks at a 'bottom-up' example, Marie Skłodowska-Curie Individual Fellowships, the focus is also on funding research that will make a contribution to economy and society, and that will develop the career of researcher (in both the academic and non-academic sense), primarily by imparting transferable skills that enhance employability:

> The goal of Individual Fellowships is to enhance the creative and innovative potential of experienced researchers wishing to diversify their individual competence in terms of skill acquisition at multi- or interdisciplinary level through advanced training, international and intersectoral mobility.[11]

Unquestionably, the acquisition of empirical research skills for legal scholars falls squarely within what is envisaged here.

---

[10] Horizon 2020, 'Societal Challenges' <http://ec.europa.eu/programmes/horizon2020/en/h2020-section/societal-challenges> accessed 13 July 2015.

[11] Horizon 2020, 'Research and Innovation:Individual Fellowships' <https://ec.europa.eu/research/participants/portal4/desktop/en/opportunities/h2020/calls/h2020-msca-if-2015.html> accessed 13 July 2015.

In sum, what I have argued is that, for legal scholars, engaging in empirical research is an intellectual and educational good in itself, and is a pragmatic career move in terms of publication and funding. If we accept, for now, that this is the case, why are so few of us in law schools doing empirical research?

III – Why Not?

To answer this question, I will simply refer to the Nuffield report published in 2006. Although the report studied the UK only, its findings also, I argue, applied and still apply to Ireland.[12] I will briefly highlight some of the key findings of the report, which point to significant limitations in the development of empirical legal scholarship, before going on to discuss how these might be addressed.

In chapter 4, the report refers to the failings of law schools in carrying out, and training students and early career researchers to carry out, empirical research. The report notes that law schools have traditionally been dominated by a focus on text-based doctrinal work, particularly at undergraduate level. Whilst there has been a move towards providing more 'skills' training in Ireland for undergraduate law students (for example, most law schools now incorporate mooting as part of the core curriculum), courses tend to focus on the skills that fit with traditional doctrinal research (locating and utilising case law, legal writing and advocacy) and there are few law schools in the UK or Ireland that offer comprehensive and systematic training in empirical methods for undergraduate students.

This inevitably leads to a problem of self-replication. Law graduates who pursue academic careers, or, initially, postgraduate study, and who have little, if any, experience of empirical research, tend to drift to what they know; doctrinal legal issues. The self-replication problem means that finding adequate supervision for empirical research projects is often extremely difficult; traditional legal academics tend to prefer supervising traditional legal academic research projects.

The wider institutional context of the University is not helpful, either. To carry out quality empirical legal research, greater support from, and linkages with, cognate disciplines in which empirical techniques are already embedded would be enormously helpful. Professor Malcom Grant, then-Provost and President of University College London, is quoted in the Nuffield Report

---

[12] Indeed, in conversation with some of those involved in the preparation of the Report, the view was prevalent that its findings apply *still* to law schools in the UK.

stating that 'university departments still reflect a Victorian "brigading" of knowledge into law, philosophy, biology, medicine and so on'.[13] The academic institution, as a whole, should be concerned with how to provide training in research skills to research students and academics that is broad, encompassing, and transcends narrow disciplinary boundaries, but, as the Nuffield Report states, also has 'relevance to the specific context in which they will be working and on the kinds of research that they are most likely to be undertaking'.[14] Not easy; but what worthwhile ever is? The next section moves on to look at examples of what kinds of work I am trying to describe here, drawing on personal experience.

IV – What Do I Mean?

Research Issue/Design

The starting point for many (most?) pieces of UK or Irish legal research, including PhDs is: the law on X is flawed and needs reform; here are some examples from the US/Canada/Australia, etc., on what is required.[15] This is a perfectly defensible way to design a research project, and, in many instances, is the best way to address the research issue. However, my fear is that the limitations in academic legal training, outlined above, have resulted in the consideration of a relatively narrow range of options when it comes to research design.[16] As legal academics, by and large, tend to only 'dabble in' empirical research, they also tend to have little or no understanding of what amounts to a *coherent* research design. One frequently comes across research proposals that promise 'interviews' or 'surveys' but convey absolutely no sense of what these 'empirics' will add to, or why they are necessary for, an understanding of the research issue. The lack of training also shows up in a frequent lack of understanding of the expenditure of time, effort, and resources, and the challenges that arise, in the context of empirical data collection. Collecting data may well have a value in and of itself (it usually does), but a good research design collects data in order to meet a clearly-defined and justifiable objective. Few of us have the luxury of being able to simply add in an empirical element because it might look good on a funding proposal.

---

[13] Nuffield Report (n 1) 35.
[14] ibid 36.
[15] The dominance of common law jurisdictions as points of reference is understandable, but perhaps too limiting.
[16] For texts on research design see (n 2) above. A text I like very much, although it was written quite a while ago now, is Catherine Hakim, *Research Design: Successful Designs for Social and Economic Research* (2nd edn, Routledge 2000).

For the remainder of this chapter, I am going to focus on two forms of empirical research;[17] the collection of survey data (quantitative) and interview data (qualitative).[18] Here, I will briefly comment on some of the challenges in carrying out this kind of research.[19] I will move to discussing practical examples in the next section.

If the research design incorporates an empirical angle, carrying out interviews as opposed to quantitative surveys, in terms of the financial resources required, will often be the more practical option, particularly for a PhD student. However, access to the respondents required to address the research issue is key. Two issues must be addressed in the research design. First, how will the respondents be accessed? Frequently, this will hinge on 'gatekeepers', who can leverage access for the researcher. Contacts and networks are important here,[20] and PhD supervisors should be called upon for assistance. Secondly, there must be a 'plan B'; what will happen if you cannot get access to the required respondents? In this sense, a research design that depends on interviewing, say, the judges of the EU Court of Justice is very high risk. The same applies if the target population is extremely vulnerable (victims of abuse, for example). In both cases, it must be assessed first if the research issue can be addressed *without* such access; would a retired judge, or a judicial assistant, suffice? Would a representative of an organisation working with victims of abuse be able to give adequate information?

Irrespective of who the target respondents are, qualitative research involves a huge element of managing relationships, and a careful and thorough consideration of ethical concerns (in terms of the research design itself, and data collection and retention). With qualitative research, there are many software packages that aid with analysis (NVivo is among the best known) and use of one of these will speed things up dramatically in terms of looking for connections and themes in interview data. However, old-fashioned

---

[17] I will justify this by pleading the inevitable space constraints, but (full disclosure,) whilst I am a legal academic with a PhD in Sociology, I am still a legal academic, and so I am reluctant to talk about techniques beyond those I have personally employed.

[18] There are, of course, different ways of interviewing for research projects, ranging from relatively informal, 'go with the flow' conversations to highly-structured, closed-response interviews, where all respondents are asked the same questions and asked to choose from a set number of responses (see extensive discussion in Patton, n 1). In this chapter, I will refer to 'semi-structured' interviews, where the same general *areas of information* are collected from, and the same *broad questions* are asked of, each interviewee. This allow for comparative analysis, but also a degree of flexibility in getting information and opinion from the interviewees.

[19] For a fuller account, see the chapter by Fiona de Londras in this volume.

[20] Attending conferences and seminars as early as possible in the PhD process is a huge advantage.

preparation for interviews, listening, and being able to engage your respondent, remain fundamental. Most researchers need time and experience to develop good interview skills and techniques (and, frankly, some never do).[21] Do not think this is an 'easy option'; to do properly, it takes a lot of preparation, time, and energy.

Sample Size and Resources

There is one fundamental issue that always concerns researchers in relation to interviews: how many do I need to do? It is a question that is dependent utterly on the research issue and design; there is no 'minimum/maximum threshold'. If the research is looking at the daily work experience of Supreme Court justices, five interviews might be considered hugely valuable; if the research looks at the work experience of city bus drivers, a larger sample might be required (due to much wider variations in age and ethnicity, for example). The preoccupation with this issue, I think, comes down to concerns about 'generalising' results: if I only interview five people, how can that be of value? It is important here to distinguish between qualitative and quantitative research. For the quantitative researcher, the idea is to be able to sample cases that are typical in specified ways of the population. If the sample is correctly drawn, then the results are deemed to be applicable (generalisable) to the specified population. Therefore, sample sizes and response rates are important. When doing interviews, or qualitative research more generally, however, the generalisation is not about populations, but about *theoretical propositions* in situations where *context* is important and situations cannot be manipulated in the manner of a laboratory experiment.[22] Therefore the basis of any 'generalisation' is not about the 'typicality' of the case, but the existence of particular *processes*, in particular *contexts*, which may *influence behaviours and actions*.

It is this need for adequate sample size that, generally, results in survey research being resource intensive. Surveys are quite blunt instruments. What the researcher gains in terms of numbers of responses (and 'generalisability') must be set against what is lost (compared with interviews) in term of nuance and depth. Furthermore, surveys are generally a 'one-shot' deal, whereas one can often (though not always) return to an interviewee for clarification, etc. Thus, the design of the survey is crucial and, as a result, getting it right is quite time-consuming. Unlike in an interview situation, there is no space for

---

[21] I would always recommend that researchers ease themselves in to interviewing - never interview the key informants first, but try and do some 'fact-finding' interviews to get into the swing.
[22] Yin (n 2) ch 2.

the researcher to explain questions to, or resolve any confusion on the part of, the respondent.[23] Survey questionnaires should always be piloted and, based on results, revised. Ideally, this process should be repeated as often as is feasible.

Questionnaires also need to be disseminated to the target population (which itself has to be carefully defined as part of the research design). Obviously, surveys can now be relatively easily disseminated online, often at no cost to the researcher. This seems like an easy option and it is, undoubtedly, a help to researchers, especially if the object is to collect relatively simple descriptive data. However, it should be noted that easier dissemination can result in greater levels of 'response fatigue', making it easier to reach a target population but harder to get that population to engage. Even where a survey is going out online, some sort of relationship with the target population (perhaps via a 'gatekeeper') is likely to result in higher response rates. It should also be noted that many free methods of survey dissemination offer little in the way of analytics. If the researcher wants to analyse the data in a relatively sophisticated way (going beyond the descriptive to look at statistical correlations, for example) s/he may end up having to re-input the results (manually!) into a data analysis package.[24]

Data analysis is the step that probably requires most in terms of training. Crudely, what the researcher needs to be clear on is the relationship between an outcome — the dependent variable — and one or more explanatory factors — the independent variable(s). I will illustrate this with an example, below. Survey data analysis is dependent on being comfortable with relevant software (like SPSS or Stata) and this, again, takes time, effort, and training.

One thing academic lawyers tend not to do is use existing data ('secondary data'). Criminologists are very comfortable in using data collected by others, most obviously official crime statistics, but it is not very common to see company lawyers using the Companies Registration Office data, or consumer lawyers referencing statistics from the Financial Ombudsman. A broader

---

[23] Unless, of course, surveys are administered face-to-face.

[24] For example, one might simply be looking to count how many university law lecturers use PowerPoint presentations (descriptive). If the object, though, is to investigate statistical correlations between using PowerPoint presentations and student results, a much more sophisticated method of data collection and analysis (controlling for all sorts of other influences, such as class sizes, etc.) would be required. This level of analysis would almost certainly require a more detailed method of dissemination and analysis than is typically offered by free dissemination services.

focus on the types of research we could do should also entail a wider appreciation of the tools available to us to carry this out.

V – EXAMPLES: OUT IN THE FIELD

In this section, I am going to give some practical examples of empirical work I have carried out. The narcissism inherent in this I explain simply by saying it is easier to speak to work one has carried out personally! What will become clear is that I have engaged in mixed methods approaches. This might be one of the advantages of coming from a discipline without a long tradition of using empirical methods; one does not become overly concerned about being classified (pigeon-holed?) as a 'qualitative' or 'quantitative' scholar. This can be observed in other disciplines, but our (relative) ignorance in this sphere may mean legal academics are more willing to embrace, utilise, and move between, different methods.

Interview Data

I have primarily worked on qualitative projects, usually focussing on interviews. A number of these are exemplified by a project I worked on in 2011-12; a study of the legal aspects of the posting of workers in the EU and Norway.[25] The project was funded by the European Commission and involved the leaders co-ordinating 27 national reports on the implementation and operation of EU rules on posting, and producing two reports for the Commission on the results of the project.[26] The objectives of the studies were to establish how effectively the Directive on posting was operating and being enforced, and to suggest ways in which enforcement might be improved. A questionnaire to guide the interviews was designed by the project leaders and provided to all the national researchers. This was not to be rigidly adhered to in a 'tick the box' fashion, but all researchers were required to seek out information that would broadly cover the themes laid out in the questionnaire. In total, ten interviews were carried out in Ireland; in my view, and in the view of the project leaders, this yielded more than enough information to meet the goals of the project.[27]

---

[25] 'Posted workers' are workers who are employed in one Member State but are sent ('posted') by their employer to work on a temporary basis in another Member State. The legislation that covers the posting of workers is Directive 96/71/EC of the European Parliament and of the Council of 16 December 1996 concerning the posting of workers in the framework of the provision of services [1996] OJ L 18/1.

[26] Employment, Social Affairs and Inclusion <http://ec.europa.eu/social/main.jsp?catId=471> accessed 13 July 2015; the Irish report contributed to *Complementary study on the legal aspects of the posting of workers in the framework of the provision of services in the European Union* (2012).

[27] Note that one could easily envisage a project, with broadly similar aims, that would focus on the experiences of posted workers themselves. This would ideally still require the 'elite' perspective,

The interviews (as is common in research related to employment rights) were to be with relevant persons in employer representative groups, trade unions, the government (and, notably, the Department of Jobs, Enterprise and Innovation), and the labour inspectorate. Thus, the interviews were to be with 'elites'; respondents that could be expected to have insights into both policy and practice, and could be expected to provide an overview of the issues. Moreover, all of the researchers in the 27 Member States would have more or less similar respondents to 'target'. 'Elite' interviews have advantages from the researcher's point of view. Generally, the respondents will have expertise in the issue and will be used to articulating their views. However, securing access can often be difficult, preparation is crucial (the researcher must be comfortable with the issue at hand, or respondents can lose patience, or, worse, spend the interview outlining basic information, which is probably readily accessible), and the researcher must always be alert to the 'agenda' of the respondent, and the fact that responses may be guarded. Thus, the ability to make the respondent comfortable with the process and the ability to steer the discussion are crucial skills a researcher must master. Also, the researcher must be open to the interview going down unexpected lines. An overly rigid adherence to the research design must be avoided; there is a balance to be struck between getting the information deemed to be required, and being open to views and opinions that do not fit the hypothesis!

The majority of interviews I carried out for my PhD research, by contrast, were not with 'elites', but with 'ordinary' workers.[28] For example, I conducted more than 30 interviews with city bus drivers, retail store workers, and local authority employees over the course of many visits to the various workplaces. This type of interviewing requires using the same basic skills of interviewing outlined above (section II.i), but there are subtle differences. Frequently, those not in 'elite' roles (here this would equate to, for example, organisational management positions) can be wary of what might be seen as 'intrusive' questions about their personal experience, or, even more frequently, bemused as to why a researcher would want to know about their day-to-day experiences. Such respondents are also less likely to

---

but would also need interviews with a representative sample of workers. Such a project, to my mind, would need more than ten interviews to be robust.

[28] M Doherty, 'Does the Union Still Make Us Strong? Irish Trade Union Membership in the Partnership Era' (PhD thesis, Trinity College Dublin 2007). Examples of the use of the data can be seen in M Doherty, 'When the Working Day is Through: The End of Work as Identity?' (2009) 23(1) Work Employment and Society 84; M Doherty, 'Mind the Gap - National and Local Partnership in the Irish Public Sector' (2010) 41 Industrial Relations Journal 461.

be used to articulating their views to strangers.[29] Again, managing the personal interaction is crucial. It depends on the nature of the target population, of course, but I have always found that the vast majority of people really do like to talk about their experiences, even if they have to be coaxed a little initially. Perhaps more than is the case with 'elite' interviews, the question of how the observer affects what is observed is very important. The researcher must be sensitive to the extent to which social worlds are changed by his or her intrusion. So, the role of the researcher requires both detachment and personal involvement. The term 'reflexivity' emphasises the importance of self-awareness, political/cultural consciousness, ownership of one's own perspective, and the ideological origins of one's voice and perspective. This means recording all the key choices and assumptions made throughout the process of framing the questions, data collection, and the generation of organising ideas or frameworks, for example through extensive diary notes and recorded reflections throughout the research periods.[30]

Equally, it means being aware that the members of the unit under investigation will attempt to put the researcher in a social space; the researcher must therefore be aware of how s/he is being identified. For example, a researcher may well choose to dress differently when going to interview bus drivers at a garage than when going to speak to employees of a corporate bank at the employer's HQ.[31] Practical issues of location can also be significant. For my research, I decided early on to interview respondents at their place of work. The logistical difficulties of finding a neutral space to carry out interviews with multiple respondents, living in dispersed locations, were considerable. However, there were some methodological advantages to this too; gaining cooperation was perhaps easier as respondents did not have to give up their free time before or after work, and respondents were able to illustrate points visually for me (by pointing out physical aspects of the workplace and so on).

Survey Data
The most significant piece of quantitative research I have carried out alone was for my PhD thesis, which sought to measure member participation in

---

[29] Let me be very clear that I am *not* saying such respondents are less likely to be articulate!
[30] R Whipp, 'Qualitative Methods: Technique or Size?' in K Whitfield and G Strauss (eds), *Researching the World of Work* (Cornell University Press 1998).
[31] Bitter personal experience, too, has taught that, when interviewing bus drivers, it is not a good idea to blame being late on travelling by bus.

trade unions.³² For this research, both qualitative (described, in part, above) and quantitative methodologies were employed. I designed a survey questionnaire and distributed 360 across the workplaces (physically, not online). I received 129 useable responses, giving a response rate of 36%; acceptable for this kind of survey.³³ In this part of the research, the aim was to discover what, if any, impact various explanatory factors (independent variables) had on members' union participation (the dependent variable). The independent variables were derived from a study of the literature on trade union participation and included factors like working time, belief in trade unionism, job satisfaction, gender, age, etc. Virtually all the concepts were evaluated through the employment of scaling; the use of a composite measure of a concept, a measure composed of information derived from several questions or indicators.³⁴ Scales are created by converting the information contained in several relatively specific indicators into one new and more abstract variable. So, for example, rather than simply ask respondents whether or not they were 'satisfied with their job', I asked a series of questions as to whether they were satisfied with their pay, physical work environment, their task, the pace of work and so on. This enables the use of multiple indicators to develop more valid measures, increasing reliability and enabling greater precision. The majority of the scales were Likert scales with closed responses ranging from 'strongly agree' to 'strongly disagree'.

This was a sociological thesis and the primary aims were to identify the factors that affected the extent of worker participation in their unions, and to identify which of these had the greatest effect. However, quite clearly the data also revealed matters of significance for labour law; for example, what *legal supports* might increase worker participation in trade unions? One of the key findings from the data was that 'satisfaction with the workplace union representative' had a very strong positive effect on levels of participation.³⁵ Thus, we might argue that robust legal protection for workplace union representatives would be significant in boosting union participation levels; this might require strong anti-victimisation laws, for example, or statutory support for paid time-off, leave, and education and training for workplace representatives.³⁶ Naturally, of course, if the public

---

³² (n 27).

³³ de Vaus (n 2).

³⁴ ibid ch 11.

³⁵ 'Satisfaction with the workplace union representative' was again a composite variable - the survey asked a number of specific questions (does the workplace representative keep the workers informed of developments in the organisation; does s/he adequately address members' grievances, etc.).

³⁶ So, in Ireland, we see protection against unfair dismissal that is related to trade union membership

policy objective is to *reduce* workplace support for trade unions, statutory supports of this kind would be removed or not enacted.

VI – Conclusions: What Next?

I will begin this concluding section with another confession. In my PhD research, both the survey and interview data strongly pointed to a view on the part of workers that their employers did not keep them adequately informed about significant business decisions, and changes in work practices and organisation, which impacted heavily on their working lives. Furthermore, both the survey and interview data strongly suggested that workers felt changes were implemented without adequate consultation with them or their representatives. At the time the data collection was carried out in 2003-2004, Ireland was in the process of transposing Directive 2002/14 on the Information and Consultation of Workers. In the concluding chapter of the thesis, I pointed out that the implementation of this directive, and the subsequent operation of the legislation, would be crucial in addressing the problem of the lack of worker voice and involvement identified in the thesis. I also pointed out that there was great scope for empirical studies that would track the effectiveness of the legislation in the years ahead… which leads to the confession. There was indeed such scope, and some excellent empirical studies were carried out following the enactment of the Employees (Provision of Information and Consultation) Act 2006…all of them by scholars in business schools…it is not always easy to practise what one preaches![37]

Nonetheless, I will conclude with some brief reflections on how empirical legal research might be better supported into the future. Somewhat depressingly, one could look to the conclusions and recommendations (Chapter 5) of the Nuffield report and simply list these off again. I will look briefly at some improvements that could take place in three areas.

Money Talks: Institutional And Resource Support

Over the medium/long-term, it is important that those viewing empirical legal research as being important advocate for some sort of 'targeted' funding

---

or activities; Unfair Dismissals Act 1977, s 6(2)(a) (as amended). In the UK, we see the Trade Union and Labour Relations (Consolidation) Act 1992, s 168, allows union officials paid time off from work in order to carry out certain union-related duties.

[37] See, for example, T Dundon et al, 'Employer Occupation of Regulatory Space of the Employee Information and Consultation (I&C) Directive in Liberal Market Economies' (2014) 28(1) Work, Employment and Society 21; N Cullinane et al, 'Regulating for Mutual Gains? Non-union Employee Representation and the Information and Consultation Directive' (2014) 25(6) International Journal of Human Resource Management 810.

for empirical legal projects. In an ideal world, 'ring-fenced' funds for empirical legal work, initially on a pilot basis perhaps, but at least for a period of time in order to allow such research to gain a foothold, would be established by funding bodies and Higher Education Institutions (HEIs). Encouraging this type of research can also, however, be achieved more subtly, for example by funding calls privileging empirical legal approaches. An obvious starting place is to incentivise such research at doctoral level, via scholarships and bursaries. Additionally, a careful initial targeting of projects around key national strategic policy areas might be a way to 'sell' the idea to public funding bodies; in Ireland, for example, empirical legal research funding could be linked to core *areas* of foreign direct investment, on which the national economy is so dependent, such as financial services or pharmaceuticals, or to vital *processes* such as dispute resolution or public procurement procedures.

At the level of individual HEIs (or, ideally, clusters of HEIs), a re-thinking of resource allocation that actively promotes the reality (as opposed to the rhetoric) of multi- or interdisciplinary teaching and research is crucial. It must be recognised that such activities require time, dedication, and effort that must be accounted for in resource allocation models. Quite simply, those engaging, for example, in cross-discipline teaching initiatives or postgraduate supervision must be given time and space outside of the 'normal' workload model to participate in these properly, and departments and schools that engage in such activities must be encouraged, supported and, indeed, privileged by institutional resource allocation models. This all might subsequently lead to the promotion of cross-faculty staff recruitment, which is currently neither usual nor easy given the sharp disciplinary boundaries that persist in typical HEIs, but which could contribute to the establishment of a virtuous circle.

Law Schools: Time To Get Serious?

At a recent Socio-Legal Studies Association Conference, I mentioned to a colleague that there were some mixed student responses to a second-year undergraduate module on innovation in legal practice being piloted as part of the LL.B programme in my university. His immediate response was that second year was too late – by then the students had already been 'captured' by orthodox legal teaching! There is a real need for those serious about empirical legal research training to embed this in the undergraduate curriculum. There are various means by which this might be done. Explicit 'empirical skills' modules could form part of the curriculum, or be incorporated into existing legal skills courses. Importantly, to me, 'core' modules should not focus exclusively on doctrinal material, but should incorporate and encourage empirical perspectives (in lectures and/or tutorials). Crucially, before students ever get to looking at qualitative and quantitative research techniques, the possibility of applying an empirical perspective to 'traditional' legal materials should be emphasised. For example, why not more empirical research on contracts, focusing less on the legal principles outlined in court cases and more on the types of clauses contracts in different settings (commercial, employment, land, etc.) actually contain?[38] Equally, one could look at decisions of tribunals or other non-court decision-making bodies in various settings (e.g. personal injury, employment, social welfare) to categorise and explore information about the types of claimants, the nature of the disputes, and so on.[39]

It would also be a huge step forward if greater teaching and research collaboration between different units in HEIs could be promoted. Law students, for example, should have access to, and be encouraged to take, options in other disciplines, and vice versa. This, ideally, should be in some sort of structured fashion, perhaps organised thematically. For example, students taking Family Law might be encouraged to take related modules in psychology, social studies, or sociology; those studying EU Law might be encouraged to take modules in politics or economics, and so on.[40] In terms of research, similarly, legal academics should be encouraged, and incentivised, to target links with colleagues in different disciplines researching in similar thematic areas.

Law Students

As noted in the introduction, this chapter was intended to be both a 'call to arms' and a practical guide for those interested in pursuing empirical legal research. The various institutional changes I have suggested are important for systematically developing, supporting and sustaining a cohort of skilled and engaged empirical legal researchers. However, for any law student or legal researcher reading this, it is probably best not to wait for all, or any, of these to take place. The first steps are to reflect openly on the possibilities for your own research interests, to talk to your colleagues in other disciplines, and, most importantly, to be brave and seek adventure!

---

[38] See, for example, J Davey and C Kelly, 'Romalpa and Contractual Innovation' (2015) 42 Journal of Law and Society 358.

[39] For research on the Labour Court (which, despite its moniker, is an employment tribunal), for example, see M Doherty, 'Representation, Bargaining and the Law: Where Next for the Unions?' (2009) 60 NILQ 282.

[40] Again, this would have to be incentivised by resource allocation modules.

CHAPTER 9

Participatory Research: Some Provocations for Doctoral Students in Law

Fiona de LONDRAS[*]

Participatory research is a challenging but rewarding approach that can greatly enhance a piece of legal research, including doctoral work, when done well. The concept of participatory research is instinctively attractive to many researchers, but one's initial enthusiasm can tend to waiver somewhat when the reality of doing participatory research dawns. As an approach to research, participatory research is time consuming, sometimes difficult, often expensive, and not always entirely successful.[1] It does not 'suit' all research projects or, indeed, all researchers. Doing it well requires patience, curiosity, sometimes a thick skin, and always an intellectual openness to being persuaded by the views of others, to recognising authority in experience and 'perspective', and to coming to previously unanticipated conclusions. The purpose of this chapter is not to outline how one does the different possible forms of participatory research that are available.[2] Rather, it is to encourage

---

[*] Chair of Global Legal Studies, University of Birmingham
Email: f.delondras@bham.ac.uk
This chapter was originally presented at a conference on legal method for doctoral students in the University of Limerick in September 2014. My thanks go to Jennifer Schweppe and Shane Kilcommins for their invitation and their hospitality. Thanks to Sinead McEneaney for discussions on authority and Montaigne. The usual disclaimer applies.

[1] This is not unique to participatory research by doctoral students. For a little perspective, read the wide range of reflections on experiences (good and bad) of doing socio-legal work, including a lot of participatory research, in Simon Halliday and Patrick Schmidt (eds), *Conducting Law and Society Research: Reflections on Methods and Practices* (Cambridge University Press 2009).

[2] On method, there is now a wide range of possible resources for graduate students in law. These include Peter Kane and Herbert Kritzer, *The Oxford Handbook of Empirical Legal Research* (Oxford University Press 2010); Reza Banaker and Max Travers (eds), *Theory and Method in Socio-Legal Research* (Hart Publishing 2005); Martha LA Fineman, 'Feminist Theory and Law' (1995) 18 Harvard Journal of Law and Public Policy 349; Ian Ward, *Introduction to Critical Legal Theory* (Routledge 2004); Mathias Siems, *Comparative Law* (Cambridge University Press 2014); as well as the many social sciences and humanities handbooks that are available.

the reader (typically a doctoral student in law) to consider the potential and the pitfalls of participatory research.

In this context, participatory research can be broadly understood to be research that involves the participation of others apart from the primary researcher and his or her team. This participation can happen at various points in the research: conception of the project, through empirical research involving participants, in testing hypotheses etc. It thus encompasses co-design of research, co-production of research, and the incorporation of 'stakeholder' perspectives in research. This chapter will focus on this latter understanding. Participatory research is not always necessary or appropriate, and it is often the case that, even where empirical insights would be useful in a project, someone else has already done appropriate empirical research that is available for consultation and incorporation so that the doctoral researcher does not have to 'reinvent the wheel'. However, that is not always the case and, in those situations, participatory research may be useful.

I – WHY DO PARTICIPATORY RESEARCH?

Participatory research can be understood as both an approach and as a set of methodological possibilities. Thinking about it as an approach, first, is important, as it helps the researcher to decide whether participatory research 'fits' with the overall aims and objectives of the research being undertaken.

In my view, participatory research is best done by a researcher who recognises the value of incorporating the people whose 'real world' is being studied into a research project.[3] This is quite an important cognitive shift for a researcher in a (traditionally desk-based) discipline such as law to make, and is certainly fundamental to being a successful practitioner of participatory research. The recognition that 'experience matters' can come from a number of possible starting points. Here, I will canvas only three of these which might arise for doctoral students. There are, of course, many more, but these three are not uncommon across legal research.

The first starting point is quite pragmatic: there are some areas regulated by law (or in which law and legal researchers are interested) where information is so "hard to reach" as to make it almost impossible to research certain questions without engagement. One can, of course, still do legal doctrinal research without such engagement (at least where there are 'hard laws' to study), but any research that is interested in effectiveness, implementation,

---

[3] See also, Andrew Cornwall and Rachel Jewkes, 'What is Participatory Research?' (1995) 41(12) Soc Sci Med 1667.

diagnosis of the problem, reform, meaningful comparison, and policy change is likely to need to engage in some way in participatory research in order to be successful. We might think here of two areas, popular among doctoral candidates, in which the challenge of 'hard to reach' information tends to arise: security and intelligence, and family law.

Security and intelligence is, of course, a field in which much information about how law actually works and (perhaps more importantly) *whether* it works is held by so-called 'information monopolies'; it is a field in which secrecy is both a practice and often a necessity. Any researcher who is interested in the real-world workings of things like intelligence oversight, data protection, security services organisation, counter-extremism, and counter-terrorism more generally, is likely to need to secure the participation of stakeholders in order to get a complete picture. Stakeholders here are widely defined: intelligence and security practitioners, the security industry, policy makers and politicians, NGOs, activists, community and religious leaders, IT specialists, and security professionals might all be potential participants. All will have different pieces of information and different perspectives to bring, and, depending on the research question being pursued, there might be a need to secure the participation of stakeholders from all or some of these categories, and indeed others! There may also be a need to see these categories as broadly defined. Take the concept of a 'security professional', for example. In the counter-terrorism field, that is broad indeed: it includes, of course, police officers and counter terrorism specialists within civilian and military organizations, but it can also include bankers (who have security obligations relating to the disruption of terrorist financing flows), and people who work on airport security and check-in (who have *de facto* passport, visa, and other security-related obligations). Precisely whom one needs to speak to will depend on the project being pursued, but a broad understanding of the possibilities is fundamental.

Another area in which information is hard to reach, albeit often for other reasons, is that of family law. This is because much of family law takes place in private, whether that is in *in camera* courts, or in mediation, or in the everyday choices and familial regulation engaged in by private persons without the formal institutional intervention of the state or of 'law' per se. In the family law context, then, some research questions can only be answered in a meaningful and rigorous way if participatory research is engaged in. Take, for example, questions relating to restrictions on testamentary freedom (as much a question of family law as of the law of succession or property law). If one wanted to explore whether statutory restrictions on testamentary freedom are *necessary,* one would need to first understand how and why people choose to divide their estates in their wills. This is a question that requires exploration *before law*, i.e. before (in Ireland at least) the law intervenes to ensure that a spouse cannot be disinherited, or that children must be given proper provision.[4] And so one needs to get the perspectives of people on how and why they divide up their estates in their wills. One might also, perhaps, want to acquire the views of legal professionals, who tend to be involved in advising people on the legal possibilities in dividing their estates in order to see how they perceive clients' reactions to being informed of the requirements of the relevant law. A doctrinal analysis of statute can only take one so far in answering questions about testamentary freedom: only engaging with people who do (and who don't) make wills can shed light on what the *actual* decision-making processes around testamentary freedom might be, which can then feed into assessments of whether statutory regulation (i.e. limitation) of testamentary freedom is necessary. The necessary information is 'hard to reach'; participatory research helps us to acquire it.

In some ways, this feeds into a second standpoint that might encourage a researcher towards participatory research: the belief that we cannot understand law or make any really meaningful observations about it unless we also understand how it works *in the everyday*: i.e. the socio-legal approach. A commitment to socio-legal research does not necessitate participatory research: socio-legal research is a broad church and there are many ways of engaging in socio-legal study.[5] What all of these modes of engagement share, however, is a socio-legal commitment to understanding law in context.

That context can come from an interdisciplinary framework, and from finding ways of incorporating the everyday realities of living with, in, under, outside, and against law, into the legal query. Fundamental to socio-legal approaches is seeing law as only one of a broader set of social, political and humanities theories and approaches, and the rejection of law's sometimes-assumed particularity, difference, and distinctiveness.[6] It is this that tends to open the socio-legal researcher up to the possibilities of engaging in qualitative and quantitative methodologies such as empiricism, oral history and testimony, statistical analysis, and participatory research. This does not make socio-legal work 'superior' to doctrinal legal research; nor does it make it inferior

---

[4] Succession Act 1965.
[5] See, for example, Reza Banaker and Max Travers (eds), *Theory and Method in Socio-Legal Research* (Hart Publishing 2005).
[6] See, for example, Mariano Croce, 'All Law is Plural: Legal Pluralism and the Distinctiveness of Law' (2012) 44 The Journal of Legal Pluralism and Unofficial Law 1.

to or in any way less 'scholarly' than doctrinal legal research. It simply makes it different.

The third standpoint from which we might draw a realisation that we ought to recognise the perspectives of those being studied is a fundamentally critical one that disputes the traditional (and traditionally masculinist) conceptualisation of 'authority' in law. As lawyers, we are often (or at least, we *were* often) taught that authority resides in a limited repository of sources: positive law ('of course'), parliamentary debate, case law, 'high' debate and 'high' theory (compare, for example, the authority assigned in a typical undergraduate legal education to St Thomas Aquinas or John Finnis with that assigned to Catharine MacKinnon or Judith Butler).

What these structures of thinking and of teaching law implicitly (or, indeed, sometimes explicitly) tell us is that what *doesn't* matter is experience, authenticity, or lived truth. Oliver Wendell Holmes may well have said that "the life of law…has been experience",[7] but what he meant by that — and he was not alone — is a kind of rarefied experience refracted by professional expertise and, by implication therefrom, class, education, gender, race and socio-economic resources. This maps on to, for example, the enduring nature of "the man on the Clapham omnibus"[8] and the mythological autonomous liberal white male[9] as the central subject of law. Critical discourse on law recognises this for what it is: an exclusionary, explicatory and organisational supra structure from which typical (considered by law as 'atypical') experiences of power (-lessness), life (and death), resource (poverty), subjectivity (and objectivity) are excluded. The law, understood by reference only to its 'classical' constructions, is impoverished, according to these critical perspectives, and so proposed reforms, claims of meta-juridical principles, or empirical diagnoses accounting only for these classical perspectives are inadequate. The response to this is to recognise as authoritative a far broader range of sources including 'testimony' (not refracted through a juridical process), experience, and voice. Thus, fundamentally critical perspectives (including feminist legal theory, critical race theory, third world perspectives, and post-colonial discourses) often use participatory research methods to enrich — and, arguably, to correct — the narrative from the narrowness of 'traditional' legal research.

---

[7] Oliver Wendell Holmes, *The Common Law* (MacMillan & Co 1881).

[8] *McQuire v Western Morning News* [1903] 2 KB 100, 109 (Collin MR). This continues to be used as shorthand for "the reasonable man" today. See, for example, *Healthcare at Home Limited v Common Services Agency Limited* [2014] UKSC 49, [1]-[4].

[9] See Martha LA Fineman, 'The Vulnerable Subject: Anchoring Equality in the Human Condition' (2008) 29(1) Yale Journal of Law & Feminism 1, for a critique and alternative construction.

None of the foregoing is intended to claim superiority in method, standpoint or outputs for participatory research methods. Rather, it is to say: if any of these starting points resonate with you as a researcher and with your research question, then keep on reading. Participatory research might well be for you.

II – Which Participants?

If the first step in deciding on research method is always to ask 'why might I do my research this way?', then the second is surely to ask 'how can I do my research this way?'. This is always a complex query, reflected in the wide range of aids and guides to methodology now available to the typical graduate student.[10] The 'how?' question inevitably has different elements to it, but before addressing it, a key one of these as it relates to participatory research ('which participants?'), I want to reassure you that the answer to the 'how?' question will never be perfect.

It is in the nature of all research that we make mistakes:[11] we go down pathways of enquiry that prove unfruitful or ill-advised, we misconstrue our own research questions, we get distracted by interesting but ultimately irrelevant findings (the key, by the way, to managing this is an 'interesting stuff for after the PhD' folder on your desktop…), and we throw out almost as many words as we keep. In designing the methodology for your PhD, you will make mistakes: this is perfectly normal. However, the added dimension to bear in mind when doing participatory research is that one must strive to minimise these mistakes and not to involve participants until the method is fairly settled. There are two reasons for this.

First, the participants in your research are giving of their time and resources to engage in *your* research. Not wasting their time by being insufficiently prepared is fundamentally a matter of esteem. This is all the more so when one realises that we are often engaging with participants in order to get to their experiences: we are asking them deeply personal, revelatory, sometimes upsetting questions that can expose the participant's vulnerability in a way that disempowers. Before asking someone else to engage in the performative activities of telling, being heard, and then being 'retold' as a research finding or part of a data set, we must be sure we need the information for which we are asking. This is, of course, part of the reason why university

---

[10] See, for example, Gina Wisker, *The Postgraduate Research Handbook: Succeed with your MA, MPhil, EdD and PhD* (2nd edn, Palgrave 2007).

[11] Think, for example, of the classic form of exploring an idea, often resulting in the discovery of category, cognitive and other mistakes: the essay (*essayer*). The classical exemplar is the essays of Michel de Montaigne *Les Essais* (1570-1592)).

ethics processes (which you must ensure you engage with before you do *any* participatory research)[12] are often so onerous. The 'system' is designed to make sure that we ask people to reveal only what we really need from them for the purposes of our research.

Secondly, the researcher rarely, if ever, gets a second 'bite of the cherry' with a research participant (with obvious exceptions in longitudinal studies, for example). The stakeholder is likely to only be interviewed once; the focus group dynamic cannot be recreated to follow up on a point you missed the first time; a community consultation meeting cannot be recalled because you discover later that it would have been really useful to ask different or additional questions. The researcher cannot risk losing the participant by being underprepared. Thus, while methodological adjustments are not at all unusual, all possible steps should be taken to avoid them vis-à-vis the participants in your research themselves.[13]

And so this brings us to the core concern of this part of the chapter: which participants will you involve? Deciding on this is a key stage in the research design process, which is usefully approached by starting with three key questions:

1. What do I need to know?

2. What do I want to achieve?

3. Who has the relevant *power* by reference to questions (1) and (2) above?

Starting with these questions allows the researcher to think about where *power* (as it matters within their project) lies. In this respect, power has to be seen in a broad and often informal sense. Power is knowledge, influence, experience, ability to bring about change, ability to recruit other participants to the project and so on. Identifying participants through paying attention to power is entirely appropriate to participatory research, which, at its best, distributes power among the researcher and the participants.[14]

---

[12] See, for example, Hope Davidson and Jennifer Schweppe, 'An Introduction to Research Ethics in Legal Scholarship' in Chapter 11 of this volume.

[13] David Silverman, *Doing Qualitative Research* (4th edn, Sage 2013) ch 12.

[14] Probst and Hagmann, 'Understanding Participatory Research in the Context of Natural Resource Management' (2003) Agricultural Research and Extension Network (AgREN) Paper No. 130 <www.odi.org.uk/networks/agren/papers/agrenpaper_130.pdf> Accessed 29 February 2016.

These are a couple of ways of thinking about identifying potential participants through the prism of power, not all of which will be appropriate to all research contexts. Arnstein tells us to think about who has power when important decisions are being made, and then argues that the method of involving these people in the research can take the form of placation, consultation, informing, delegating power, ceding control, or creating a partnership.[15] In truth, Arnstein's construction reflects the fact that participatory research sometimes comes from a somewhat cynical or instrumental motivation. This may be more common in research projects intended to, for example, consider major infrastructural changes in which community 'buy in' is required (these are some of the earlier kinds of contexts for participatory research 'in the real world'), but academic research in law is perhaps less likely to 'need' participation in this way. More common at the doctoral level, perhaps is an approach to participatory research that aligns more with Biggs' construction: contractual, consultative, collaborative, and collegial.[16] As ever, the decision about what role the participatory research will take — and who the researcher will involve as participants — will also be determined by very practical considerations such as time (setting up and doing interviews is very time consuming), the fact that such work can be costly (the costs of travel, equipment, transcription, and data storage are all relevant considerations), and the researcher's skills, not only in formal interview technique, but also in striking up a rapport.

Knowing what you want (and need) from your participants is key to identifying which participants you want in your research. Thinking about power and purpose as outlined above can help us to make sure that we do that. The processes of selection and recruitment of participants then follows, and this is often very challenging. There are various different approaches to recruitment that might be taken and outlining them is not the purpose of this chapter. However, what matters (especially from the point of view of establishing the appropriateness of your approach at the *viva voce* examination) is that approach you take *makes sense* by reference to the purposes of your participatory research *per se* and the types of participants you need to fulfill those purposes.

---

[15] Sherry Arnstein, 'A Ladder of Citizen Participation' (1969) 35(4) Journal of the American Planning Association 216.

[16] Biggs, *Resource-Poor Farmer Participation in Research: A Synthesis of Experiences from National Agricultural Research Systems* (OFCOR, Comparative Study No. 3, International Service for National Agricultural Research 1989).

III – What Form of Participation?

Having decided that you want to do participatory research, and having identified which participants you want to recruit, you must then decide on what form (or forms) of participation will be used in your project. In this respect, it is wise to think about what forms of participation are most sensible by reference to both the participants you will recruit *and* the function of the participation. It is trite to remark that not all forms of participation will be appropriate for all participants. Children or people for whom communication is challenging will need a different participatory format to, for example, high-level experts in the field for whom no conventionally-understood communication challenges arise. So, too, might status be an appropriate consideration. There are some people who, by virtue of their status, cannot reasonably be expected to participate in, for example, a focus group. In a project about 'leadership', for example, one might secure the participation of people as diverse as heads of state and leaders of local GAA clubs. While the Chairman of the local juvenile GAA club might be reasonably invited to participate in a focus group, one wonders whether the President of Ireland would be? In these matters, a little common sense, personal judgement, and consultation with your doctoral supervisor go a long way.

The range of possible participatory methods is vast, particularly where one takes to heart the observation drawn from socio-legal studies that humanities and social sciences methodologies and approaches can be applied to legal enquiry.[17] When we cast the net widely, we see that methods as diverse as surveys, interviews, walking,[18] music-making, art and ethnography all present as possibilities. What they all have in common is that they require training, care, precision, and preparation. The purpose of this chapter is not to regurgitate the vast literatures on the technicalities of different methodological approaches. Rather, I want to suggest something that may at first seem obvious, but is in fact vital and often overlooked: the method(s) of participation you engage with should be chosen because they best suit the purposes of participation in the particular project you are engaged in, and the characteristics, resources and availability of the participants. There is no one right way to do participatory research: there is only the appropriate way to do it for your project. That should then be executed according to best

---

[17] Reza Banaker and Max Travers (eds), *Theory and Method in Socio-Legal Research* (Hart Publishing 2005).

[18] Yes, really. See Kate Moles, 'A Walk in Thirdspace, Place, Methods and Walking' (2008) 13(4) Sociological Research Online 2 <www.socresonline.org.uk/13/4/2.html>.

methodological practice and the highest possible standards of ethics for that particular approach.

That said, it may be instructive to briefly consider what, from my experience of supervising and examining doctoral research, seem to be three commonly-used methods of participatory research utilised legal research by reference to common motivations for engaging in participatory research at all. The three common forms are interviews, focus groups, and surveys or questionnaires. As the chart below indicates, the researcher gets different things from each of these methods, although the observations below are also variable depending on, for example, the quantity of participants, the quality of the research instrument used, and the motivations of the participants.

	Interview	Focus Group	Survey/ Questionnaire
Reaching 'personal' information	✓	✓	✓
Acquiring 'hard to reach' information	✓	✓	
Enhancing depth of knowledge	✓	✓	
Determining importance of issues	✓	✓	✓
Acquiring generalizable information			✓
Enhancing originality	✓	✓	✓

Common PR Methods and their Benefits

IV – Reaching 'Personal' Information

There are some things that people may not want to be in the public domain because they are sensitive or personal to them, but which are nonetheless important to your research question. An example is the sexual orientation of politicians, which an individual politician may not want to be known publically but which may be important to a project about perceived legitimacy and representativeness in parliamentary democracy.[19]

---

[19] On the role of representativeness in representative democracy, see House of Commons, *Speaker's Conference on Parliamentary Representation: Final Report* (Stationery Office 2010) <www.publications.parliament.uk/pa/spconf/239/23902.htm> accessed 22 December 2015.

Sensitive information may be 'reachable' through participatory research by using any one of interviews, focus groups, or surveys and questionnaires, although not all such information will emerge in every one of these circumstances. Let us return to the example of sexual orientation. Whether a parliamentarian 'reveals' her sexual orientation in any one of these given scenarios will very much depend on the circumstances. With all of these approaches the participant is likely to need first to be convinced that information about her sexual orientation is *material* to your research project: in other words, gathering this sensitive information is not gratuitous but rather is connected to the enquiry with which you are concerned. Indeed, in most universities the ethics approval process will endeavour to ensure that this is the case.

The regulation of your project will also be important to the participant. Here, we might think about what kinds of systems are in place to store and protect the data that you acquire. Will the information be securely stored? If so, for how long? Will it then be destroyed, and if so, by whom? Is the process anonymous? If not anonymous, is it confidential? (Remembering, of course, that anonymity and confidentiality are not the same thing). Can you, as a researcher, be trusted not to 'leak' the information? Again, all of these regulatory matters will be germane in each of the scenarios of interview, focus group, and survey or questionnaire, and this underlines the importance of explaining clearly, honestly, and comprehensively, what will be done with the data gathered by the researcher.

Finally, the particular dynamics of the method as experienced by the participant will make a difference. If you use a survey or questionnaire, the politician in our example might feel able to 'trust' the system of data collection more or less depending on things as diverse as whether you ask for her email address to submit an online questionnaire ('can this be traced back to me?'), how you have structured the questionnaire ('does this person seem like a credible researcher?'), the rules as to anonymity or confidentiality you have outlined in the information and consent sheets, and the extent to which the participant maintains a right to withdraw from the project. In a focus group, it may well depend on who else is in that focus group, and *their* trustworthiness in the eyes of the participant. Interviews offer a whole other scale of possibility, not only in the potential to 'follow up' on questions, but also in the ability to use environment in order to trigger questions, follow ups, or conversation points that can build trust and engagement (e.g. family photos in offices or homes, where interviews sometimes take place).[20]

---

[20] On selecting your instrument or approach see, for example, David Silverman, *Doing Qualitative Research* (4th edn, Sage 2013).

Thus, all three modes can be situations in which sensitive information can be reached, but the range of elements that go into creating the right environment for participants to reveal it is vast. All of these things should be taken into account when deciding on method.

V – Acquiring 'Hard To Reach' Information

Not all information is available in the public domain, sometimes because of the sensitive nature of the information in question. Things like numbers of covert surveillance operations being undertaken on suspected terrorists in any given city at a particular point in time are an example. Where the right participants can be recruited, participatory research offers a pathway to acquiring such information.[21] Here, however, surveys or questionnaires seem less likely to be successful than interviews or focus groups.[22] This is largely because the bonds of trust required for the participant to disclose the information cannot really be developed through a survey or questionnaire. Instead the perceived trustworthiness of the researcher, which is a subjective judgement that can be ascertained by the participant through personal interaction, is more likely to arise in interview and focus group situations. The 'entry questions' that you ask—often 'softer' questions — and the tone of the interview or focus group that you set by your introduction, preparation, explanation of the project, and overall appearance of 'competence' are important here. So too is intellectual agility: can you, as a researcher, see 'openings' in the discussion to ask questions that might lead to this information? Are you sufficiently well read in the area to be able to pick up on 'cues' within answers and discussions that suggest natural 'question points' to enter into these areas of conversation? In a focus group, have you gathered together appropriate participants in the same focus group, or have you created a mixture of people in which the hard to reach information will not be disclosed because of insufficient homogeneity? If you were researching security oversight, for example, would you put intelligence officers, pacifist politicians who are vociferous critics of the intelligence services, and rights-oriented NGOs

---

[21] Recruiting the 'right' participants can be very difficult, especially where they are part of 'hard to reach' participant groups. For an overview, albeit in a medical context, see, for example, Billie Bonevski, Madeleine Randell, Chris Paul, Kathy Chapman, Laura Twyman, Jamie Bryant, Irena Brozen and Clare Hughes, 'Reaching the Hard-to-Reach: A Systemic Review of Strategies for Improving Health and Medical Research with Socially Disadvantaged Groups' (2014) 14(42) BMC Medical Research Methodology <http://bmcmedresmethodol.biomedcentral.com/articles/10.1186/1471-2288-14-42> accessed 22 December 2015.

[22] On focus groups, see, for example, Sue Wilkinson, 'Focus group methodology: a review' (1998) 1(3) International Journal of Social Research Methodology 181.

in the same focus group? If you did, what would you think the potential for acquiring 'hard to reach' information would be?

VI – Enhancing Depth of Knowledge

All three of these popular approaches to participatory research are extremely useful when one wants to enhance the depth of one's knowledge. Here we might think, particularly, of the step change in knowing what the law *is* (which we can ascertain from desk research) and knowing how the law *works* (which we can ascertain from participatory research). Shifting from a formal to a rounded knowledge base in this way is an exercise in deepening knowledge, and participatory research is very useful from this perspective. However, participatory research should not be used to deepen knowledge where that knowledge is available through other forms like, for example, doing better or more extensive desk research. There are two reasons. First, participants might well be annoyed to be asked to tell you what you should be able to find out for yourself and their buy-in to you and your research may be eradicated. Secondly, participatory research gives you *perspectives*, whereas, if you seek knowledge that is verifiable (e.g. what the law on income tax in the Czech Republic is), then it must be acquired in a manner that lends itself to objective verification, or 'fact checking' to use a simpler term.

VII – Determining Importance of Issues

It is a truism that sometimes the things we think are really important on a review of the traditional legal sources are actually not particularly important 'in the real world', and that which *is* important cannot always be discerned from traditional legal research. To say that something is not important in the world of the practitioner, or the person experiencing law, is not to say that it is unimportant from a doctrinal point of view, or that it is undeserving of study. But it *is* a finding that can raise lots of issues for exploration within a research project. Similarly, determining the importance of issues can lead to unanticipated discoveries, which is also a finding that opens up multiple research possibilities. All three of the popular methods outlined above can allow for ascertaining the relative importance of issues, although, where a questionnaire or survey is used, it is important to ensure that your list of issues always includes an 'other' option and asks the participant to expand on this. Otherwise you greatly reduce the possibility of discovering unanticipated knowledge.

VIII – Acquiring Generalisable Information

As already mentioned, participatory research often produces perspectives of the particular research participants so that generalisability can be difficult.

This is not a reason not to do participatory research; it is, rather, a warning about the kinds of claims that one might make and claim are underpinned by the findings of participatory research. The researcher does not always seek generalisable information — nor must one — but it is not wholly uncommon, in my experience, to see general claims asserted on the basis of particular data ascertained from a small sample in a selective schema of participatory research. Unless surveys and questionnaires are done on a very large scale (either in terms of absolute numbers or in terms of the proportion of the target group of participants who take part), for example, their findings should be qualified by reference to the number of participants. So, survey and questionnaire data may be generalisable, although it often is not at doctoral level because students are necessarily working within short time frames and with limited resources. Interviews and focus groups will almost never lead to generalisable information. This does not make their findings less valuable — remember the reflections above about authority and recognising the authority of experience and perspective — but as already noted it does necessitate care in how those findings are expressed.

IX – Conclusion

Originality is, of course, the Holy Grail of doctoral students. That the candidate has made an original contribution to knowledge is, at core, the basic requirement for being awarded the degree for which you have studied for at least (and often far more than) three years. Originality is achievable in many means: there is no one right way to establish it. Certainly a well-constructed, curious, intelligent research question that pushes the boundaries of existing knowledge is more or less essential, but so is how one pursues the fundamental task of the PhD: pursuing that question through a well-designed research project. In doing that, your choice of methodological approach is important, and participatory research can be an excellent framework for the acquisition of original knowledge, which is then processed, considered, analysed and marshaled into an argument that constitutes an original contribution to knowledge. Participatory research can lend a new kind of authority to assumed knowledge, present real-world heterodoxies to doctrinal orthodoxy, enrich a set of findings, and greatly enhance the originality and practicability of research findings. However, all of this can only be achieved if two conditions are met: (i) the research enquiry justifies the methodology, and (ii) the researcher engages seriously and carefully with the process and the participants.

CHAPTER 10

Empirical Studies in Contract – The Way Forward

Sally WHEELER*

I – INTRODUCTION

In this chapter, I examine several of the various different types of empirical studies in contract. They reveal that contract, as a nomenclature for exchange, matters as both an initial ordering mechanism and a resolution mechanism but not necessarily in the way that strictly legal models might suggest.[1] My starting point is the foundational work of Stewart Macaulay and I concentrate, for obvious reasons, on studies which have hitherto received little traction in the UK,[2] but which, in my view, have innovative and replicable methods and important findings that expand the picture we have of contract law in empirical settings. These studies reveal the new life that has been breathed into the area by the advent of the internet, both in terms of the contractual practices studied and the methodologies that can be employed for data collection.

I have deliberately excluded studies based exclusively in law and economics. This is partly for reasons of space, as studies that are testing or constructing predictive economic models dominate empirical studies in law in the US,[3] and so are simply too numerous to comment on, and partly for reasons of intellectual integrity. This chapter is about research methods for the empirical study of contract law and the findings that those studies produce; be they that contract is not used in the way formal legal doctrine

---

* Professor and Head of the School of Law, Queen's University Belfast.
[1] S Macaulay, 'Contracts, New Legal Realism, and Improving the Navigation of *The Yellow Submarine*' (2006) 80 Tulane Law Review 1161.
[2] This does mean that I do not discuss some of the well-known 'classics' in the area, such as H Beale and T Dugdale, 'Contracts Between Businessmen: Planning and the Use of Contractual Remedies' (1975) B J Law and Soc 45.
[3] Z Eigen, 'Empirical Studies in Contract' (2012) 8 Annual Review of Law and Social Science 291, 297. In his survey of studies from 2005 to Jan 2012, Eigen found that economic theories were dominant in framing the questions that researchers asked. Eigen's point is really a statement of the status quo. For an explanation of the status quo, see D Smith and B King, 'Contracts as Organizations' (2009) 51 Arizona L R 1.

thinks it is or that distinct social norms surround the adoption and use of contract as an organizational mechanism. It should be unsurprising that a chapter with this starting point does not engage with studies the starting point of which are neoclassical economics, principal and agency theory, and incomplete contract. There may well be much in this work for the development of economic theory, but little, I suspect, for research in contract law. This is not always an easy line to tread; included are a series of studies on attitudes to breaching contracts which have their roots in appraising the doctrine of efficient breach. I suspect that Stewart Macaulay would not approve![4] However, these studies are included because they reveal some of the social norms around decisions to perform or to breach contracts and so add to our picture of the lived world of contract transactions.

I divide empirical studies on contract into two groups depending on the nature of their relationship with the doctrinal construction of contract law that tends to be put forward, certainly in the context of the teaching of law, in both law schools and business schools. In the first group are those studies that are closest to the doctrinal model. They seek, essentially, to explain the 'gap' between the 'real deal' (the commercial relationship that exists between the parties) and the 'paper deal' (the formal legal contract between the parties), as Stewart Macaulay so eloquently put it,[5] with the expectation being that the paper deal confirms to the doctrinal model. Within that first group, I look at the methodology and findings of studies within four distinct areas of contract; planning, terms, breach of contract and dispute resolution. In the second group are studies which focus, not on contract as it is defined by law, but on broader ideas of exchange and the norms of that exchange. This is not a uniformly accepted categorisation nor, indeed, the only way of constructing a categorisation.[6] Kim, for example, would push these two categories together and posit a single category of 'relationship or relational' on the grounds that they are looking at 'contract law as governing relations rather than transactions'.[7] This does fit, in a shallow sense, much of

---

[4] S Macaulay, 'Almost Everything That I Did Want to Know About Contract Litigation: A Comment on Galanter' (2001) Wis L Rev 629, 637. Macaulay's view of the idea of efficient breach was that it was an elegant theory, about which far too much was written, which was unlikely to have any foundation in the real world of contract practice.
[5] S Macaulay, 'The Real and the Paper Deal: Empirical Pictures of Relationships, Complexity and the Urge for Transparent Simple Rules' (2003) 66 Modern Law Review 44.
[6] Eigen (n 3) 294-95.
[7] N Kim, *Wrap Contracts* (Oxford University Press 2013) 11.

Macaulay's work, even though his opening question for his original 1963 paper was 'What good is contract law'.[8]

The norms that are revealed by Macaulay are ones which tell us about the character of the individuals involved, but convey little about the nature of the transactions they are undertaking, or about the wider social norms that frame their interactions. However, this is not necessarily a feature present in many of the studies placed in the first category. Studies in the two groups are doing fundamentally different things from different starting points. The first group of studies acknowledge and work from contract law principles, whether they discuss individual, transactional or broader social norms, whilst the second group see those contract law principles as merely part of a much more complex picture of social relations; and it is social relations in the context of exchange that is their starting point. As will become clear from the text below, this is the major difference between a Macaulay-inspired approach to empirical legal studies in contract and an Ian Macneil-inspired approach to the same area. Macneil himself dealt in abstractions, rather than empirical analysis,[9] but his theoretical position that all contracts are, to one degree or another, relational, as exchange takes place in a relational context, has inspired the studies in the second group.

II – THE FIRST GROUP — IN THE STEPS OF STEWART MACAULAY

Macaulay was using a traditional legal definition of contract that sees contract not as a mechanism for achieving an efficient allocation of resources, as an economist would have it, but as the device that facilitates, and encapsulates the terms of, the exchange. To facilitate exchange, a contract must do two things: it must try to capture an element of rational planning by offering a risk-based solution for future contingencies, and it must include legal sanctions to either induce performance or compensate for non-performance. 'Do not get me wrong — reading cases is important. It is just not enough.'[10] This is a comment made by Macaulay while reviewing Gulati and Scott's

---

[8] S Macaulay, 'Non-Contractual Relations in Business: A Preliminary Study' (1963) 28 American Soc Rev 1.

[9] For many, the most detailed statement of Macneil's work is his monograph; I Macneil, *The New Social Contract: An Enquiry into Modern Contractual Relations* (Yale Uni Press 1980). He began to produce US law review articles in the mid-1970s, but his work had its roots much earlier in his career. See I Macneil, *Contract: Instruments for Social Cooperation* (F B Rothman 1968), and I Macneil, 'The Tanzania Hire-Purchase Act' (1966) 2 East Africa L J 84.

[10] S Macaulay, 'Notes on the Margins of Lawyering, in Three and Half Minutes' (2011) 40 Hofstra L Rev 25, 37.

The Three and a Half Minute Transaction.[11] This is an important and relatively recent work in the trajectory of empirical scholarship on contract and it is a volume that I return to below. Any account or examination of scholarship in this area naturally begins with Macaulay.[12] His 1963 study was situated in the machinery manufacturing industry of Wisconsin. The primary research question asked was when contract was used in this industry and when it was not. Macaulay conducted the empirical part of his research by means of a snowball sample beginning with personal contacts. By the end of project, he had contact with 68 lawyers and business executives from 43 manufacturing firms and 6 law firms. Macaulay was keen to point out, in subsequent years, that the study was never intended to produce a representative sample, something which he regarded as impossible, but by being located in just one industry, he satisfied himself that the sample could be said to have kept inconsistency to a minimum.[13]

Macaulay's concern for 'replication' and 'representativeness', albeit expressed as recently as 2009,[14] is somewhat out of kilter with the tenor of debate and description of methodology and method in contemporary socio-legal studies. His concern for representativeness might be seen as a defence to the attacks on empirical socio-legal studies, in as much as they offer nothing of theoretical significance to legal theory,[15] are based on anecdotalism

---

[11] Macaulay's review was part of a workshop devoted to Gulati and Scott's project at Hofstra Law School, see M Gulati and R Scott, 'The Three and a Half Minute Transaction: Boilerplate and the Limits of Contract Design' (2011) 40 Hofstra L Rev 1. Gulati and Scott subsequently published a more extensive and developed version of their work in *The 3½ Minute Transaction* (Chicago Uni Press 2013).

[12] Macaulay (n 8). The enduring importance and popularity of this article is clear from the fact that it is currently the 4th most highly cited paper in Sociology from the 1960s, though not necessarily the most highly cited in the decade of its publication, the 1960s <http://kieranhealy.org/blog/archives/2014/11/15/top-ten-by-decade/> accessed 25 August 2015. See also, J Jacobs, 'ASR's Greatest Hits' (2005) 70 Am Soc Rev 1. Within the legal cannon, some 30 years after publication it was heralded as the 15th most-cited law review article of all time, see F Shapiro, 'The Most-Cited Law Review Articles Revisited' (1996) 71 Chi Kent L Rev 751.

[13] Macaulay (n 1).

[14] 'Stewart Macaulay and "Non-Contractual Relations in Business"' in S Halliday and P Schmidt, *Conducting Law and Society Research* (CUP 2009) 14. Much of Macaulay's concern about the legitimacy in terms of representativeness of his informants seems to come from the fact that his father-in-law arranged his initial contacts. In modern parlance, his father-in-law would be styled as a gate keeper!

[15] This is a point particularly close to Macaulay's heart, see his reference to Grant Gilmore's critique of his 1963 study in *The Death of Contract* in S Macaulay, 'An Empirical View of Contract' (1985) Wisconsin Law Review 465. It is a point he repeats in many of his later law review articles.

and 'poorly theorized accounts of social institutions',[16] and are methodologically unsophisticated.[17] However, this critique has been reduced to a whimper in recent years, as socio-legal studies has become the predominant expression[18] for research in law in the UK at least. Moreover, within UK socio-legal studies, and this is at least partly true of the US Law and Society movement as well,[19] empirical legal studies take many different forms, with the emphasis being on theoretical development rather than being in any way representative of particular phenomena or practice — the ethnographic, the actor network theory inspired, content analysis based with grounded theory, are all well-used methodologies[20] — often using much smaller samples than Macaulay, with the achievement of data saturation the key target. It is recognized that empirical studies, whether qualitative or quantitative in nature, provide 'information of a different character from that which can be obtained through other methods of research. Empirical study answers questions about law that cannot be answered in any other way'.[21]

Contract As Planning

Macaulay's findings were that his sample of manufacturers only partially used contract law in setting up their exchanges and very rarely used contract law subsequently to adjust or enforce their exchanges. His interest in exchange planning was met by findings that machinery manufacturers did not completely plan their exchanges. Gaps were left to be filled in later during the performance of the exchange. The presence of 'non-contractual relations' meant that disputes were avoided. These non-contractual relations were based around ideas of good faith in business, such as industry-wide customs,

---

[16] N Lacey, 'Normative Reconstruction in Socio-Legal Theory' (1996) 5 Social and Legal Studies 131.

[17] F Cownie, *Legal Academics: Culture and Identities* (Hart Publishing 2004) 51-55.

[18] See R Collier, 'We're All Socio-Legal Now – Legal Education, Scholarship and the Global Knowledge Economy: Reflections on the UK Experience' (2004) 26 Sydney L R 503 for a summary of this debate and C Boyd, 'In Defense of Empirical Legal Studies' (2015) 63 Buffalo Law Review 363 for a defence of empirical legal studies against the type of attack referred to in the text above.

[19] Within the US Law and Society community, quantitative studies have more traction and the subgroup that is the Empirical Legal Studies movement is almost entirely dominated by scholarship based on large data sets assembled in the US. For empirical confirmation of the US situation in relation to the balance between qualitative and quantitative studies, see Eigen (n 3) 302.

[20] F Cownie and A Bradney, 'Socio-Legal Studies: A Challenge to the Doctrinal Approach' and M Burton, 'Doing Empirical Research: Exploring the Decision-Making of Magistrates and Juries' in D Watkins and M Burton (eds), *Research Methods in Law* (Routledge 2013) 34 and 55 respectively.

[21] A Bradney, 'The Place of Empirical Legal Research in the Law School Curriculum' in P Cane and H Kritzer (eds), *The Oxford Handbook of Empirical Legal Research* (OUP 2013) 1025, 1033.

past dealings and personal relations between actors in different organizations, and ideas of reputation, both personal and professional. The focus was on ensuring that business continued between the parties to the exchange. Macaulay explains that there was a view that the formalities of contract could get in the way of creating a good exchange relationship between business units. Contract was of more assistance in explaining detailed product specifications and requirements within the firm than in securing inter-firm exchanges. Macaulay's account of business exchanges taking place in the world of manufacturing in Wisconsin takes us back to the pre-globalization era. The business world is a much bigger place than it was in 1963. There are likely to be far fewer 'local' deals enhanced by personal relationships as production industries have gradually relocated to economies with low labour and other external costs,[22] introducing the dimension of contracting across national boundaries. In the 1963 context, Macaulay identifies two behavioural norms that are considered to be more important than the rational planning of an exchange: being seen as having and supporting a good product; and not 'welching' on a deal. The question of why some transactions are more formal than others in terms of the contract entered into is not one that Macaulay seeks to answer. Nor is he telling us that contract law does not matter. Rather, he is explaining that contract law matters, but perhaps not as much as we might have thought, and in very different ways to those highlighted by the doctrinal model. Macaulay is looking at categories of doctrinal contract law to see how far the 'paper deal is the real deal'.

It is this concern with planning, understood in terms of the legal categories identified as relevant to contract formation and adjustment, that underscores the collation of these studies into this first group. An example of this first group of studies would be Esser's avowed replication of Macaulay's work:[23] despite his engagement with the literature on transaction-cost economics and the sociology of institutionalisation, as well as a nod to the relational contract theory of Macneil,[24] Esser's primary reference point for his study is doctrinal contract law. He is concerned with drawing attention to the structures of contract law in the books, recognizing that, since Macaulay conducted his study, the UCC has been adopted by all US states apart from Louisiana, and pointing out the gap that exists between the picture of contract offered there, and the deals that the parties make in the course of business. The contexts for

---

[22] On this, see the findings of John Esser in relation to industry structures in Wisconsin, discussed later in this text, in J Esser, 'Institutionalising Industry: The Changing Forms of Contract' (1996) 21 Law and Social Inquiry 593.
[23] ibid.
[24] ibid 597-603.

his assertion that the deal in books is not the same as the deal in action are his findings around the presence of 'partner' status between the contracting parties and industry structure. Partner status is a descriptor for a long term and exclusive trading relationship which would allow the parties to order, reorder and change the specifications of products regularly.[25] The industry structures he found demonstrated a prevalence of practices such as 'just in time' delivery and enhanced service standards.

In *The Three and a Half Minute Transaction*,[26] Gulati and Scott are concerned with sovereign debt contracts and, in particular, the *pari passu*[27] provision that their analysis of over 1500 contracts made in the last 60 years reveals nearly all of them contain. Their book is a three-stage examination of the status of this provision, using documentary analysis of existing contracts, doctrinal legal analysis and interview data. It is the combination of these three methods that allows the authors to tell the story in the way that they do. Their first discovery is that, in a historical sense, no-one knows why the *pari passu* provision ever entered sovereign debt contracts or remained there as a 'harmless relic'.[28] At the second stage, they focus on the interpretation of the provision by a Belgian commercial court[29] in 2000, which, through its use of injunctive relief, gave effect to the clause in favour of Elliot Associates, a hedge fund, against Euroclear, in circumstances where both were creditors of the Peruvian Government and holding their bonds. This interpretation sparked heated debate in the international financial community, protestations as to its incorrectness, and demands for reforms,[30] but it has gained traction and popularity. The final stage of Galati and Scott's research is their finding that the *pari passu* clause is still contained in sovereign debt contracts and has become more pervasive rather than less;[31] it is, in the parlance of contract lawyers, 'sticky'. This is not what would intuitively be expected. They then interview lawyers, based primarily, but not entirely exclusively, in London

---

[25] Consider the position of the protagonists in *Baird Textile Holdings v Marks and Spencer PLC* [2001] EWCA Civ 274 and the discussion, inter alia, in S Mouzas and D Ford 'Managing Relationships in Showery Weather: The Role of Umbrella Agreements' (2006) 59 J of Business Research 1248, and S Mouzas and M Furmston, 'From Contract to Umbrella Agreement' (2008) 67 CLJ 37.

[26] Gulati and Scott (n 11).

[27] *Pari passu* is the name given to the principle that creditors in the same class rank equally to each other.

[28] Gulati and Scott (n 11) 11, 25.

[29] Elliot Assocs, No 2000QR92 (Ct. App. Brussels, 8th Chamber, 26 September 2000).

[30] Gulati and Scott (n 11) 11-17, 21-32.

[31] Gulati and Scott (n 11 at p 55) estimate from their documentary analysis that, in the 1950s, 63% of contracts included the clause, but in the decade after the Brussels ruling, usage of the clause became almost universal, see p 74.

and New York,[32] who draft these contracts, to find out why the clause had not been redrafted to deal with its current problematic interpretation.[33]

Sovereign debt contracts are standard form or adhesive contracts that have been in existence for many years, with adaptive changes rather than wholesale changes, and are used to regulate the relationships of experienced parties. Scott and Gulati examine several popular hypotheses around contract drafting and the use of standard form contracts[34] to explain the lack of change, but reject the explanatory power of each one. They consider the idea that a standard form contract represents collected wisdom as to current best practice, as ambiguous and weak terms are drafted out over time; that uniformity in standard form contracts reduces the price of the contract subject matter and imbeds a cost against innovation; that changing a standard form contract invites the other contracting party to enter into negotiations which be costly; and finally that changing a standard form contract invites a court to conclude that the parties concur with the correctness of a previous tribunal's decision; in this case, the decision of the Brussels Court, referred to above, in 2000.

These hypotheses all have a certain attraction in explaining the fondness commercial parties have for standard form contracts, and, indeed, they combined to form the responses of many of Gulati and Scott's interviewees. However, none of them fit what has occurred in relation to these sovereign debt arrangements. It is hard to argue for 'collected wisdom' in circumstances where no-one seems to know why the *pari passu* provision was ever included or what it means. There is no evidence to suggest that a departure from the 'industry' standard terms has affected bond pricing and, indeed, there is evidence to the contrary; Gulati and Scott did note some term variance, but it had not affected pricing structures. As far as term innovation attracting costly negotiations, again Gulati and Scott found evidence in their document analysis of term evolution over the years, but no evidence of lengthy negotiations. As far as the view of a tribunal of changes in standard terms is concerned, it is surely more likely to be the case that the view taken is that, in not changing their contract, the parties are impliedly acknowledging the

---

[32] Sovereign debt work is the province of a small number of elite law firms based primarily in the US and UK but with some work going to lawyers based in Paris and Frankfurt, see ibid at p55 for a full methodology statement of the qualitative part of this research.

[33] Perhaps it is their focus on interviewing lawyers in a small number of firms (they did interview 200 or so individuals!) or perhaps it is evidence of the dominance of quantitative methodology in US law and Society work but Gulati and Scott refer to their methodology as being seen 'as a naïve technique' by some readers, see ibid 11.

[34] ibid 33-44.

correctness of the most recent judicial interpretation. Gulati and Scott argue that what explains the continued inclusion of the *pari passu* provision are the dynamics and economics of elite law firm practice. They find risk aversion and herd behaviour amongst lawyers — no law firm or individual lawyer wants to initiate a term change first and without the prior action of a regulatory or official body such as the IMF or the Bank of England. Law firms have commodified contracts at this level; innovation in contract terms risked requiring the whole contract to be at least checked for unforeseen or negative impacts on other terms, and clients were unwilling to pay for this level of 'lawyering'.[35] Gulati and Scott go on to tell a fascinating story about elite law firms and legal practice which is really beyond the scope of this chapter. Ultimately, however, while they tell us much that questions the theory of 'sticky' terms in standard form contracts, they are unable to prove concretely why this particular term has survived, and even prospered, in the light of an adverse ruling about its meaning.[36]

Are Contracts Read?

Marotta-Wurgler supplies a considerable amount of insight into the contents of contracts, rather than the use of contracts. She conducted two large scale pieces of work on the contents of standard form contracts used by software sellers,[37] known as 'end user license agreements' (EULAs) and the extent to which they are accessed and read by consumers.[38] Standard form contracts in the context of software purchases are particularly adhesive, in that their terms are often not visible to the purchaser until after they have completed their purchase. However, not all software purchase contracts fall into the shrink-wrap category, and Marotta-Wurgler's second study examines, inter alia, the

---

[35] ibid 89-93.

[36] A Boyack, 'The Three and a Half Minute Transaction: What Sticky Boilerplate Reveals About Contract Law and Practice' (2013) 35 Whittier L R 1.

[37] F Marotta-Wurgler, 'What's in a Standard Form Contract? An Empirical Analysis of Software License Agreements' (2007) 4 J Empirical Legal Studies 677, 'Unfair' Dispute Resolution Clauses: Much Ado about Nothing?' in O Ben-Shahar (ed), *Boilerplate* (CUP 2007), 'Competition and the Quality of Standard Form Contracts: A Test Using Software License Agreements' (2008) 5 J Empirical Legal Studies 447, 'Are 'Pay Now, Terms Later' Contracts Worse for Buyers? Evidence from Software License Agreement' (2009) 38 J of Legal Studies 309, F Marotta-Wurgler and R Taylor, 'Set in Stone: Change and Innovation in Consumer Standard-Form Contracts' (2013) 88 New York Uni Law Rev 240.

[38] F Marotta-Wurgler, 'Will Increased Disclosure Help? Evaluating the Recommendations of the ALI's 'Principles of the Law of Software Contracts'' (2011) 78 Uni of Chicago Law Review 165, 'Does Contract Disclosure Matter?' (2012) 168 J Inst and Theoretical Econ 94 and Y Bakos, F Marotta-Wurgler and D Trossen, 'Does Anyone Read the Fine Print? Consumer Attention to Standard-Form Contracts' (2014) 43 J Leg Stud 1.

differences in consumer behaviour when browse wrap contracts, which provide hyperlinks from the seller's website, are used.[39]

The first study that Marotta-Wurgler reported was an examination of 647 EULAs collected from software sellers. Against a backdrop of the default provisions set out in UCC Art 2, the terms of the EULAs were coded using a bias indexing methodology, to ascertain the distance the contract had moved from the default provisions towards either pro-seller or pro-buyer bias from the Art 2 standard,[40] in the opinion of the researcher. It is this link to the concerns of doctrinal contract law that places Marotta-Wurgler's work in the first category of studies. Her findings are presented using statistical regression techniques, but this does not detract from the fact that it is a study about the presence or absence of particular contract terms as defined by classical contract law. EULAs were revealed to be more pro-seller than pro-buyer, with an average regression of -4.85 from the UCC Art 2 standard, so in non-statistical terms, an average of five terms worse than the Art 2 default position would be. There was variation between what Marotta-Wurgler identified as the core terms of the EULAs, giving lie to the idea that standard form contracts are uniform or almost uniform. The most pro-buyer contracts were the ones that were the hardest to find for the consumer in terms of the number of clicks required to access them. The conclusion that we can draw is that software package sellers were not hiding one-sided pro-seller contracts behind relative inaccessibility.[41]

In her second study, Marotta-Wurgler accessed clickstream data that enabled her to track the visits of nearly 47,500 households to the websites of 81 software sellers for a period of one month. The context for this study was provided by the American Law Institute's proposals in 2009 for enhanced disclosure by increased accessibility to the terms of software sale contracts.[42] Her conclusion was that clickwrap contracts were read marginally more frequently than browse wrap contracts, despite clickwrap contracts being available only after purchase on a 'pay now, terms later' basis. However,

---

[39] ibid.

[40] 23 roughly equivalent terms, although their equivalence is a matter of subjective judgment. EULAs were scored on the basis that those that were enhanced for the buyer above the UCC Art 2 standard received a score of 1, those that were pro-seller received a score of -1 and those that matched the Art 2 standard received a score of zero. See D Schwarcz, 'Reevaluating Standardized Insurance Policies' (2011) 78 U Chi L Rev 1263, where the same methodology is used to measure the contents of home insurance policies against a particular standard derived from the ISO Homeowners 3 policy.

[41] Marotta-Wurgler (n 37).

[42] American Law Institute, *Principles of the Law, Software Contracts* (American Law Institute 2009).

more startling, perhaps, was the finding that the total rate of readership of EULAs[43] was no more than 1%, whatever the sales contract type. A study of Eigen's[44] can be added to the readership puzzle. It broadly supports Marotta-Wurgler's finding on how little reading of contracts there is by consumer purchasers, actually establishing a link between a high level of supplied information and a lack of reading. However, a more significant finding in the context of this study was that there was a link between the reading of contract terms and the subsequent performance of the contract in a positive sense. Eigen's study involved 1400 participants being asked to fill in an internet based survey on work and employment. The contract involved a long and rather cumbersome survey in exchange for a free, but low value and commercially available, DVD. As Eigen acknowledges there are potential weaknesses in the design of his experiment[45] — the correlation between reading the contract and performing the contractual obligation might be skewed because the contract was with a research team and not a commercial actor and participants might have chosen to do the survey regardless of being informed that it was a contractual requirement to do so.

Marotta-Wurgler is offering an empirical, essentially descriptive, assessment of the contents of standard form contracts and consumer behaviour. She is not offering a normative critique of those terms based upon unfairness, as she accepts without comment the default standard of UCC Art 2. Her findings are hugely important for the way in which law and legal structures respond to standard form contracts. They also exemplify the critique referred to earlier, which, while it attaches to socio-legal studies in general, is primarily aimed at studies that share the characteristics of this first group. By focusing on the gap between what legal doctrinal structures point to and what parties actually do, the studies do not take forward a project to construct a new edifice of

---

[43] There was no determinative test employed in this study for whether an EULA agreement had indeed been read. Marotta-Wurgler's proxy for readership was an accessing of the EULA page for at least one second. Given their complexity of language and their length, actual readership may be considerably lower than 1%. For the use of a more determinative test of readability based on the Flesch readability scale and its constituent parts, see F Marotta-Wurgler and R Taylor, 'Set in Stone: Change and Innovation in Consumer Standard-Form Contracts' (2013) 88 New York Uni Law Rev 240, which was an empirical assessment of EULAs over time (2003-2010). See also M Rustad and T Koenig, 'Wolves of the World Wide Web: Reforming Social Networks' Contracting Practices' (2014) 49 Wake Forest L Rev 1431, 1464. This study concluded, also through use of the Flesch readability scale, that the terms of use provided by social networking sites were less readable than standards set for readability for Texas healthcare provider agreements and insurance policies in New Jersey and Delaware.

[44] Z Eigen, 'Experimental Evidence of the Relationship between Reading the Fine Print and Performance of Form-Contract Terms' (2012) 168 J of Inst and Theo Econ 124.

[45] ibid 168.

contract, for example, based on an understanding of the alternative concepts and structures that the parties do use.[46] This is because their analysis goes no further than observing that formal doctrine is not as relevant to actual contract practice as has been previously assumed.[47]

Ideas About Breach

Wilkinson-Ryan and Baron[48] used a vignette-based study, mounted on the internet to explore ideas about breach of contract. Their starting point was that, despite contract being promise based, contract remedies for breach of contract do not recognise any moral gradations around breach of promise. This is not a novel observation in itself,[49] but what the study does that is novel is to explore how this sits with 'common-sense' ideas of contract and promise. Their study was distributed to 500 mainly-US respondents, representative of the adult US population in terms of age, income and education, but not gender.[50] These respondents were asked for their responses to a series of scenarios which involved either breach of contract to achieve a gain or breach of contract to avoid loss. For example, one of the scenarios is about a kitchen refurbishment contractor and presents the study participants with one of two alternatives to which they have been randomly assigned and where they have to choose, on an eight-point scale, the level of damages they would award. In one of the alternatives, the price of materials rises dramatically, to the point where the contractor will make a loss and the contractor decides to breach the contract to take profitable work. In the second alternative, the contractor hears that there is more profitable work available and breaches his contract to take it. The participants assigned higher damages in the breach to gain variation.

The differential between the level of damages awarded, again penalizing the breach-to-gain contract breaker more heavily, increased dramatically when, in a subsequent scenario, the participants were allowed to choose the level of

---

[46] E Zamir and Y Farkash, 'Standard Form Contracts: Empirical Studies, Normative Implications, and the Fragmentation of Legal Scholarship' (2015) 12 Jerusalem Review of Legal Studies 137-170.

[47] R Cotterrell, *The Sociology of Law* (Butterworths 1992).

[48] T Wilkinson-Ryan and J Baron, 'Moral Judgment and Moral Heuristics in Breach of Contract' (2009) 4 J of Emp Legal Studies 405.

[49] C Fried, *Contract as Promise* (Harvard Uni Press 1981) and D Kimel, *From Promise to Contract* (Hart Publishing 2003). These two authors approach the link between contract and promise in very different ways and reach very different conclusions. Their differences notwithstanding, they remain the best interrogators of this point.

[50] The sample was drawn from a bigger panel of people who had signed up to do surveys and participate in studies on the internet. Whilst it was possible for Wilkinson-Ryan to balance her sample for most demographics, women pre-dominated on the original larger panel.

damages awarded. Participants were also asked to comment on whether the contract should be fulfilled or not. Three-quarters of the participants wanted the contract to be fulfilled and two-thirds of the participants thought that the contractor should be legally obliged to fulfil the contract by performance. Wilkinson-Ryan and Baron conclude, unsurprisingly, from this that their participants saw a contractual promise as a promise to perform and not a promise to perform or do something as valuable as performance i.e. pay expectation damages. This type of study does not involve the norms of reputation or continuing business relations, making it an informative but partial picture. In a subsequent study, Wilkinson-Ryan[51] looked at mortgage default decisions during the US sub-prime crisis, where credit rating and reputation are both present as contextual factors. She found that the social importance attached to fulfilling a contractual promise declined as default became more normalised within society, and lenders were seen as predatory at worst and greedy at best. This would suggest that behaviour around breach of contract, while there might be a 'moral' view of it, has to be seen in its various contexts.

Eigen's study on the reading of contracts, reported above,[52] also offers a contribution to our understanding of breach of contract and, in particular, what motivates promisors to perform or to breach their contract. Eigen set his survey up in such a way that online participants would find completion cumbersome and time consuming.[53] When participants inevitably decided to stop completing the survey and tried to exit, they received a message asking them to complete it and reminding them that they clicked to sign a contract to this effect. The participants were randomly assigned one of four messages that made this appeal in different ways; legally, morally, instrumentally and socially. The legal appeal was to point out that non-completion was a breach of contract, the moral appeal referred to the making of a binding promise and the importance of keeping one's word, the instrumental appeal pointed out that the DVD would not be supplied if the task was not completed, and the social appeal was an appeal to conformity with the norm — would-be defaulters were told that a high number of other respondents had completed the task.[54] Participants that received the moral

---

[51] T Wilkinson-Ryan, 'Breaching the Mortgage Contract: The Behavioral Economics of Strategic Default' (2011) 64 V and L R 1547.

[52] Eigen (n 44) and Z Eigen, 'When and Why Individuals Obey Contracts: Experimental Evidence of Consent, Compliance, Promise, and Performance' (2012) J of Legal Studies 67.

[53] Eigen 'When and Why Individuals Obey Contracts' (n 52) 78-79. The survey had 480 questions, each opening on a separate web page, 321 of which were multiple-choice questions. There were no default answers offered.

[54] Eigen (n 44) 81.

prompt carried on to answer significantly more questions than those participants that had received any of the other prompts. Again, this is a study without any of the supporting contexts that might be imaginable in a business or even consumer transaction — at all times the participants know the survey is being conducted by a research team. Nevertheless, this does indicate again that contracts are seen as binding as a matter of morality, rather than anything else.

Contract and Dispute Resolution

Macaulay makes the point[55] that contracting practices amongst private individuals, corporate actors and governments exist within the wider world drawn by law and society research. We have to see business practice as taking place in a world in which the use of law and lawyers is not free and may, even for parties to a business transaction, be prohibitively expensive. Resorting to formal legal dispute resolution methods in terms of court action, or, as in the case of contract, to the pre-agreed sanctions in the parties' agreement, may not be appropriate for other strategic reasons that the parties have identified, such as reputation or the preservation of a continuing business relationship.

The meticulous analyses provided by Bernstein in relation to dispute resolution in the cotton industry and the grain and feed industry[56] illustrate this. Bernstein's finding was that, notwithstanding the presence of what doctrinal lawyers would consider a relationship involving a legally enforceable contract, business relationships were subject to two separate governance mechanisms — one formal, employing legal mechanisms, and one informal, based on social norms and relationships. Which governance mechanism prevailed depended on whether the business dealings between the parties were on-going or not. If they were on-going then the parties employed strategies she called 'relationship-preserving norms'. It was important to the parties that they employed these norms and not a neutral third party, as would be the case in any litigation before a judge or arbitrator, and there was an explicit recognition that these norms, such as splitting the

---

[55] Macaulay (n 1). See also, however, Macaulay's acknowledgement that factors such as the failure by an industry to introduce arbitration schemes and disruptions to patterns of competition might result in increased litigation, L Kenworthy, S Macaulay and J Rogers '"The More Things Change....": Business Litigation and Governance in the American Automobile Industry' (1996) 21 Law and Social Inq 631.

[56] L Bernstein, 'Merchant Law in a Merchant Court: Rethinking the Code's Search for Immanent Business Norms' (1996) 144 Univ Pennsylvania L R 1765 and 'Private Commercial Law in the Cotton Industry: Creating Co-operation Through Rules, Norms and Institutions' (2001) 99 Michigan L Rev 1724.

difference, would differ from the ones contained in the written form of any agreement. Only once the relationship between the parties has broken down, do they resort to their legal rights under the contract and seek third party enforcement of them.

Dietz[57] in his study of contracting in a transnational sense adds to this picture of the relationship between contract, business based sanctions, and enforcement of legal sanctions. He looked at software development contracts between German purchasers and Bulgarian, Romanian and Indian developers, as a series of three cases studies with interviews, not only with the contract parties, but also with trade associations and chambers of commerce. What he found was that the German purchasing firms entered into very detailed contracts, which also set German law as the appropriate adjudicatory mechanism, but even as they entered these arrangements, they knew that they were not enforceable against developers in other countries, either as a device for securing performance or protecting the intellectual property rights they had purchased. The presence of a contract between the parties instead provided a basis for communication between them regarding technical specifications and cultural expectations around delivery etc. In a sense, the contract was being used to create social norms where there was no shared cultural language or experience. Added to this was the ability of the German purchasers to interact directly with the developers' computer systems via the internet, so that, through monitoring, they were almost co-producers of the product.

Investment in a contract was also required as a signifier for third parties that the purchaser might deal with, such as banks, insurance companies and the revenue authorities, that its business relationships were legitimate. It was seen as an important protection for managers in relation to shareholders; in the event that a transaction failed in some way, managers would be in a position to point to appropriate planning on their part.[58] Performance of the contractual obligation was actually secured through reliance on reputational networks. These came, in part, from the references that developers supplied of previous satisfied customers and in part from foreign trade chambers. The involvement of other customers, who themselves have no financial interest in the satisfaction or otherwise of subsequent customers, represents a layering up of reputational capital;

---

[57] T Dietz, 'Contract Law, Relational Contracts, and Reputational Networks in International Trade: An Empirical Investigation into Cross-Border Contracts in the Software Industry' (2012) 37 Law and Social Inquiry 25.

[58] ibid 38-39.

previous customers giving a developer a falsely positive reference would lose considerable professional reputation in their own community. Officially, foreign trade chambers exercise an order brokering service only between German purchasing companies and their foreign members. Dietz's work reveals the existence of an informal information exchange network, which both parties — customer and developer — recognised was hugely significant in terms of securing business through the maintenance of a good track record of delivering quality products in a timely fashion.

III – THE SECOND GROUP — FOLLOWING IAN MACNEIL

Macaulay exhorted those who are thinking of undertaking empirical work on contract, not to do so without first considering Macneil and his contribution to contract scholarship.[59] Macneil views all exchanges as contracts irrespective of whether the formalities required by contract doctrine are present. His philosophy of contract is one which sees contract as social behaviour rooted in co-operation, rather than the more adversarial paradigm which is favoured by contract doctrine, the function of which is to plan exchange into the future.[60] Within this notion of co-operation, the parties retain their separate goals; the significance of this is that Macneil believes that co-operation is key, not to the conclusion of the transaction, but to the attainment of separate goals. Macneil's contract norms are grafted onto his first and second level relations, which he sees as necessary for exchange behaviour to occur. At the first level, there is the common bond of 'society' — shared meanings, language etc. — and at the second level, there are the political bonds of polite society, which contain exchange behaviour among utility-maximizing individuals within the market place, and prevent them from simply stealing from each other. At the third level come Macneil's external and internal norms. Macneil's concern is with moving legal analysis of exchange-based relationships beyond the idea of the simple, regulated transaction towards identifying the norms that govern such transactions when they are viewed as continuing relationships between the parties. External norms are those restraints on behaviour which result from legal strictures or trade association rules. Internal norms, of which Macneil identified ten, are linked to external norms, and are the behaviours which

---

[59] S Macaulay, 'Relational Contracts Floating on a Sea of Custom? Thoughts About the Ideas of Ian Macneil and Lisa Bernstein' (2000) 94 Northwestern University L R 755. Macneil was equally complimentary about Macaulay's contribution to his own scholarship, describing Macaulay's 1963 article (n 8) as a 'demolition effort' that cleared the way for relational contract theory, I Macneil, 'Relational Contract: What We Do and Do Not Know' (1985) Wis L Rev 483, 509.

[60] Macneil (n 9).

underscore contract behaviour by encouraging co-operative attitudes between the parties.

The distinction between exchange and the formalities of contract that Macneil endorses is particularly important in the context of *umbrella contracts*. The idea of umbrella or framework agreements has recently become popular in management and economics literature and it is beginning to have resonance within legal research as well. As the name suggests, this is an arrangement where the parties recognise that they are engaged in a business relationship in which there are likely to be numerous individual exchanges over time between them. The umbrella or framework agreement does not exist to shape immediate decisions arising from the relationship but instead to set out jointly agreed principles which will provide flexibility in business dealings between the two in the future. In all likelihood, the parties to an umbrella agreement are basing their agreement on norms which either come from their own previous dealings or are known to be in common usage in their field of interest. The parties are planning how they will react to future changes of circumstances. The agreement may contain a myriad of options, many of which will not be drawn upon unless particular circumstances occur. An umbrella agreement does not contain fixed obligations but rather a series of agreed options and ideas, which are used to underpin renegotiations and adjustments according to future circumstances. By using an umbrella agreement, the parties are indicating that they will not resort to litigation but will negotiate their way past obstacles and difficulties using the norms that they agreed upon at the outset. This is a typical site for Macneil-inspired research, but one which classic contract law would struggle to accept as coming within its definition of contract.[61]

It is not easy for lawyers in particular to work with Macneil's descriptive vocabulary.[62] Much of it is confusing and alien to the world in which one might expect it to have the most traction; contract lawyers. Terms such as 'presentation', 'social matrix' and 'solidarity' are not part of contract law's terminological family. This lexicon may sound more familiar to a scholar rooted in the disciplines of sociology or management perhaps. It is perhaps not surprising that Macneil's work has appealed more to academics rooted in those disciplines who have used relational contract theory, in particular its ideas of trust and reciprocity, to examine co-operation and long-term

---

[61] (n 25).
[62] J Feinman, 'The Reception of Ian Macneil's Work on Contract in the USA' in D Campbell (ed), *The Relational Theory of Contract: Selected Works of Ian Macneil* (Sweet and Maxwell 2001) 59, 63.

relationships between firms.[63] In so far as Macneil's ideas penetrate the world of lawyers whose focus is the doctrinal model of contract law, their engagement with him is around the dichotomy between discrete and relational contracts. The most common approach to the question of the discrete contract is to situate it at the opposite end of a spectrum to relational contract. Macneil hints at the existence of such a spectrum,[64] and while it is not something that he develops,[65] it remains part of his thinking, if only as something which has purely mythical force.[66] The most comprehensive and sophisticated discussion of the spectrum idea occurs in Campbell's work[67] and, as his analysis makes clear, what Macneil means by this idea of a discrete to relational spectrum is not a device for plotting contracts by type, from spot to supply, say, or for mapping individual contract scenarios, but a mechanism by which we can examine contract at a macro level. This is the only way that Macneil's assertion[68] that 'every contract ... involves relations apart from the exchange of goods itself. Thus every contract is ... partially a relational contract ... relations other than a discrete exchange' cannot contradict his later statement that 'discrete exchange will always be a comparatively rare phenomenon because it performs only the transfer of control function and is only minimally related to physical production of goods and services'.[69] In the first statement, Macneil is talking about individual contracts and in the second, his focus is on economic ordering within society at a macro level. He is using the journey from discrete to relational to give a sociological account of how society evolves and then works.[70] If an economy was dependent on discrete contracts (a discrete economy, as Macneil describes it)[71] as its primary method of facilitating

---

[63] D Smith and B King, 'Contracts as Organizations' (2009) 51 Arizona L Rev 1.

[64] I Macneil, 'The Many Futures of Contracts' (1974) 47 Southern California Law Review 691, 737f.

[65] I Macneil, 'Relational Contract Theory as Sociology: A Reply to Professors Lindenberg and de Vos' (1987) 143 J of Institutional and Theoretical Economics 272.

[66] I Macneil, 'Relational Contract Theory: Challenges and Queries' (1999) 94 Northwestern Univ L Rev 877, 894f.

[67] D Campbell, 'The Relational Constitution of the Discrete Contract' in D Campbell and P Vincent-Jones (eds), *Contract and Economic Organisation* (Dartmouth 1996) 40; D Campbell, 'Ian Macneil and the Relational Theory of Contract' in D Campbell (ed), (n 62) and D Campbell, 'What Do We Mean by the Non-Use of Contract?' in J Braucher, J Kidwell, W C Whitford (eds), *Revisiting the Contracts Scholarship of Stewart Macaulay* (Hart Publishing 2013) 159.

[68] Macneil (n 9) 10.

[69] I Macneil, 'Relational Contract: What We Do and Do Not Know' (1985) Wis L R 483, 488.

[70] R Scott, 'The Promise and Peril of Relational Contract Theory' in J Braucher et al (n 67) 105, 114-115.

[71] Macneil (n 69) 490.

exchange, productivity would be very low and transaction costs would be very high.[72]

Macneil never intended that the label 'discrete' should be appended to particular contract scenarios, but rather that these interactions should be seen as more or less relational. This is clear from his use of marriage as an example of a relationship that can be more or less transactional, depending, presumably, on the wishes of the parties involved and the nature of their relationship.[73] At the level of individual contract scenarios, Macneil's concern is with moving the legal analysis of exchange-based relationships beyond the idea of the simple regulated transaction, towards identifying the norms that govern such transactions when they are viewed as continuing relationships between the parties. Macneil's internal contract norms will determine how an exchange works in practice. The suggestion is that some norms will come to the fore when exchanges are more discrete, namely 'implementation of planning' and 'effectuation of consent'; while others, such as role integrity and solidarity, will be more evident in exchanges that are more relational. Factors that are present in the party's relationship with each other, but not included in the contract between them, will become part of their obligation to each other. All ten of the norms that Macneil identifies will be present to some degree or another in each exchange. Of these ten norms, five hold special significance with Macneil's scheme. These are *role integrity* and *propriety of means*, which come straight from the list of ten, and three others, which are a combination of the remaining eight. These three are *preservation of the relation* (an expansion of *contractual solidarity* and *flexibility*), *harmonization of relational conflict* (derived from *flexibility* and *harmonization of the social matrix*) and the *supra-contractual norm* (produced from the *harmonization of the social matrix*).[74] These will be generated in the relationship over time.

Macneil's norms and contextualisation of exchange practices have been used to examine, inter alia, what underpins ideas of trust in contract relationships between business actors. A project which demonstrates this is that undertaken by a collaborative team of researchers from Parma, Cambridge University

---

[72] S Wheeler, 'What Ian Macneil Might Have Said About Using eBay?' in D Campbell, L Mulcahy and S Wheeler (eds), *Changing Concepts of Contract* (Palgrave Macmillan 2013) 38.
[73] Macneil (n 65).
[74] I Macneil, 'Values in Contract: Internal and External' (1983) 78 Northwestern University L Review 340 and R Spediel, 'The Characteristics and Challenges of Relational Contracts' (1999) 94 Northwestern Univ L Rev 823.

and Hamberg-Harburg Universities.[75] Their inquiry spanned three countries — Britain, Italy and Germany — and two industries selected for their different operating contexts in terms of competition within their respective sectors and their involvement with trade and other business associations — mining machinery manufacture and kitchen furniture manufacture. 62 firms across the three jurisdictions participated in interviews and released both qualitative and quantitative information about their business practices. Among the project's many findings, two are particularly interesting. The supporting institutional environment that the parties find themselves in affects behaviour around trust and co-operation, and the presence of relational factors, such as trade and business associations, codified contract conditions and industrial standards, all assist in creating trust and co-operation. In contrast to Macaulay's findings, informal contract practices, such as the absence of a written agreement, were more likely to result in the parties using formal redress mechanisms. The presence of formalised contract relations (for example, in Germany) was considerably less likely to result in court proceedings between the parties. Trust between the parties was built through the use of legal mechanisms, rather than through the non-observance of legal mechanisms.

The once-natural division of arrangements into public and private has been increasingly challenged by the ordering and governing arrangements that many developed societies have adopted in recent years. Legal structures commonly used to order private relationships can be transplanted into the public sector, where they are used in quite a different way. The legacy of New Public Management is a series of arrangements, for a bewildering range of government-provided services and functions, and of services and functions that are provided by private sector actors on behalf of government, which use the language of contract to describe the relationship between the governor and the governed irrespective of whether the arrangements in question are legally enforceable as contracts. Macneil's emphasis on context is the key here to seeing these contractual relationships as forming a constitution in which procedures for monitoring service provision, incentivising performance, and imposing administrative sanctions are laid out.

---

[75] S Deakin, T Goodwin and A Hughes, 'Contract Law, Trust Relations and Incentives for Co-operation: A Comparative Study' in S Deakin and J Michie (eds), *Contracts, Co-operation, and Competition* (OUP 1997) 328.

The best study in terms of the breadth of material covered and the quality of analysis is that of Vincent-Jones.[76] His work in this field began in the early 1990s, with several empirically grounded projects on the use of compulsory competitive tendering in local government. Since then, he has followed the use of contract by the state to achieve certain policy goals, such as increasing citizen choice or modifying citizen behaviour, in areas as diverse as the behaviour of school children and the delivery of welfare services. The account that results from this bears the fruit of years of painstaking empirical work by presenting hugely rich qualitative data. Vincent-Jones' work addresses important policy issues about citizen-state relationships that are beyond the scope of this chapter and, in many ways, that is the primary purpose of his work.

Of interest to empirical legal studies is the way in which Vincent-Jones uses the Macneil model of exchange to define the three categories of contract into which he divides these relationships, eschewing the more familiar model of legally enforceable contracts on the one hand and non-enforceable contracts on the other. Without the encumbrance of using legal enforceability as the feature on which classification depends, he is able to employ a broad, threefold functional classification into administrative contracts, economic contracts, and social control contracts. His aim is to compare the norms of these arrangements with the norms identified by Macneil. Vincent-Jones observes that the idea of contract as a mutual arrangement, which the parties can adjust in order to achieve wealth-maximisation, is not applicable to public sector contracting, which is insufficiently flexible to adapt to changing circumstances. Reciprocity, which underpins trust, is not present because, often, the resources on the state side of the contract are insufficient to address the needs of the citizen. In many of the relationships, but particularly those involving social control contracts, the norm of consent is missing. In Vincent-Jones' view, it is because of the absence of so many of Macneil's norms that public sector contracting in its current forms fails to deliver on its policy objectives and fails the test of legitimacy. Vincent-Jones does suggest remedial steps that could be taken, but what is important here is the depth and richness of analysis he is able to achieve by using Macneil's contract norms in a setting which goes well beyond interactions between business actors, into a world that classic contract law would not recognise as contractual.

---

[76] P Vincent-Jones, *The New Public Contracting* (OUP 2006) and 'Relational Contract and Social Learning in Hybrid Organization' in Campbell, Mulcahy and Wheeler (n 72) 216.

IV – CONCLUSION

In this chapter, I have examined a number of empirical studies in contract that use the work of the two leading scholars, in my view, in this field – Stewart Macaulay and Ian Macneil. These studies, which have thus far achieved little traction in Europe or the US,[77] were chosen because they employ research methods that are replicable by lone scholars or postgraduate students. I have set out their methodology in some detail, not least to show that, while studies using Macaulay's methods of 'asking those in the field' persist,[78] there are some that are using the power of the internet and the habitat of the experimental psychologist – the lab – to push empirical studies in this area forward. The internet has distinct attractions and further potential as a research tool for contract-related projects that want to interact with a general pool of respondents mapped onto particular demographic characteristics, rather than a specialist group of participants. It is largely free to use, it reduces perceptions of 'capture' by the interviewer, and it allows participants to interact with the study at hand in their own environment. This reduces the possibility of behaviour change that might be introduced by a lab setting. However, a lab setting does reduce the possibility of participants misunderstanding what is required of them as it allows for face-to-face interaction.[79] Both the laboratory and the internet offer a new dimension to empirical studies that is relatively under-explored.

There are some areas of contract that we now know very much more about than we did, thanks to the data produced by empirical studies. They give us, at best, a different picture of the landscape and, at worst, a basis for asking further questions about incomplete pictures. Standard form contracts and the reading of those contracts is one area where we know as much as we do about contract planning in the business world, because of the findings of a number of recent studies. The world in which many of us domiciled in the EU find ourselves as consumers is very different from the world that these studies describe because of the impact of EU level and domestic level legislation. However, regardless of this, these studies give us valuable information to feed into contract design and future law reform initiatives. There are other areas of contract that we still know very little about. Gender is one such area. Despite empirical findings that women pay more for consumer services, including credit and borrowing facilities, we know very little about the world

---

[77] See, for example, the recent book-length treatment of standard form contracts by Radin, which, while an excellent volume on its own terms, gives barely a nod in the direction of empirical work in the area; M Radin, *Boilerplate* (Princeton Univ Press 2013).

[78] Gulati and Scott (n 11) and Deakin, Goodwin and Hughes (n 75), for example.

[79] See Eigen (n 44) 71-72 for a more detailed discussion of these points.

of gender and contract. We suspect that the relational values of women may differ from men, despite the obvious caveat of stereo-typing! But we do not know whether this then maps onto a different attitude to contract negotiation and standard form contracts, for example.[80] In a similar vein, we know very little about the effect of socio-economic status on contract negotiation, the traction of standard form contracts and views on breach, despite the efforts of Eigen to the contrary.[81] There would appear to be some ground for future studies to plough here!

---

[80] A Schmitz, 'Sex Matters: Considering Gender in Consumer Contracting' (2013) 19 Cardozo J of Law and Gender 437.
[81] Z Eigen, 'The Devil in the Details: The Interrelationship Among Citizenship, Rule of Law and Form-Adhesive Contracts' (2008) 41 Connecticut Law Review 381.

Chapter 11

An Introduction to Research Ethics in Legal Scholarship

*Hope DAVIDSON and Jennifer SCHWEPPE**

I – Introduction

In this edited collection, a number of the authors have discussed the role, importance and possibilities associated with empirical research in law (Doherty; de Londras; Wheeler). Prior to engaging in empirical research, it is vitally important that you, as a researcher, consider the ethical implications of your research, in order to fully protect both your research participants and yourself. These considerations will usually be submitted to an institutional Research Ethics Committee (REC) or Institutional Review Board (IRB).[1] This chapter will first briefly detail the context to this process, explaining the evolution and fundamental principles of research ethics. It will then go on to set out some of the issues that you might face as a researcher, and the issues that you will need to consider in determining what (if any) ethical implications there are for your research. In this context, it will address some issues which are perhaps most particular to research in law.

II – Context

Research ethics frameworks are well established in the field of clinical trials. The regulation of behavioural ethics, or ethics in the social sciences, is a much more recent consideration, though that is, of course, not to say that social scientists were not concerned with the ethics of their research; merely that it was not universally regulated until more recently.[2] Indeed criticisms are made by social scientists that, because regulation emanated from the

---

* Hope Davidson is a PhD researcher in the School of Law, University of Limerick. Jennifer Schweppe is a lecturer in the School of Law, University of Limerick.
[1] For the purposes of this chapter, we will use the term Research Ethics Committee (REC) as it is most commonly used in an Irish context.
[2] The 1975 revision of the Declaration of Helsinki created Research Ethics Committees. World Medical Association General Assembly, *Declaration of Helsinki: Ethical principles for Medical Research Involving Human Subjects, Finland 1964* para 23 <www.wma.net/en/30publications/10policies/b3/> accessed 7 March 2016.

biomedical sphere, there has been an attempt to shoehorn behavioural research in to a clinical model into which it does not necessarily fit.[3]

As a law student, you are more likely to be concerned with behavioural research than biomedical, although of course you may find yourself on multi-disciplinary research projects as you progress through your career. If you intend to conduct interviews, surveys, questionnaires, observational studies, or in some cases, use existing data, you will need to consider the ethical implications of your research, and obtain ethical approval from the relevant REC in your institution. Without such approval, you cannot begin the empirical stages of your research. Further, the consideration of the ethical implications of your research, and the obtaining of approval for that research also forms a critical part of many funding applications.[4]

III – A Brief History of Research Ethics

The requirement to consider the ethical implications of research has as we have said its origins in the biomedical sciences. Up until the middle of the last century, research had come to be regarded as an 'unqualified and unquestioned good' due to the 'potential benefit to be gained for society'.[5] As Brazier observes, many of us would not be alive today but for the advances made in research involving human beings.[6]

The benefits gained, however, were not without a cost to the participants, and to society as a whole. The now infamous Nuremberg Trials in 1947 revealed some of the harsher realities of research carried out on human beings. In Nazi concentration camps, prisoners were exposed to extreme cold, low-pressure chambers, malaria, and typhus in order to gain information that might prove useful to the treatment of soldiers.[7] At the infamous trial of the doctors, ten principles, which came to be known as the Nuremberg Code,[8] were set out governing future research on human beings. The principles require full, free and informed consent on the part of participants; a scientific basis for the

---

[3] M Israel, *Research Ethics and Integrity for Social Scientists* (2nd edn, Sage 2105).
[4] See for instance the Irish Research Council postgraduate, postdoctoral and other research funding opportunities <www.research.ie> accessed 7 March 2016.
[5] D Madden, *Medicine Ethics and the Law* (2nd edn, Bloomsbury 2011) 569.
[6] M Brazier, 'Exploitation and Enrichment: The Paradox of Medical Experimentation' (2008) 3(3) Journal of Medical Ethics 180.
[7] ibid. That the Nazis were far from alone in committing atrocities in medicine's name is well known within the medical profession and the bioethics community, but less well publicised more generally.
[8] *Trials of War Criminals before the Nuremberg Military Tribunals under Control Council No.10*, Vol.2 181-82 (US Government Printing Office 1949).

need for the research; and that the benefits to the research outweigh the risks. These principles in full are as follows:

1. The voluntary consent of the human subject is absolutely essential. The duty and responsibility for ascertaining the quality of the consent rests upon each individual who initiates, directs or engages in the experiment;

2. The experiment should be such as to yield fruitful results for the good of society, unprocurable by other methods or means of study, and not random and unnecessary in nature;

3. The experiment should be so designed and based on the results of animal experimentation and a knowledge of the natural history of the disease or other problem under study, that the anticipated results will justify the performance of the experiment;

4. The experiment should be so conducted as to avoid all unnecessary physical and mental suffering and injury;

5. No experiment should be conducted, where there is an *a priori* reason to believe that death or disabling injury will occur; except, perhaps, in those experiments where the experimental physicians also serve as subjects;

6. The degree of risk to be taken should never exceed that determined by the humanitarian importance of the problem to be solved by the experiment;

7. Proper preparations should be made and adequate facilities provided to protect the experimental subject against even remote possibilities of injury, disability, or death;

8. The experiment should be conducted only by scientifically qualified persons. The highest degree of skill and care should be required through all stages of the experiment of those who conduct or engage in the experiment;

9. During the course of the experiment, the human subject should be at liberty to bring the experiment to an end, if he has reached the physical or mental state, where continuation of the experiment seemed to him to be impossible;

10. During the course of the experiment, the scientist in charge must be prepared to terminate the experiment at any stage, if he has probable cause to believe, in the exercise of the good faith, superior skill and careful judgement required of him, that a continuation of the experiment is likely to result in injury, disability, or death to the experimental subject.[9]

While the Code itself was hugely important in terms of setting down expected standards for future research, its effect was largely symbolic, as it was largely ignored by medical professionals[10] who equated the incidents to which it gave rise with war crimes.[11] It was however, subsequently adopted and expanded upon comprehensively[12] by the World Medical Association in the Declaration of Helsinki in 1964.[13] The Declaration has had nine revisions to date, the latest of which was in Brazil in 2013.[14] For present purposes, an important creation of the second revision of the Declaration was the creation of Research Ethics Committees[15]

Ethically Problematic Research in the Biomedical Sciences

In the years that followed the drawing up of the Declaration of Helsinki a number of high profile public health scandals emerged in the public domain in the United States. The most famous of these was the Tuskegee Syphilis Trial,[16] in which the participants, who were largely socio-economically disadvantaged African-Americans, were left medically untreated for syphilis indefinitely, so that researchers could map the natural course of the disease. In 1966 an influential article by Henry Beecher, a highly regarded anaesthetist from Harvard University, was published in the *New England Journal of*

---

[9] ibid.

[10] H Biggs, *Healthcare Research Ethics and the Law: Regulation, Review and Responsibility* (Routledge-Cavendish 2010) 26.

[11] D Madden, *Medicine Ethics and the Law* (2nd edn, Bloomsbury 2011) 576.

[12] Biggs (n 10).

[13] World Medical Association General Assembly (n 2).

[14] ibid.

[15] ibid para 23, 'The research protocol must be submitted for consideration, comment, guidance and approval to the concerned research ethics committee before the study begins'.

[16] In a study in Tuskegee, Alabama between 1932- 1972, African-American men enrolled in a study of the natural history of syphilis. Over half the men had syphilis, though they were not told of this, and other men contracted it during the study. During the study effective treatments became available but were not provided to the men, who were in the main poor and uneducated, and doctors were actively discouraged from treating them. A public apology was given by President Clinton in 1997 <www.cdc.gov/tuskegee/timeline.htm> accessed 7 March 2016.

Medicine.[17] In it he outlined 22 examples of medical experiments which posed a risk to participants, including the Jewish Chronic Disease Hospital Study[18] and the Willowbrook hepatitis scandal (1956-8).[19] These revelations led, in 1978, to the U.S Department of Health, Education and Welfare publishing the now infamous Belmont Report or *Ethical Principles and Guidelines for the Protection of Human Subjects of Research*.[20]

The Belmont Report distilled three principles by which research was to be governed: *respect for persons, beneficence* and *justice*. Respect for persons required that people were to be treated as individual autonomous agents, and that those with diminished autonomy were entitled to protection.[21] Beneficence was a duty to maximise benefits and minimise potential harm to research participants. Justice required that equals be treated equally, and therefore that no grouping be selected for research by virtue of ease of access for the researchers on account of the subjects' vulnerability.

Ethically Problematic Research in the Humanities and Social Sciences

Though perhaps some of the highest profile and publically known research scandals are from the biomedical sciences, involving as they did the physical health of largely disadvantaged and vulnerable communities, the social sciences were not without blemish.

---

[17] Regarded by some as the single most influential article written on the subject of experimentation involving human subjects. H Beecher, 'Ethics and Clinical Research' (1966) 274 *New England Journal of Medicine* 1354-60.

[18] The study involved injecting live liver cancer cells in to elderly and vulnerable adults. A Smith Iltis, 'Human subjects research: Ethics and Compliance' in A Smith Iltis (ed), *Research Ethics* (Routledge 2006) 3, M Israel, *Research Ethics and Integrity for Social Scientists* (2nd edn, Sage 2105) 33.

[19] The study involved the deliberate infection of disabled children in a care home with viral hepatitis to monitor the progression of the disease. While arguably it met ethical standards of the day in that it was granted ethical approval by the New York University School of Medicine, it subsequently transpired that the information given to the parents of the children was incomplete, and furthermore, that they were more likely to secure a place for their child in the institution if they consented to participation in the research. Biggs (n 10) 22 and A Smith Iltis (n 18) 3.

[20] National Commission for the Protection of Human Subjects of Biomedical and Behavioral Research, *The Belmont Report, Ethical Principles and Guidelines for the Protection of Human Subjects of Research* (Dept of Health, Education and Welfare 1978) https://repository.library.georgetown.edu/handle/10822/779133 accessed 8 March 2016.

[21] This was one of the areas, for instance, that the Nuremberg Code had not addressed.

The Milgram studies at Yale University in the 1960's,[22] for example were ultimately found to have involved 'multiple deceptions' and 'emotional discomfort, manipulation and coercion'[23] of research participants. The research project aimed to examine the extent to which an individual would obey an authority figure who required them to perform tasks which conflicted with their own belief system. In one of the studies, participant 'teachers' were required to administer electric shocks remotely to participant 'students' (who unbeknownst to them, were actors) in another room, with the actor 'students' making appropriate anguished sounds all the way up to the administration of an apparently fatal dose of electricity. As Biggs observes, the Milgram experiments have become synonymous with unethical research practices, primarily due to the levels of deception involved, and the distress caused to the research participants.[24]

While the Milgram study was clearly ethically questionable given the lack of consideration for the participants, the Tearoom Trade study[25] highlights further potential issues which might arise in the context of research in the social sciences, that is, how to appropriately strike the balance between research which has benefit to society, and ensuring that the research does not infringe on the rights of participants. As part of the Tearoom Trade study, between 1965 and 1968, Laud Humphreys conducted research on casual sexual encounters between consenting homosexuals in public places. He played the role of 'watch queen' or lookout at the public facilities of a St Louis Park. While he subsequently disclosed his research to some of the parties involved, with others he kept their vehicle licence plates and followed up with them a year later (in disguise) while conducting an anonymous public health survey. From an ethical perspective, what we should consider is that the research took place in a public place, the researcher went to considerable lengths to ensure the confidentiality of the participants, and it was unclear as to what harm (if any) emerged from the study.[26] However, again, the issue of deception is present here; further, the participants were unknowingly part of the research process and thus unable to give informed consent to participating in the process.

---

[22] M Israel (n 18) 33. The studies have been the subject of a number of films, including most recently *Experimenter* (2015) starring Peter Sarsgaard and Winona Ryder.
[23] Biggs (n 10) 24.
[24] Biggs (n 10) 25.
[25] L Humphreys, *Tearoom Trade: Impersonal Sex in Public Places* (Aldine Publishing Company, 1975)) as cited in J DuBois, 'Ethics in Behavioural and Social Science Research' in A Smith Iltis (ed), *Research Ethics* (Routledge 2006).
[26] M Israel (n 18) 35, 101, '[S]ome argue deceptive experiments and covert research might be justified in particular situations by reference to the balance of risk and public benefit'.

In order to protect both the participant and the researcher in research projects, third level institutions now have Institutional Review Boards or Research Ethics Committees (RECs) to oversee the conduct of research. While it is sometimes felt that such bodies constitute an impediment to research and a block to academic freedom, it is interesting to note that the Milgram study has, for instance, been replicated and approved by Research Ethics Committees,[27] with certain controls and more ethical methodology.[28] As we have noted, RECs were created by the second revision of the Declaration of Helsinki in 1975.[29] While, at first, they were predominately only present in hospital settings, now most third level institutions will have their own dedicated research ethics framework, with at least one REC present — and sometimes more than one where the size and disciplinary differences in the institution vary considerably.

IV – Applying for Research Ethics Approval

Before you begin your empirical research, you will need to seek and obtain ethical approval from your faculty REC. This section of our chapter will describe some of the issues that you may have to consider when applying for such approval, though of course each project will require a new and considered approach to framing the ethical considerations in the research. What is important to note in this context is that there are varying disciplinary norms in the context of research ethics; and for this reason, these differing norms may vary between RECs in a single institution and between different institutions in Ireland. Perhaps one of the reasons for this is that there is no national policy in relation to research ethics (though there is one in the context of research integrity)[30] and so institutions and RECs operate according to their own individual policies.

The function of the Research Ethics Committee is to satisfy itself that, where ethical issues arise in the context of your research, you have addressed these concerns and are fully aware of your obligations in relation to your

---

[27] World Medical Association General Assembly (n 2) para 23, 'The research protocol must be submitted for consideration, comment, guidance and approval to the concerned research ethics committee before the study begins'.

[28] Biggs (n 10) 25. In a replicated study in 2007, the fake shocks administered were far less than the stated fake fatal doses in the original experiment and the research participants were counselled and de-briefed immediately after the experiment and re-assured that the persons involved were unharmed. See also, M Israel (n 18) 34.

[29] World Medical Association General Assembly (n 2) para 23.

[30] Irish Universities Association, *National policy statement on Ensuring Research Integrity in Ireland* (June 2014) www.iua.ie/publication/view/national-policy-statement-on-ensuring-research-integrity-in-ireland/accessed 7 March 2016.

participants. They also must be satisfied that the potential benefits of the research outweigh the risks involved — risks that might relate to your participants, but also to you as an individual, or to your institution and its reputation. In replying to your application, the REC may approve your application; may provisionally approve it subject to minor corrections or clarifications; or may reject your application, if it raises ethical issues that are insurmountable. The consequences for the latter can be utterly devastating for a research project, which means that a carefully considered application is crucial to the timely progress of your research.

It is important to note that, while RECs are designed to facilitate and not to hinder research, they are bound to perform the function of protecting *both* the participants and the researcher in the research process. The remainder of this chapter will discuss some of the principle issues you will have to consider when applying for research ethics approval. However, when engaging with this process, you should work closely with your supervisor or research team, and always be cognisant of the institutional guidelines that apply to you.

Do I Need to Apply for Research Ethics Approval?

The first question that should be asked is, do I need to apply for research ethics approval. As a general rule of thumb, if your research involves engaging with human participants (either physically or remotely, e.g., by use of web-based surveys), or collecting or using data which is not otherwise accessible to the general public, you will need to apply for research ethics approval.

In conducting an empirically based project in law, you are perhaps most likely to be engaging in research involving surveys, questionnaires, focus groups or interviews; or perhaps the use of data not accessible publically.[31] Importantly, any research that involves patients or those employed by the HSE, who are accessed in their capacity as either patients or employees, must be referred to the Health Service Executive and not institutional RECs.

There are some issues that might arise in this context in relation to legal research that may not be particularly relevant in other disciplines. First,

---

[31] 'The Digital Repository of Ireland is a national trusted digital repository for Ireland's social and cultural data and may be of assistance in terms of providing access to data *already publically available*. The repository links together and preserves both historical and contemporary data held by Irish institutions, providing a central internet access point and interactive multimedia tools. As a national e-infrastructure for the future of education and research in the humanities and social sciences, DRI is available for use by the public, students and scholars' <www.dri.ie/> accessed 6 March 2016.

there may be information which is not publically available, but rather accessible only through a freedom of information request, or through a formal request to a government department. We would advise that, in these circumstances, as the public have a *right* to the information, there is no need for REC approval.[32] Secondly, what about either courtroom or parliamentary observations? The latter is rather simple to deal with. As the Dáil and Seanad debates are available publically through the official website <www.oireachtas.ie>,[33] there is no need to apply for approval to analyse the content of the debates. What, then, if one were to conduct research on the theatre of the debating chamber, including the body language and movement of speakers? This is slightly more complex, but again, as debates are generally publically available to view on Oireachtas TV, this should be unproblematic from an ethical perspective.

In the context of research conducted in a courtroom or similar settings, the situation is not as clear. Let us take, for example, a situation where a researcher is in a courtroom listening to the content of legal arguments and decisions of the court. In this case, as this is information which is being read into the public record, there is no need to apply for research ethics approval. Where you are retrospectively seeking to retrieve transcripts from cases, again, as this is simply a written account of that which is a matter of public record, this is largely unproblematic from an ethical perspective — though it may cost you a significant amount if you are required to pay for the information to be transcribed. What, then, about research on the theatre of the courtroom? Though this may be more problematic, again, given the public nature of the space and the expectation that those involved have of being observed (e.g. by journalists, other lawyers etc.), this arguably does not require ethics approval, though, again, it may be worth confirming this with your REC. It is this 'expectation' of observation, we argue, that makes this observation different to, for example, observing people's use of a public bathroom (as we saw in the Milgram experiments).

Finally, the use of the internet for the purposes of research throws up some interesting questions in the context of research ethics. Where an individual comments or posts in a public forum, where there is no expectation of privacy — such as Twitter — there are no ethical concerns in relation to analysing and utilising data. However, on websites where there is an expectation of privacy — such as on Facebook — ethical concerns do arise.

---

[32] That said, it might be no harm to write to your REC and confirm that this is the case.

[33] Though the alternative website <www.kildarestreet.ie> accessed 6 March 2016 is a much more user friendly and searchable website containing the same material.

Similarly, where individuals comment and discuss issues on websites or forums which are password protected, ethical issues will need to be addressed and you should seek guidance from your faculty REC on this.

Ethical Issues A: Research Participants

Informed Consent

Where you are engaging directly with your research participants, the key principle to consider is their ability to give informed consent to their participation. To be valid in law, a consent must voluntary, informed, and made by a person who has the capacity to give that consent. Thus, this principle has two aspects: first, that the individual is innately capable of giving consent; and second, that you have provided the individual with all the information they require to engage fully in the process and to know what is involved.

In relation to the first issue, the first question is whether there is a particular or potential vulnerability in the participant group. Often, in assessing the ethical implications of research, the Committee or the application form will make presumptions as to vulnerability in considering the question of whether the participant will have the ability to understand what participation involves. Where these presumptions are made, and you intend accessing that community, you will first need to get Garda Clearance. This can be a lengthy process, so it is advisable to do this at the earliest possible stage.

Presumptions as to incapacity are often made in relation to those who are under the age of 18[34] or over the age of 65. Sometimes, you may wish to rebut this presumption — if, for example, you were interviewing judges of the Supreme Court, one can simply say that while the participants may well be over the age of 65, given their position as members of the bench, we can assume that they are fully capable of giving consent to being interviewed for a research project. Where your research participants have an intellectual or developmental disability, or diminished capacity for other reasons, you will need to consider if they can consent to participating, and if not, who will give consent on their part? At present under Irish law there is no legal framework for a person who lacks decision-making capacity to participate in research,

---

[34] The age limit may vary depending on the institution or the context – for example, the age limit is 16 rather than 18 in the context of clinical trials. http://www.hse.ie/eng/about/Who/qualityandpatientsafety/National_Consent_Policy/consenttrainerresource/trainerfiles/NationalConsentPolicyM2014.pdf accessed 8 March 2016.

outside of clinical trials.[35] In practice what this means is that concerns in relation to balancing risks and benefits are particularly acute in this regard. In relation to people with little English, you may need to set out whether an interpreter or a translator will be required, and then consider the further ethical implications that this involves given the requirements of confidentiality.

If your research involves children (or indeed university students under 18) you will need to provide your signed agreement to the institution's Child Protection Policy to the REC along with your application form and potentially evidence of having obtained Garda clearance. You will need to indicate how you will deal with incidental findings such as child abuse or welfare and safety issues.[36] You will need to go in to some detail on how you will access and interact with the participants, obtain consent from a parent or guardian and, as your participant will not be able to legally consent, an age appropriate *assent* needs to be provided by the minor. If you are accessing those under the age of 18, it is best to do so in a formal setting, such as a school or a youth group. In the case of the former, you will need to provide an information sheet and consent form to the Board of Management and the principal, and in the case of the latter, the same documentation needs to be addressed to those with responsibility for the project.

The second category of circumstances in which there may be concerns regarding the ability of individuals to freely give consent is where they are in a setting in which they are in the protection, control or influence of others, or where there is a power dynamic involved — for example, if an individual is in care, in prison, or in a teacher/pupil relationship with the researcher. You will need to carefully consider how to manage this situation to ensure that the participants are freely consenting to participating, that they do not feel under a moral, legal or any other obligation to do so, and that there are no sanctions or preferential treatments for participation (as for example, in the Willowbrook study). Similarly, where a gatekeeper is required to access the group (see below), it must be made clear that they are under no obligation to participate, and that their participation or refusal to participate will not be made known to the gatekeeper in question.

---

[35] National Consent Policy, http://www.hse.ie/eng/about/Who/qualityandpatientsafety/National_Consent_Policy/consenttrainerresource/trainerfiles/NationalConsentPolicyM2014.pdf accessed 8 March 2016.

[36] University of Limerick, *Child Protection Guidelines: Protocols and Procedures* (University of Limerick,. 2010) available at <http://www.ulsites.ul.ie/researchethics/sites/default/files//Child%20Protection%20Guidelines.doc> accessed 8 March 2016.

The second principle to consider in this context is the level and amount of information provided to the participants, and that it is provided in an accessible way. The single biggest reason for which ethical approval applications fail (outside clerical errors) is a failure to inform the participants of what the study entails — a failure, therefore, to fulfill the informed part of the informed consent process. The primary means of overcoming this is by providing an information letter which details the nature of the study, what is involved when an individual agrees to participate, and what the risks and benefits are to the participant for engaging. You must also provide a consent form which details the rights and obligations the participants have in relation to their participation, which your participants must sign prior to you engaging with them. Critically, both the information sheet and the consent form must highlight the entirely voluntary nature of the process, and the circumstances under which an individual can withdraw. A clear plan as to what will happen to the data collected in the event of a withdrawal from a study must be made out for the REC. It is also important that this is written in a manner which is appropriate to the participants involved: an information letter and consent form for the Chief Justice may be technical and use legal jargon, while it would be utterly inappropriate to send the same information to participants with high levels of literacy issues.

Giving an informed consent is also dependent on the participant receiving full information on the study and how the data will be used. It is important to be specific about this and data may only be used for the purpose stated in your information sheet. If you intend to publish your research in an academic journal, or deliver a conference paper using the data collected, this needs to be clearly stated — while it is possible to return to your participants to seek further consents to different uses for the research, this is not ideal, and indeed in some cases not possible. You must also clearly set out how you propose to record the information — do you propose to use an audio recording device or a video? In the case of the latter, particular ethical issues arise in terms of the use of an individual's image, giving rise to the requirement for very clear information and consent processes.

All that said, in certain contexts it will be either impossible or inappropriate to obtain a signed consent form from individuals. The classic example of this is in the context of an anonymous online survey. In anonymous or online surveys, consent is not required because participation in the survey implies consent to be involved and the answers given are entirely anonymous from the point of collection (as distinct from data which is de-identified or anonymised after collection). Here, while you will provide all the information that you would usually do in an information sheet to participants on the email of invitation and/or the first page of the survey, researchers will commonly then set out the key principles usually contained in a consent form followed by a statement such as "By completing this survey, I hereby consent to engaging in the project".

Finally, you will need to address the question of anonymity and confidentiality, and whether or not this is offered and/or guaranteed to participants. If you cannot guarantee anonymity, you should not promise it. For example, in the context of a focus group, it would be impossible to guarantee anonymity, though you should still guarantee confidentiality in relation to personal records. In some circumstances, it will be inappropriate or indeed impossible to guarantee confidentiality of participation — if you were to interview, for example, the Director of Public Prosecutions, the Attorney General and the Garda Commissioner, it would be very clear who that person is. Further, while in some circumstances you may decide not to name an individual, it may still be possible to identify them — consider for example, a research project which were to assess the perspectives of female members of the Supreme Court bench on judicial diversity: there are only three such members, and if you were lucky enough to speak to all three it would be perfectly clear that they all participated (though you may still anonymise their responses).

Accessing Research Participants: Gatekeepers

You will need to clearly set out in your application form how you intend to access your participants: will you contact them directly; advertise at an appropriate venue (such as the offices of a civil society organisation); or use snowball sampling, whereby research participants identify further research participants. In some circumstances, which probably apply most particularly in the context of empirical legal studies, you may need to seek express permission from a gatekeeper to access your participant pool. In an Irish context, it is good practice to assume that you will need to seek permission from the Chief Justice to access members of the judiciary; from the Garda Commissioner to access either members of An Garda Síochána or its civilian staff; or from the Head of the Prison Services to access prison staff.

Ethical Issues B: Research Subject Matter

The *subject matter* section deals with the nature of the material to be discussed. Here, you are directly focused on how engaging in the subject matter of the research will impact on the participant. Are you, for example, proposing to discuss sensitive personal or political issues? If so, will this cause distress to the participant, and how to you propose to protect the participant in these circumstances? In some cases, it might be appropriate, for example, to give referral information to the participants on counselling or support services: in some cases, indeed, it may be appropriate to directly provide such support to participants following their participation.

In the context of legal or criminological research most particularly, you may be asking participants about their engagement in illegal activities. This may be anything from illicit drug-taking to more serious forms of criminal activity. You must be very clear to both yourself and the participant as to when you are legally obliged to report such behavior, and when you can assure confidentiality. For your own protection and for that of your research participants it is good practice to restrict yourself to your actual research question and to avoid getting in to the detail or particulars of any offence. You should caution participants that if you are required by a court to disclose information provided by them you will have to do so. As a general rule, if the information disclosed would cause harm to the participant or other persons, that information should be reported — you should seek advice from your faculty REC and supervisor in this situation.

You might also be speaking with participants about subject matter which, while in an interview context may appear to be relatively benign, when published in the context of a wider research project, may cause embarrassment or regret to the participant. Again, by being careful regarding the information provided to your research participant in relation to the research, and ensuring that the research is published in such a way as to ensure that their personal details are in no way identifiable, this should ensure that the research is ethically sound. Further, in all of these contexts, it is of course critical to stress that a subject can withdraw at any time from the interview process.

Ethical Issues C: Research Procedures

Finally, the *research procedures* then ask whether, in engaging with the research, the participant will be put at any risk. More commonly associated with research in the biomedical sciences rather than in the social sciences, here questions are asked as to whether the research involves the deception of participants, the offering of large inducements to participate, or physical or invasive treatments. Sometimes this will not be immediately apparent on the face of the research: some behavioural studies, such as The Tearoom Trade study, for instance, or perhaps research involving teenage drinking habits, will involve mild deception, in that participants would moderate their behaviour if they knew they were participating in a study, thus invalidating the study. Typically, in such studies RECs would require evidence of a de-briefing session following the completion of the research.

Data Protection

If you are engaging in empirical research, regardless of the ethical implications of the research, you will need to address the data protection implications of the data you collect. You will need to follow the data protection guidelines as set out in the Data Protection Acts 1998 and 2003. There are eight data rules in relation to data protection for researchers which require a researcher to:

1. Obtain and process the information fairly;

2. Keep it only for one or more specified and lawful purposes;

3. Process it only in ways compatible with the purposes for which it was given to you initially;

4. Keep it safe and secure;

5. Keep it accurate and up-to-date;

6. Ensure that it is adequate, relevant and not excessive;

7. Retain it no longer than is necessary for the specified purpose or purposes;

8. Give a copy of his/her personal data to any individual, on request.[37]

To ensure that you comply with the provisions of the Acts, data should be anonymised as soon as possible. Once fully anonymised the data can be stored on a password protected computer (though institutional guidelines vary as to how long your data should be stored, and where it should be stored), and you must give assurances that you will comply with these guidelines, storing the data in a secure location following completion of research. Further, you cannot retain data for an indeterminate amount of time. Again, institutional guidelines vary as to the length of time you must retain your data, following which you must securely destroy it. In the case of anonymised data, it is your responsibility to ensure that the identifying codes are stored in a separate location. A further consideration in data storage is consent to archiving data which is of manifestly social or cultural importance, in which case different considerations may apply. Again, your institution will

---

[37] Office of the Data Protection Commissioner "The Data Protection Rules" available at https://www.dataprotection.ie/docs/Data-Protection-Rules/y/21.htm accessed 8 March 2016.

have or should have guidelines as to the circumstances in which this type of data can be stored indefinitely.

V – Conclusion

The process of securing ethics approval for an empirically based project can be time-consuming and, in some cases, where your research is ethically unproblematic, can seem unnecessary. However, without ethics approval, you simply cannot begin this stage of your research. Further, in filling out your ethics form, and working through the ethical implications of your research, your research as a whole will inevitably be more robust, and you and your participants better protected.

Index

A

Act of Union (1800) 74
American Law Institute 172
Analogous reasoning 9–10
Anglo Irish Treaty 74
Anglo Irish War *see* Irish War of Independence
Anglo Norman settlements 72–3
Anthropological Whiggism 60
Arthur Cox Foundation 82

B

Belmont Report 191
Biomedical sciences, research ethics in 190–1
Black-letter analysis *see* Doctrinal legal methodology
Breach of contracts 174–6
Brehon law 72, 77

C

CBL *see* Community-based learning (CBL)
Centre for Legal Education 98
Child Protection Policy 197
Civic engagement 90, 96
Civil society organisations *see* Non-governmental organisations (NGOs)
Community-based learning (CBL) 90–2
  importance of reflection 97–9
  practical reflections on 99–101
Community-based research (CBR)
  and civil society organisations 94–5
  community engagement 90–2
  and community partners 89–91, 93, 96, 99–105
  description 92–3
  and non-governmental organisations (NGOs) 94–5
  overview 89–90
  potential of 104–5
  and practical matters 103–4
  practical reflections on 99–102
  question of impact 95–7
  and reflective writing 97–9
  and unmet legal need 94
Community/cultural normative systems 119
Community engagement 90–2
Community partners, and CBR 89–91, 93, 96, 99–105
Companies Act 1963 31, 36
Companies Registration Office data 140
Comparative law
  deconstruction of 48–54
  description 43
  improving 47–8
  and intellectual freedom 50–4
  and knowledge progression 44–5
  overview 39–42
  practical challenges of 54
  purpose of 45–7
  theoretical core of 42–8
  understanding of 43–4
Contract(s)
  breach of 174–6
  contents of 171–4
  and dispute resolution 176–8
  overview 163–5
  as planning 167–71
  and spectrum idea 180
  umbrella 179

Contract governance 117
Co-operation, and trust 182
Corporate governance 117
Court of Chancery 77
Court of Common Pleas 77
Court of Criminal Appeal 36, 78
Court of Exchequer 77
Courts Service 31
Critical Legal Studies 24
Customary/cultural normative orders 119

D

Data analysis 140
Data protection 201–2
Declaration of Helsinki (1964) 190
Deductive reasoning 8–10, 13–15, 34
Dispute resolution, and contracts 176–8
Doctrinal legal methodology
  advantages and disadvantages of 28–30
  application of 37–8
  challenges of 14–18
  challenges to 27–8
  definition of 22–6
  description 26–7
  importance of 13–14
  overview 7–9, 22
  process of 30–5
  properties of 9–13
  and reasoning (*see* Reasoning)
  starting points for 35–7
Doctrinal research, and socio-legal methodology 112–16
Droit idéal relatif (ideal relative law) 43

E

Economic arguments 115
Economic/capitalist normative orders 119
Empirical legal research
  institutional and resource support 145–6
  interview data 141–3
  and law schools 146–7
  and law students 147
  overview 131
  publication and funding 133–6
  purpose of 131–7
  research issue/design 137–9
  sample size and resources 139–41
  skills and employability 132–3
  survey data 143–5
Employability, and empirical legal research 132–3
Employees (Provision of Information and Consultation) Act 2006 145
'Employment-based' PhD scheme 102
End user license agreements (EULAs) 171–3
Erasmus-style partnerships 92
Ethical issues
  gatekeepers 199
  informed consent 196–9
  research procedures 200
  subject matter 199–200
Ethically problematic research
  in biomedical sciences 190–1
  in humanities and social sciences 191–3
EULAs *see* End user license agreements (EULAs)
Euroclear 169
External *vs.* internal legal history 61–3

F

Facebook 195
Fact-finding approach 27
Feminist legal theories 113
Financial Ombudsman 140
Framework agreements *see* Umbrella contracts
Functional normative systems 119

Funding, and empirical legal research 133–6

G

Garda Clearance 196–7
Gatekeepers 199
Generalisable information, and participatory research 161–2
Governmentality 127
Group work 100

H

HEIs *see* Higher Education Institutions (HEIs)
Higher Education Institutions (HEIs) 146
Historical jurisprudence 58
Honorable Society of King's Inns 78
Horizon 2020 programme 135
Humanities, research ethics in 191–3
Hunt Report 95

I

Incorporated Council of Law Reporting 78
Inductive reasoning 8–10, 34
Information
    acquiring generalisable 161–2
    acquiring 'hard to reach' 160–1
    monopolies 151
    reaching 'personal' 158–60
Information and Consultation of Workers 145
Informed consent 196–9
Insistent discourse 95
Institutional competence arguments 115
Institutional Review Board (IRB) *see* Research Ethics Committee (REC)
Intellectual freedom, and comparative law 50–4

interdisciplinary research 124
Internal conventional perspective 122, 127
Internal *vs.* external legal history 61–3
International legal norms 120
Interview research data 132, 138, 141–3
IPRT *see* Irish Penal Reform Trust (IPRT)
The Irish Association of Law Teachers 78
Irish Council of Law Reporting *see* Incorporated Council of Law Reporting
Irish Electoral Act 1923 62
Irish Free State Constitution 74
Irish Free State 82, 85–6
Irish High Court 83
Irish Legal History Society 82–3
Irish Penal Reform Trust (IPRT) 99–102
Irish Public Records Office 77, 79
Irish Reports
    Common Law (1867–1878) 78
    Equity (1867–1878) 78
    1894-present 78
Irish Research Council 102
Irish Tax Reports 78
Irish War of Independence 85

J

Judicial administration arguments 115
Judicial reasoning 115–16

K

Knowledge enhancement 161
Knowledge progression, and comparative law 44–5

L

Law and Society module 99–100
Law journals 84–6

Law Library 79
Law office history 61, 63
Law Reform Commission 124
Law Reports (Ireland) (1878–1893) 78
Law schools, and empirical legal research 146–7
Law Society of Ireland 82, 84
Law students, and empirical legal research 147
'Lawyer's history' approach 63
Legal consciousness 120–2
Legal embryology 66
Legal historical materials
  archive sources 79–81
  case reports 77–9
  law journals 84–6
  overview 71–2
  statutes 72–7
  textbooks 81–4
Legal history methodology
  internal *vs.* external 61–3
  Maine on 58–61
  overview 57
  pitfalls in 63–7
  and presentism/Whig history 63–4
  Savigny on 58–61
  as search for truth 66–7
  as source of authority 64–6
  things to remember 67–9
Legal need, and CBR 94
Legal pluralism 118–20
Legal realism 116–17
Legal reasoning 8–14, 16–18, 23, 113, 125
LexisNexis 31
Likert scales 144

M

Macaulay's methodology 165–78
Macneil's methodology 178–83
Marie Skłodowska-Curie Individual Fellowships 135

Marriage Act (No. 2) 1537 75
Material facts 32–3
Mental Health Act 2001 37
Milgram study 192–3, 195
Monopolies, information 151

N

National Archives of Ireland 79–80
National Archives of the United Kingdom 80
Nazis 188
New Public Management 182
NGOs *see* Non-governmental organisations (NGOs)
NILQ *see* Northern Ireland Legal Quarterly* (NILQ)
Non-contractual relations 167
Non-governmental organisations (NGOs) 94–5
Northern/Irish Feminist Judgment Project 114
Nuffield Report 131, 136–7, 145
Nuremberg Code 188
Nuremberg Trials 188
NVivo (software package) 138

O

Oireachtas, Acts of Parliament 74
Oireachtas TV 31, 195

P

Pareto efficiency 126
Pari passu provision 169–71
Participatory research
  acquiring generalisable information 161–2
  acquiring 'hard to reach' information 160–1
  determining importance of issues 161
  enhancing depth of knowledge 161

Index

form of participation 157–8
overview 149–50
participants 154–6
purpose of 150–4
reaching 'personal' information 158–60
Partner status 169
Posted workers 141
Poynings' Act of 1495 73, 75
Presentism/Whig history 63–4
Pro bono legal activities 94
PRONI *see* Public Record Office of Northern Ireland (PRONI)
Publication, and empirical legal research 133–6
Public interest law 95
Public Interest Law Alliance 99
Public Record Office of Northern Ireland (PRONI) 79–80

Q

Qualitative interview data 132, 138, 141–3
Quantitative survey questionnaires 132, 138–40, 143–5
Question of impact 95–7

R

Reasoning
analogous 9–10
deductive 8–10, 13–15, 34
doctrinal legal 8–14, 16–18, 23, 113, 125
inductive 8–10, 34
REC *see* Research Ethics Committee (REC)
REF *see* Research Excellence Framework (REF)
Reflective writing, and CBR 97–9
Relationship-preserving norms 176
Religious/cultural normative orders 119

Research ethics
applying for approval 193–202
in biomedical sciences 190–1
brief history of 188–93
context 187–8
data protection 201–2
gatekeepers 199
in humanities and social sciences 191–3
informed consent 196–9
overview 187
procedures 200
subject matter 199–200
Research Ethics Committee (REC) 187
Research Excellence Framework (REF) 96
Research issue/design 137–9
Research material proper sensu 52
Research procedures 200
Resources, and empirical legal research 139–41
Rule of Law 12

S

Sample size, and empirical legal research 139–41
Skills, and empirical legal research 132–3
Sliding scale of methods 49–50
Social sciences, research ethics in 191–3
Socio-legal functionalism approach 47
Socio-legal methodology
challenges of 122–6
definition 108–10
and doctrinal research 112–16
framing questions 110–12
and legal consciousness 120–2
and legal pluralism 118–20
and legal realism 116–17
overview 107–8

pitfalls of 126–8
Socio-Legal Studies Association
 Conference 109, 146
Software development contracts 177
Sovereign debt contracts 170
Spectrum idea, and contracts 180
Stakeholders 151, 155
Statute Law Revision Act
 2007 76
 2015 76
 2005 (Pre-1922) 76
 1962 (Pre-Union Irish Statutes) 76
Statute Law Revision Project 76
Survey questionnaire 132, 138–40,
 143–5
Systems Theory 24

T

Tax Code 52
Taxonomic stock-taking 8
Tearoom Trade study 192, 200
Textbooks, and legal historical materials 81–4
Theoretical core, of comparative law 42–8
Traditional doctrinal analysis *see* Doctrinal legal methodology
Transferable skills 132

Trust, and co-operation 182
Tudor period 77
Tuskegee Syphilis Trial 190
Twitter 195

U

Umbrella contracts 179
United Kingdom Feminist Judgments
 Project 113
US Law and Society movement 167

V

Volksgeist 59

W

Welfare bureaucracy 121
Westlaw 31
Whig history/presentism 63–4
Women's Court of Canada 113
World Medical Association 190

Y

'Year Books' 77